T0201453

The Art of Feature Engineering

When working with a data set, machine learning engineers might train a model but find that the results are not as good as they need. To get better results, they can try to improve the model or collect more data, but there is another avenue: feature engineering. The feature engineering process can help improve results by modifying the data's features to better capture the nature of the problem. This process is partly an art and partly a palette of tricks and recipes. This practical guide to feature engineering is an essential addition to any data scientist's or machine learning engineer's toolbox, providing new ideas on how to improve the performance of a machine learning solution. Beginning with the basic concepts and techniques of feature engineering, the text builds up to a unique cross-domain approach that spans data on graphs, texts, time series and images, with fully worked-out case studies. Key topics include binning, out-of-fold estimation, feature selection, dimensionality reduction and encoding variable-length data. The full source code for the case studies is available on a companion website as Python Jupyter notebooks.

PABLO DUBOUE is the director of Textualization Software Ltd. and is passionate about improving society through technology. He has a PhD in computer science from Columbia University and was part of the IBM Watson team that beat the "Jeopardy!" champions in 2011. He splits his time between teaching machine learning, doing open research, contributing to free software projects, and consulting for start-ups. He has taught in three different countries and done joint research with more than 50 coauthors. Recent career highlights include a best paper award in the Canadian AI Conference industrial track and consulting for a start-up acquired by Intel Corp.

The Art of Feature Engineering
Essentials for Machine Learning

PABLO DUBOUE
Textualization Software Ltd

CAMBRIDGE
UNIVERSITY PRESS

CAMBRIDGE
UNIVERSITY PRESS

University Printing House, Cambridge CB2 8BS, United Kingdom

One Liberty Plaza, 20th Floor, New York, NY 10006, USA

477 Williamstown Road, Port Melbourne, VIC 3207, Australia

314–321, 3rd Floor, Plot 3, Splendor Forum, Jasola District Centre,
New Delhi – 110025, India

79 Anson Road, #06–04/06, Singapore 079906

Cambridge University Press is part of the University of Cambridge.

It furthers the University's mission by disseminating knowledge in the pursuit of
education, learning, and research at the highest international levels of excellence.

www.cambridge.org
Information on this title: www.cambridge.org/9781108709385
DOI: 10.1017/9781108671682

First published 2020

Printed in the United Kingdom by TJ International, Padstow Cornwall

A catalogue record for this publication is available from the British Library.

Library of Congress Cataloging-in-Publication Data
Names: Duboue, Pablo, 1976– author.
Title: The art of feature engineering : essentials for machine learning /
Pablo Duboue, Textualization Software Ltd.
Description: First edition. | Cambridge ; New York, NY :
Cambridge University Press, 2020. |
Includes bibliographical references and index.
Identifiers: LCCN 2019060140 (print) | LCCN 2019060141 (ebook) |
ISBN 9781108709385 (paperback) | ISBN 9781108671682 (epub)
Subjects: LCSH: Machine learning. | Python (Computer program language)
Classification: LCC Q325.5 .D83 2020 (print) | LCC Q325.5 (ebook) |
DDC 006.3/1–dc23
LC record available at https://lccn.loc.gov/2019060140
LC ebook record available at https://lccn.loc.gov/2019060141

ISBN 978-1-108-70938-5 Paperback

A la Universidad Nacional de Córdoba, que me formó en virtud y letras.[†]

---

† Dedicated to National University of Córdoba, which taught me character and knowledge.

Contents

Preface

There are as many reasons to write books as there are books written. In the case of this book, it was driven by a desire to both help practitioners and structure information scattered in a variety of formats. The end result is yours to judge. Preliminary feedback indicates it errs on the side of too much material rather than covering only material for which there are clear intuitions or consensus. It seems that, as a matter of personal taste, I would rather have more tools in a toolbox than a few general tools. The case studies are a different matter. Some reviewers have liked them quite a bit. Others have not seen the point of having them. All I can say is that there was a substantive effort behind putting them together. People have different learning styles. Some learn by seeing others do things. If you are in that group, here you have many end-to-end examples of somebody doing feature engineering. Hopefully, it will help the concepts click.

If you think you would have written about the topic in a different way; feature engineering needs more detailed treatment beyond the anecdotal. If you leave these pages with the intention of writing your own material, I will consider the effort of putting together this book to be a success.

My interest with feature engineering started while working together with David Gondek and the rest of the "Jeopardy!" team at IBM TJ Watson Research Center in the late 2000s. The process and ideas in this book draw heavily from that experience. The error analysis sessions chaired by David Ferrucci were a gruelling two days of looking at problem after problem and brainstorming ideas of how to address them. It was a very stressful time; hopefully, this book will help you profit from that experience without having to endure it. Even though it has been years since we worked together, this book exists thanks to their efforts that transcend the show itself.

After leaving IBM, during the years I have been consulting, I have seen countless professionals abandon promising paths due to lack of feature engineering tools. This book is for them.

My students from the 2014 course on Machine Learning over Large Datasets in the National University of Córdoba were also instrumental in the creation of this book, and the students of the 2018 graduate course in feature engineering tested an earlier version of the material. The fantastic data science community in Vancouver, particularly the one centred around the paper reading LearnDS meetup, also proved very helpful with comments, suggestions and as a source of reviewers.

This book has benefited from more than 30 full-book and book-chapter reviewers. In alphabetical order, I would like to extend my unreserved gratitude to Sampoorna Biswas, Eric Brochu, Rupert Brooks, Gavin Brown, Steven Butler, Pablo Gabriel Celayes, Claudio Conejero, Nelson Correa, Facundo Deza, Michel Galley, Lulu Huang, Max Kanter, Rahul Khopkar, Jessica Kuo, Newvick Lee, Alice Liang, Pierre Louarn, Ives Macedo, Aanchan Mohan, Kenneth Odoh, Heri Rakotomalala, Andriy Redko, David Rowley, Ivan Savov, Jason Smith, Alex Strackhan, Adrián Tichno, Chen Xi, Annie Ying, and Wlodek Zadrozny. The anonymous reviewers provided by the publisher helped grow the manuscript in a direction that better fits with existing instructional material. I thank them for their help and apologize for the lack of explicit acknowledgement. Annonymity in reviews is the cornerstone of quality scientific publishing.

The publisher has also helped move this book from concept to finished product. Kaitlin Leach's help made all the difference while navigating the intricacies of book publishing, together with Amy He, who helped me stay on track.

A book always takes a deep toll on a family. This book is unusually intertwined with family, as my wife, Annie Ying, is also a data scientist.[†] This book started during a personal sabbatical while I was accompanying her in New York on a spousal visa. She proofread every chapter and helped keep my sanity during the dark times of writing. This book would not exist without her. It would have not even been started. Annie, muchas gracias, de corazón.

[†] You might say we are a couple trying to beat the odds.

PART ONE

Fundamentals

The first part of the book focuses on domain-independent techniques and overall process. While the importance of domain expertise tends to be highlighted in machine learning tasks, many times careful data analysis can steer us away from bad assumptions and yield high-performing models without domain expertise.

Whether quality feature engineering (FE) can be achieved without tapping into deep domain expertise is a topic of debate in the field. In his talk "Data Agnosticism, Feature Engineering Without Domain Expertise" expert online competitions champion Nicholas Kridler[193] argues that "responsible data analysis and quick iterations produce high-performing predictive models" and that models will help us find features without domain expertise. We will explore this viewpoint in this part of the book.

Even if you lack domain expertise, do not underestimate the dataset expertise you will gain by working with it. In their book *Communicating with Today's Patient*, Desmond and Copeland[81] argue that in a doctor visit there are two experts at work: the expert in medicine (the doctor) and the expert on the patient's body (the patient themselves). If you follow the data analysis-centric process sketched in Chapter 1 and exemplified in Part Two, you will, over time, become an expert in your dataset, even if you do not know the domain.

1

Introduction

You have some data. You have trained a model. The results are below of what you need. You believe more work should help. Now what? You can try to improve the model. You can try to collect more data. Both are good avenues for improved results. A third avenue is to modify the features to better capture the nature of your problem. This process, feature engineering (FE), is partly an art and partly a palette of tricks and recipes. In the following chapters, I hope to expand your palette with new ideas to improve the performance of your machine learning solution.

To understand the importance of FE, I would like to draw an analogy to the techniques for solving word problems covered in mathematics textbooks. Take the following problem:

> A dog runs at 10 mph back and forth between two spouses while they run into each other for 100 feet at 5 mph. What is the total distance the dog runs?

Depending on the framing, solving this problem requires an integral (adding all the distances run by the dog) or elementary school arithmetic (calculating the time it takes the spouses to meet and the distance travelled at the dog speed for that period of time). The importance of framing is easy to overlook and hard to teach. Machine learning (referred as ML throughout this book) encounters a similar situation: most ML algorithms take a representation of the reality as vectors of "features," which are aspects of the reality over which the algorithm operates. First, choosing the right representation is key. Second, sometimes the features can be preprocessed outside of the algorithm, incorporating insights from the problem domain to better solve it. This type of operations, FE, tends to bring out performance gains beyond tweaking the algorithms themselves. This book is about these techniques and approaches.

Book Structure. This book is structured into two parts. In the first part, I[†] have sought to present FE ideas and approaches that are as much domain independent as FE can possibly be. The second part exemplifies the different techniques as used in key domains (graph data, time series, text processing, computer vision and others) through case studies. All the code and data for these case studies is available under open-source licenses at

http://artoffeatureengineering.com

This chapter covers definitions and processes. The key to FE is expanding the ML cycle (Section 1.3.1) to accommodate FE (Section 1.3.2) and, among other things, to include a data release schedule to avoid overfitting, a matter of evaluation (Section 1.2). Two types of analysis are central to this cycle, one to be done before the ML starts (Exploratory Data Analysis, Section 1.4.1) and another one after one ML cycle has concluded (Error Analysis, Section 1.4.2), which will inform the next steps in your FE process. Then we will look into two other processes related to FE: domain modelling, which helps with feature ideation (Section 1.5.1) that then results in different techniques for feature construction (Section 1.5.2). The chapter concludes with general discussions about FE particularly where it falls with respect to hyperparameter fitting and when and why to engage in a FE process (Section 1.6).

Chapter 2 discusses FE techniques that modify the features based on their behaviour as a whole. Techniques such as normalization, scaling, dealing with outliers and generating descriptive features are covered. Chapter 3 deals with the topic of feature expansion and imputation with an emphasis on computable features. Chapter 4 presents a staple of FE: the automatic reduction of features, either by pruning or by projection onto a smaller feature space. Chapter 5 concludes Part One by presenting advanced topics, including dealing with variable-length feature vectors, FE for deep learning (DL) and automatic FE (either supervised or unsupervised).

Part Two presents case studies on domains where FE is well understood and common practice. Studying these techniques can help readers working on new domains where the domain lacks such maturity. Neither of the case studies is to be taken as comprehensive instructional material on the domain; you would be better served by specific books on each domain, some of which are mentioned at the end of each chapter. Instead, the case studies are intended to help you brainstorm ideas for FE in your domain. As such, the nomenclature used might

---

[†] FE has plenty of topics still left open for debate. I have tried to separate my opinions from more established topics by using first person singular in cases where I felt you might want to take my comments with extra care. The use of first person singular is not to be less welcoming, it is to warn you to be specially critical of what you are about to read.

differ slightly from what is usual for each domain. A contribution of this book is also a dataset shared by the first four chapters specifically built to teach FE, which contains graph data, textual data, image data and timestamped data. The task is that of predicting the population of 80,000 cities and towns around the world based on different available data, and it is described in detail in Chapter 6. The domains studied are graph data, timestamped data (Chapter 7), textual data (Chapter 8), image data (Chapter 9) and other domains in Chapter 10, including video, geographical data and preference data. The chapters refer to accompanying source code implemented as Python notebooks; however, studying the code is not required to understand or follow the case studies.

How to Read this Book. This book has been written with practitioners in mind, people who have already trained models over data. With such readers in mind, there are two different situations this book can help you with:

You want to get better at FE. You have done some light FE and felt your efforts were lacking. A full light reading of Part One will give you fresh ideas of things to try. Pay special attention to the cycle proposed in Section 1.3.2 in this chapter and see if it makes sense to you. You could adapt it or develop your own cycle. It is good to have a process when doing FE; this way you can decide when to stop and how to allocate efforts and evaluation data. Then, move to Part Two and tear apart the case studies. The work presented in Part Two is intended to get the conversation started; your own opinions on the data and domains should give you plenty of ideas and criticism. I disagree with many of my own decisions in each of these case studies, as shown in the postmortems. Enticing you to come up with better ways to approach the case studies could be your fastest route to excel at FE. Hopefully, you will feel energized to give your ideas a try on the datasets and code released with the book.

You have a dataset and problem and need help with FE for it. This requires more precise reading of specific sections. If your domain is structured, approach the case study in Chapter 6 and read the linked material in Part One as needed. If your domain is sensor data, look at Chapter 9. If it is discrete data, look at Chapter 8. If it has a time component, look at Chapter 7. Alternatively, if you have too many features, look at Chapter 4. If you feel your features have a signal that is poorly captured by the ML algorithm, try a feature drill-down using the ideas in Chapter 3. If the relation of a feature value to the rest of the values and features might be important, look into Chapter 2. Finally, if you have variable length features, Section 5.1 in Chapter 5 can help you.

Background Expected from the Reader. ML practitioners come from a variety of backgrounds. The same can be said about ML researchers, which in turn means a wide variety of methods in existing work. There are many techniques that require advanced mathematics to understand them but not necessarily to use them. The explanations in these pages try to stay away from advanced topics as much as possible but the following subjects are assumed: knowledge of ML algorithms (decision trees, regression, neural networks, k-means clustering and others), knowledge of linear algebra (matrix inversion, eigenvalues and eigenvectors, matrix decomposition) and probability (correlation, covariance, independence). The last section of the chapter contains pointers to material suitable to cover these topics, if needed. Practitioners tend to be very strategic with their learning as their time is limited. Many of the techniques described in this part exceed this basic background. If the technique ends up in your critical path, references to all the source material are included in case you need to drill down deeper.

Throughout the book, I use the following abbreviations: ML for machine learning, NN for neural networks, IR for information retrieval, NLP for natural language processing and CV for computer vision.

1.1 Feature Engineering

The input to a supervised ML system is represented as a set of training examples called **instances**. Each instance in a classification or regression problem has a **target class**, or **target value,** which can be of discrete size (classification) or continuous (regression). This discussion refers to target class and classification but it also applies to target value and regression. Besides its target class, each instance contains a fixed-size vector of **features**, specific information about the instance that the practitioner doing ML expects will be useful for learning.

When approaching a ML problem, target classes and instances are usually given beforehand as part of the problem definition. They are part of what I call **raw data** (other authors use the term *variable*[134] or *attribute* vs. feature to make a similar distinction). Such raw data is normally the result of a data collection effort, sometimes through data collection hooks on a live system, with target classes obtained from the system or through human annotation (with suitable guidelines[262] and cross-annotator agreement[57]). Features themselves are not so clear cut, going from raw data to features involves extracting features following a **featurization** process (Section 1.5.2) on a **data pipeline**. This process goes hand in hand with **data cleaning** and enhancement.

Distinguishing raw data from features makes explicit the modelling decision involved in picking and assembling feature sets. If the raw data is tabular, each row can be an instance and there would be a temptation to consider each column a feature. However, deciding which columns are features and what type of preprocessing (including clustering, etc.) ought to be done on them to obtain features is a task closely tied to the problem sought to be solved. These decisions are better addressed through exploratory data analysis (Section 1.4.1), and featurization (Section 1.5.2). Therefore, a feature is defined as any value that can be computed from the raw data for the purpose of modelling the problem for a ML algorithm.[51] What makes good features and how to come up with them is discussed in the domain modelling section later in this chapter (Section 1.5.1).

The distinction between raw data and features is key and it enables the type of decisions behind successful FE. In the second part of the book, we will study examples where raw data includes graphs with hundreds of thousands of nodes, texts with millions of words and satellite images with hundreds of millions of pixels with features such as the average population of cities in a given country or whether the word "congestion" appears in a text.

Given these definitions, we are ready to define FE. The term means slightly different things for different people and I have not found an existing definition that captures the intuitions followed in this book. I therefore wrote my own definition, which follows, but beware the term might mean different things to other practitioners:

> Feature engineering is the process of representing a problem domain to make it amenable for learning techniques. This process involves the initial discovery of features and their stepwise improvement based on domain knowledge and the observed performance of a given ML algorithm over specific training data.

At its core, FE is a representation problem,[51] that is, it is the process of adjusting the representation of the data to improve the efficacy of the ML algorithms. It uses domain knowledge[195] and it might also use knowledge about the ML method itself. It is difficult, expensive and time consuming.

FE is referred to by many names, such as *data munging* or *data wrangling*,[49] or sometimes as a synonym of feature selection (which is of course limiting, as discussed in Section 4.1, in Chapter 4).

In the words of Jason Brownlee:[51]

> [Feature engineering] is an art like engineering is an art, like programming is an art, like medicine is an art. There are well defined procedures that are methodical, provable and understood.

I follow other authors[132] in considering FE as an encompassing term that includes feature generation (producing features from raw data), feature transformation (evolving existing features), feature selection (picking most important features), feature analysis (understanding feature behaviour), feature evaluation (determining feature importance) and automatic feature engineering methods (performing FE without human intervention). Note that in many circumstances, the term "feature engineering" will be used as a synonym for only one of such activities.

Examples of FE include normalizing features (Section 2.1 in Chapter 2), computing histograms (Section 2.3.1), using existing features to compute new ones (Section 3.1 in Chapter 3), imputing missing features (Section 3.2), selecting relevant features (Section 4.1 in Chapter 4), projecting the features into a smaller dimension (Section 4.3) and the rest of the techniques discussed in this book.

There is wide consensus in the field that FE is the place to add domain knowledge[49,341]; therefore, half this book describes FE in the context of domains where it is understood to be a key ingredient in learning. For example, realizing that certain feature values are not useful after a threshold (Section 6.4 in Chapter 6), or computing averages that take into account the cyclic nature of the data (Section 7.3 in Chapter 7) or grouping together words that start with the same letters (Section 8.5.2 in Chapter 8). Even custom signal processing (Section 9.8.1 in Chapter 9) is an example of using domain knowledge to modify the feature representation to present to the ML algorithm.

In the words of Yoshua Bengio:[337]

> Good input features are essential for successful ML. Feature engineering is close to 90% of effort in industrial ML.

These intuitions can also be captured at the feature ideation level, as discussed in Section 1.5.1. For example, if you think that emails that include a person in their lead photo convert better (i.e., they generate more sales), you can create a binary feature that records whether a person appears in the lead photo (how to compute such a feature is a different problem and you might need to rely on a separate ML system for it). You (if you are a domain expert) or **consulting with a domain expert** can provide information about the need to expand your available raw data. For example, if there are reasons to believe power consumption may be related to server outages in a data centre, you might want to request measurements for power consumption begin to be recorded and made available for learning and so on. As part of the FE process, the raw data should be transformed into features highlighting their relation to the target class (e.g., transform weight into BMI[171] in a health assessment task).

In the words of Andrew Ng:[337]

Coming up with features is difficult, time-consuming, requires expert knowledge. "Applied machine learning" is basically feature engineering.

FE is sensitive to the ML algorithm being used as there are certain types of features (e.g., categorical) that fare better with some algorithms (e.g., decision trees) than others (e.g., SVMs). In general, the hope is that better features will improve the performance of any ML algorithm but certain operations are more useful for certain algorithms. Whenever possible, I have tried to signal them throughout the book.

The reasons for doing FE are usually reactive: an initial transformation of the raw data into features (featurization) did not render the expected results or did not render results good enough to put them into production use. At this stage, it is common to embark on what I call *model shopping*, or what has been called by other authors *data dredging*[204] or *a random walk through algorithm land*,[193] that is, to try different ML algorithms without much intuition, just out of convenience with the ML software package. In general, the difference between ML models with similar possible decision boundaries is not substantial and after repeating this process a number of times, the chosen algorithm will most definitely overfit (even when doing cross-validation because the model will not be overfit but the decision of picking the model will be too tied to the training data). In my experience, a well-orchestrated FE process can highlight much value in the raw data, sometimes even driving its expansion (for example, adding geolocation by IP[49]).

In the words of Pedro Domingos:[84]

... some machine learning projects succeed and some fail. What makes the difference? Easily the most important factor is the features used.

A separate reason to do FE is to put the features into a more understandable light from a human perspective, with the purpose of having interpretable models. Such is the case when doing inference rather than prediction.

There are two other, more abstract, reasons. First, as Dr. Ursula Franklin said on her 1989 CBC Massey Lectures,[310] "Tools often redefine a problem." FE allows to maintain a focus on problem-solving grounded in the domain at hand. ML does not exist in isolation. Second, having a suitable toolbox can prove to be a phenomenal boost in self-confidence, a fact highlighted by Stephen King in his non-fiction work *On Writing*:[183]

[C]onstruct your own toolbox [...] Then, instead of looking at a hard job and getting discouraged, you will perhaps seize the correct tool and get immediately to work.

Finally, many types of raw data require significant FE before they can be used with ML. The domains in Part Two fall into this category. The same goes for raw data with very large number of attributes.

I will conclude with a quote from Dima Korolev regarding over-engineering:[72]

> The most productive time during the feature engineering phase is spent at the whiteboard. The most productive way to make sure it is done right is to ask the right questions about the data.

1.2 Evaluation

Before looking into ML and FE cycles, let us spend some time looking into the issue of evaluating the performance of your trained model. They say it is better to crawl in the right direction than to run in the wrong one. This applies also to ML. How you will evaluate your trained model has deep implications on your choice of model and the type of FE you can perform. Centering the evaluation metric decision based on which metrics are easily available in your ML toolkit can be a great mistake, particularly as many toolkits allow you to plug in your own metric.

We will briefly discuss metrics next, about which many books have been devoted.[169,350] We will then look into how cross-validation relates to evaluation (Section 1.2.2) and at issues related to overfitting (Section 1.2.3), before concluding with a discussion about the curse of dimensionality.

1.2.1 Metrics

As part of the problem definition, it is important to spend some time thinking about the different metrics that will be used to evaluate the results for a trained algorithm. The metrics are deeply tied to the underlying use for which you are training the model. Not all errors will have the same impact on your application. Different metrics can penalize specific errors differently. Familiarizing yourself with them can help you pick the right one for your task. We will start by looking into metrics for classification before discussing regression metrics.

A great way to understand errors and metrics is through a **contingency table** (also known as a cross-classification table), which for the case of predicting a binary class becomes the following:

		Real	
		+	−
Predicted	+	true positives	false positives
	−	false negatives	true negatives

In general, it is good to distinguish **false positives** (type I errors), where the system is predicting something that it is not there, from **false negatives** (type II errors), where the system is missing to identify something that it should. Certain applications are more tolerant of one type of errors over the other. For example, prefiltering data can be quite tolerant of type I errors. On the other hand, an application that decides to single out a person for shoplifting, however, will have very little tolerance for type I errors.

Measuring how many times a classifier outputs the right answer (**accuracy**, true positives plus true negatives over the total number of points) is usually not enough, as many interesting problems are very biased towards a background class (and thus true negatives will dominate the computation). If 95% of the time something does not happen, saying it will never happen will make you only 5% wrong, but is not at all a useful classifier.

Type I and type II errors are usually summarized as ratios. For instance, the number of true positives over the total number of labelled examples. This metric has received many names including **precision** or PPV (positive predictive value):

$$precision = \frac{|correctly\ tagged|}{|tagged|} = \frac{tp}{tp + fp}$$

Alternatively, you can focus on the false negatives. This metric is called **recall**, TPR (true positive rate) or also sensitivity:

$$recall = \frac{|correctly\ tagged|}{|should\ be\ tagged|} = \frac{tp}{tp + fn}$$

This metric will give you an idea about whether the system is missing many labels.

Other metrics can be so defined, for example, NPV (negative predictive value) and TNR (true negative ratio). If you need to have only one metric that summarizes both numbers, you can take a weighted average of them, what is called the F_β-**measure**, where the β tells you whether to favour precision rather than recall:

$$F_\beta = (1 + \beta^2) \cdot \frac{P \cdot R}{\beta^2 P + R}$$

Setting β to 1 renders the metric as F_1 or simply just F and that favours both metrics equally $(2PR/P+R)$. Another popular metric to summarize the behaviour is **area under the ROC curve** (AUC-ROC), that is, the curve under a recall vs. false positive rate (1-TNR) plot obtained by varying sensitivity parameters of the model.

Note that using F_2 versus using F_1 might significantly change the results of your evaluation. If you know nothing about your task, you can use F_1, but the more you know, the better metrics you can use (or even design). For example, in the question answering competition TREC, the script distributed by the organizers[53] computed a whopping 36 metrics on the results. Focusing only on one metric is usually preferred by higher-level decision makers, but as a practitioner working closely with ML algorithms and source data, you will be better served to consult a variety of metrics in order to build a better understanding of the behaviour of the trained model. Ultimately, I advocating for a full-fledged error analysis process (Section 1.4.2).

When comparing multiple annotations, as when having multiple annotators, metrics for inter-rater reliability can be used, for example Fleiss' kappa,[108] which measures the agreement that can be achieved above chance and the numerator measures the agreement actually observed above chance.

For regression problems, the error can be measured as a difference, but in that case negative errors might cancel with positive errors. Therefore, it is necessary to take the absolute value of the error. However, the absolute value does not produce a continuous derivative, and thus, it is customary to use the square of the errors instead, the mean squared (MSE). To have the metric in the same units as the original signal, you can take the square root of the mean of the squared errors, obtaining the RMSE. Other ways to weigh the errors are possible but less common. For example, you can use another exponent instead of powers of 2, or you can weigh negative errors different than positive errors. Note that the requirement of a continuous derivative is important if you are using the error directly as part of the optimization process of your ML algorithm (for example, to train a neural network). You can also use an error metric for algorithmic purposes and another to evaluate your results and see whether they are fit for their underlying purpose (**utility metrics**).

Finally, the metrics discussed before all deal with averages and try to summarize the behaviour of the model on its most representative case. Nevertheless, that does not address the **variance** of the results. This topic is well studied in ML, where we talk about the **bias** (learning the wrong thing; errors due to limitations of the model) versus **variance** (learning scattered points; errors due to finite data sampling and different samples produce different models).[84]

1.2.2 Cross-Validation

Cross-validation is a technique to deal with small datasets in model evaluation by reducing the loss of data allocated to testing the model. In general, this is done due to a lingering feeling that testing data is "wasted" as it is not used to estimate the parameters of your model. However, keeping data aside to understand how well your trained ML model performs on production is definitely more valuable than the marginal changes to the model that data will produce: if 20% more data produces drastic changes, then your model is not stable, and you do not have much of a model, really. Basically, you will be better served by a simpler model with fewer parameters that behaves in a stable fashion over your available data.

Moreover, the value in executing your model on test data goes hand in hand with using your model as a component inside a larger solution. A good understanding of how well your model performs on unseen data might enable you to address many of the model's shortcomings with business logic outside the model itself. Would you rather have a model that has a 5% lower RMSE but fails in obscure, not understandable ways, or one where its errors are understood, signed off and accepted by its potential users and clearly communicated to them? (Of course, if you do not know how either model behaves, you will choose the one with lower RMSE but I am trying to argue for deeper understanding of the behaviour of the models.) The process for leveraging the test data to gain such rich insights is called error analysis and it is discussed in Section 1.4.2.

In cross-validation, the rationale is to split the training data into N parts, taken at random. The system is then trained and tested N times: for each fold, the remaining $N - 1$ folds are used to train a model, which is then used to predict labels or values on the selected fold. In certain domains, care has to be taken when splitting the data so that each fold contains a full view of the data, and then the splitting is random over sets of instances rather than over all instances. For example, if training over multiple rounds of user logs, all rows for the same user should fall into the same fold. Otherwise, the evaluation will not be representative of the behaviour in production. Also, care should also be taken that all labels appear in the train set.

At the end of the process, the evaluation metric or metrics can be computed over the full, labelled dataset (micro evaluation) or as the average of the evaluation metrics over each fold (macro evaluation). I personally prefer micro evaluation as it does not depend on the number of folds but the variance of the macro evaluation is a good estimator of the stability of the model over the available data.[42]

1.2.2.1 Out-of-Fold Estimation

A great use of cross-validation, which is needed by many techniques presented in this book, including the case study in Chapter 6, is to use the fold system to compute feature transformation estimates that depend on the target variable. Without the use of cross-validation, such estimates constitute what is known as a **target leak**, a poorly constructed feature where the target class has been made available by mistake to the ML algorithm. Such target leaks are usually very unfortunate. The too-good-to-be-true evaluation numbers could get communicated widely before the target leak is discovered when trying to implement the production code that makes use of the model ("What do you mean I need the attrition rate to compute this feature? I don't know the attrition rate, that's why I'm calling your model!"). This technique of using folds for estimating feature transformation that require the target variable is known as **out-of-fold** estimation, and it is so common that it is abbreviated as OOF. Be careful to use a large number of folds, so as to have estimates that are stable enough. For an example, see Section 6.4 in Chapter 6.

1.2.3 Overfitting

Overfitting is a well-studied topic in ML. It is well-addressed in existing general ML books[234] and it is central to FE. When doing ML, we care about fitting a model to existing data, with the purpose of generalization, that is, extrapolation. Overfitting happens when the model follows too closely to the original training sample and it fails to generalize. It is the reason we always use a separate test set when training supervised learning models. Evaluating the train set will provide a view of the results that is too optimistic and not representative of the behaviour on new data.

Now, the training data and test data all constitute a *sample* of the overall population over which we plan to use the model. Sometimes, through a series of training and evaluation steps, we might gain insights about the full sample that will lead to overfitting of the ML process, not just on the testing-on-train-data sense but on trickier ways, such as choosing suboptimal models, model parameters or, central to this book, features that accidentally perform better on the sample but will underperform when applied over the actual population.

For example, imagine if you are trying to predict whether a drug will produce an adverse reaction and a patient should discontinue its use. Training data was collected during the winter and one of the questions asked was whether the patient was thirsty frequently. This question proved to be a very informative feature. You might encounter that this is positive (i.e., that the feature fires) much more often during the summer months, producing many false positives in production. At that stage we can conclude the model features were overfit to the test set.

A common misconception that I have heard from practitioners of all levels of expertise is that cross-validation is not prone to overfitting as compared to using a held-out set. That is, of course, not true; if you quiz your data repeatedly, your results get tuned to the sample rather than the overall population. That is well understood in statistics and there are techniques like the Bonferroni correction[95] that says roughly that if you use the same data to answer N questions, the statistical significance threshold has to be reduced substantially, as much as dividing it by N (making rejecting the null hypothesis much harder and therefore requiring much more extraordinary evidence for significance). I have not yet encountered a similar principle for FE, but as I advocate in the next section to use a held-out set only once, the issue falls into a matter of personal taste.

1.2.4 Curse of Dimensionality

Care must be taken when designing feature sets to escape the **curse of dimensionality**. The main issue with higher-dimensional spaces is that everything starts to become very close, even if just by chance. That is the case as meaningful differences on a few key coordinates are drowned over similar values for the remaining coordinates. Moreover, the more dimensions present in the data, the more training data needed (a rule of thumb says an absolute minimum of five training instances per dimension.)[84]

1.3 Cycles

Given a ML algorithm and some identified features, the parameters for the algorithm can be estimated from the training data and then evaluated on **unseen data**. The purpose of this book is to provide you with tools to perform several cycles iterating over the process of finding better features, a process called **feature evolution**. If the test set is consulted multiple times, that will lead to overfitting (discussed in detail in the next section), that is, to select a suboptimal model that appears to perform better than what it will perform when applied to truly fresh data (which will be tragic when deployed on a production setting). To avoid this problem, it is of uttermost importance to have a development test set to use during feature evolution and to leave enough test data for a final evaluation. Such data might be new, held-out data or freshly acquired data if you are looking into a process that continuously generates annotated data.[49]

1.3.1 ML Cycle

Building computer systems that adapt their behaviour based on available evidence is usually subdivided into several types of problems. By far, the most common type of ML problem is that of extrapolation of a function. In this context, extrapolation involves, given some known points of a function, to predict how the function will behave over a different set of points. This is the case of **supervised learning** of classifiers, discussed in the next section.

While supervised learning is the most common problem and technique, there are other problems and techniques popular within ML (see Table 1.1): **unsupervised learning** (which seeks to find structure on unannotated data), **reinforcement learning** (which uses delayed feedback to guess annotations over the data), **active learning** (that selects which data to be annotated next) and **semi-supervised learning** (that mixes annotated and unannotated data), to name a few. Most of these problems and techniques operate over representations of reality consisting of feature vectors and can benefit from the techniques discussed in this book.

At its core, a supervised ML algorithm is defined by a representation being learned, an objective function to be minimized or maximized and an

Table 1.1. *Types of ML.*

Learning Type	Goal	Example/Advantage
Supervised	Function extrapolation.	Given the behaviour of a website visitor, determine whether they are likely to purchase if offered a coupon.
Unsupervised	Find structure in unannotated data.	Group together different paradigmatic customer behaviours in a website, to help build marketing personas.
Others		
Reinforcement	Learning from past successes and mistakes.	Game AIs.
Active	Select data to be annotated next.	Needs less annotation effort than supervised.
Semi-supervised	Mix annotated and unannotated data.	Needs fewer annotations.

optimizer that guides the search over the space of potential representations.[84] For example, in a decision tree, the representation is the tree being built, the objective function is a metric of how well the tree splits the training data into homogeneous sets and the optimizer picks the feature split that improves over the worse subset. There is a recent trend in moving to an explicit representation of these three components, led by NN frameworks like TensorFlow.[1]

The ML cycle presented here (Figure 1.1) follows consensus in the field but it expands the relation between raw data and featurization. It starts with

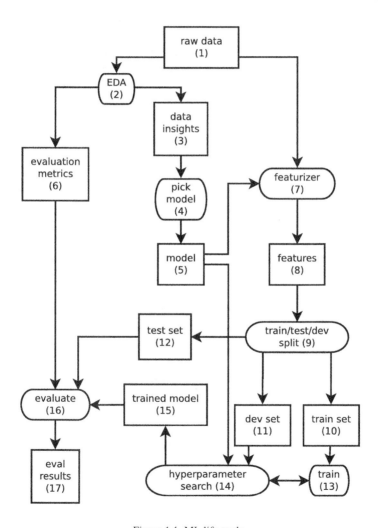

Figure 1.1 ML life cycle.

an exploratory data analysis (EDA), discussed in Section 1.4.1 and numbered (2) in the figure, on the raw data (1). From the obtained data insights (3), you ought to be able to pick (4) an ML model (5) in a more informed fashion. At this stage, the evaluation metrics should also be decided[204] (6). With the model in hand, you can proceed to generate features (8) from the raw data (7), which is then split (9) into train (10), development (11) and test sets (12). The train and test sets ought to be completely separated as we want to know how the model will predict on new data.[49] The test set should be at least 10% of the total data, with some authors[204] recommending up to 30%.[†] The model can then be trained on the train set (13). The development set, if any, is used for a hyperparameter search, which is model dependent (14). The best model from the hyperparameter search is evaluated (16) on the test set (**held-out data**). This cycle concludes with a trained model (15) together with a believable evaluation (17). Note the held-out data can only be used to test the model once. Resist what has been called "double-dipping the training data,"[49] either explicitly or by applying cross-validation repeatedly. If you want to do several cycles doing variations of different parameters of the algorithm (or its features, see next section), you should use a different (new) held-out set. Alternatively, you can use a separate evaluation set ("development test set") and acknowledge you will be overfitting your results to that set, before performing a final evaluation. Such is the approach I advocate for a full-fledged FE cycle, as discussed in the next section.

The changes from raw data to features plus the different experiments, datasets being used for evaluation (and, thus, consumed), etc., become the pedigree of your models. Care must be taken to document this process, for example, in a **log book** or lab notebook.[204] Without this, for problems that undergo a long improvement process, it is not uncommon to encounter trained models that work well in practice and there is no recollection of what data or exact process was followed to obtain them. Trade speed in executing iterations with judicious documentation as training a model is something seldom done once. Always favour **reproducible builds** over a few extra points of performance.

1.3.2 Feature Engineering Cycle

My proposed FE cycle (Algorithm 1.1) has an emphasis on building an understanding of what features work and do not work and having a **final**

[†] Very large datasets can get away with using only 1% of the training data, as long it has low variance.[235]

evaluation on held-out data (generated in line 1 of Algorithm 1.1). That final evaluation set has also been called a *confirmation set*.[204] I am proposing this methodology as a compromise when no continuous stream of newly annotated (fresh) data is available. If fresh data is available (or if you can schedule batches of test data on a **data release schedule**), you can just cycle through the whole process altogether; each evaluation on fresh data is equivalent to a full evaluation. In the proposed framework, the training data is reused on a number of cycles (line 2 of Algorithm 1.1) and thus risks overfitting. In each cycle, a fixed development set may be used or a new one split into a train set and a development set (a **bootstrap**) can be used. Cross-validation is also an option but the extra running time might not be worth it, and it complicates the error analysis. Of course, the decision is yours.

FE is an iterative process where a set of features is defined, experimented upon, evaluated and refined. As part of that process, training data is consumed and hypotheses regarding changes to the feature set are built based on the result of the experiments. For the process to be successful, a stream of unseen data is needed, otherwise, the hypothesis generated from the experiments might lead to procedural overfitting, that is, to changes to the feature representation that will not help in the general case but help for the data analyzed as part of the FE cycle.

If you do not have enough data, you can use a different split. The FE process concludes with you building in your mind an understanding of the behaviour of the features for this data, problem, and ML model.

When doing repeated ML experiments, it is useful to have a development test set[43] – a test set, independent from the train set that is used during development. This test set is also independent from the final test set. It helps avoid procedural overfit. This final test speaks better about the generalization power of the model. While this is a good idea in general, when doing heavy FE, it is mandatory as the possibility for overfitting when doing FE is greatly increased.[17]

FE cycle is not unlike the ML cycle. The key difference is in the type of processes performed in the cycle: (1) identifying good features and expanding them[17] and (2) identifying redundant/uninformative features and dropping them. Moreover, it might not be necessary to run the full train cycle to do this. Sometimes, measuring the correlation between a feature and the target class is enough, that is, you might want to consider creating a contingency table for each feature and to look for patterns in that data.[43]

Ultimately, I believe that error analysis is the leading force in FE.[44] The key is improving the understanding of each feature, for example, revisiting EDA but this time only for one feature or one feature and the target.[72] The final goal is to have a better framing of the raw data.[295]

The final output of the FE process is a data pipeline (or two if you do not have a stream of fresh data) that produces features from data.[49†] Such pipelines can be expressed as custom code or through feature manipulation formalisms such as the ones present in scikit-learn.[253]

While many quick iterations reduce the need for domain expertise,[193] if you have domain knowledge or access to people who do, this is also a great moment to incorporate domain knowledge (for example, realizing the category "late cretaceous" falls into the category "cretaceous"[267]).

If the FE process was performed without a fresh stream of test data, then I advocate for the construction of two feature sets, an optimized set (with a greater risk of overfitting) and a conservative set (maybe worse performing). In the final evaluation, both feature sets are evaluated separately (lines 5 and 6 in Algorithm 1.1). The conservative set will be used if the optimized set does not outperform it in a significant manner (line 7 in Algorithm 1.1).

Algorithm 1.1 Feature engineering life cycle. The ML cycle in the loop is the one in Figure 1.1.

Require: raw_data
Ensure: featurizer, model
1: $raw\_data_{final\_eval}, raw\_data_{feat\_eng}$ = final_eval_split(raw_data)
2: **while** not good results **do**
3:     $featurizer_C$, $model_C$, $featurizer_O$, $model_O$ =
    ML_cycle($raw\_data_{feat\_eng}$)
4: **end while**
5: $results_O$ = evaluate($model_O$, $featurizer_O(raw\_data_{final\_eval})$)
6: $results_C$ = evaluate($model_C$, $featurizer_C(raw\_data_{final\_eval})$)
7: **if** $results_O > results_C + \delta$ **then return** $featurizer_O, model_O$
8: **else return** $featurizer_C, model_C$
9: **end if**

1.4 Analysis

The FE process proposed in the last section is heavily dependent on two types of analyses described next. Exploratory data analysis (Section 1.4.1) is helpful to understand the raw data, devise features and select suitable ML algorithm

---

† Chapter 7.

and metrics. Error analysis (Section 1.4.2) seeks to understand the strength and weakness of your feature set to drill down and improve it. Note that there is a certain analyst bias in any of these tasks. Other practitioners doing similar analysis might arrive at different results.[284]

1.4.1 Exploratory Data Analysis

EDA refers to exploratory analysis of the raw data. Even without domain knowledge,[91] it is possible to analyze raw data and extract insights about the behaviour of the data, particularly as it relates to the target variable. I am among many authors[196,278] who find it to be a necessary ingredient for successful FE. You want to make sure that you have "rich enough data to distill meaningful features."[20] A good first step is to analyze the variety of values the different columns in the raw data take. Descriptive statistics such as mean, median, mode, extremes (max and min), variance, standard deviation, quartiles and visualizations such as box-plots are helpful at this stage.[239] Columns with very little variability tend to have very little explanatory power and are better off being ignored, unless the variability is highly correlated with some values of the target class. Therefore, it is good to plot correlations between the target variable and different columns. Other things to try include analyzing how your ongoing conclusions about the nature of the dataset change as you take different subsamples of the data, particularly samples segmented by time or type.[72] You might also want to check whether certain fields that look random are actually random by using standard randomness tests.[204] Again, random data ought to have no explanatory power and can be discarded. Outliers can also be found and discussed at this stage (cf., Section 2.4 in Chapter 2).[19] Similarly, you can start looking into missing values, although you might need to do a full featurization to find ways to deal with them in a principled way.

From there, you can look into the relationship between two columns or a column and the target class. Scatterplots help you visualize this graphically. Another alternative is to use summary tables (also known as pivot tables), where a categorical column is used to segment the values of a second column. Each cell in the table contains summary statistics about the values of the second column that fall into the first category value. If only counts are provided, it resembles a simplified contingency table, but other summaries (mean, standard deviation, etc.) are possible.[239] Finally, you can compute metrics about the relationships between pairs of columns by using correlation coefficients or any of the metrics presented in Section 4.1.1 in Chapter 4.

If you possess domain knowledge or have access to people who do, this is a great time to make your assumptions about the domain as explicit as possible and test whether such assumptions hold on the data at hand. Do you expect certain distribution of values to follow a normal (or any other given) distribution? State that assumption and check whether it holds. For example, using histograms (cf., Section 2.3.1 in Chapter 2) or computing representative statistics such as skewness, etc. (cf., Section 2.3).[19] You do not want to build heavily on assumptions that ultimately do not hold. All throughout FE, you need to exercise an inquisitive mindset and drill down on anything that looks suspicious. If the domain knowledge indicates a certain column ought to behave in a certain way and it does not, do not let that fact pass by without further investigation. You might unveil data extraction errors or hidden biases in the sampling. Or you might just have the wrong domain assumptions that might have deeper implications than the data columns at hand. This will also be a good moment to engage in data cleaning, for example, to check that your values are all in the same units using box-plots.[204]

Useful tools for EDA include, of course, spreadsheets such as Excel,[18] Jupyter Notebooks[188] and OpenRefine.[316] The latter, formerly GoogleRefine, can find similar names, bin numerical data and do mathematical transforms, among many other capabilities.[17] You might even want to do a data survey computing key statistical descriptors following Pyle's method from chapter 11 of *Data Preparation for Data Mining*.[263] There are also ways to visualize observations by looking at multiple variables at once: based on data similarities (clustering); based on shallow data combination (association rules); and based on deeper data combination (decision trees).[239†]

All case studies in Part Two, Chapters 6 to 9 start with an EDA process. For example, in Chapter 7, we will see a feature heatmap over different versions of the feature, reproduced here in Figure 1.2. The graph aligns features for each year, uncovering the story of the data. Missing values are shown in a checkerboard pattern. The values of the features are clustered into six classes, represented as different gradations of gray. This allows you to see how the values of a feature evolve over time. See Section 7.1.1 for further details.

1.4.2 Error Analysis

The previous discussion about approaching the behaviour of the data with suspicion takes its full force when doing **error analysis**. Plenty of analysis can be done with aggregate metrics but I feel that falls in the direction of

---

† Chapter 5.

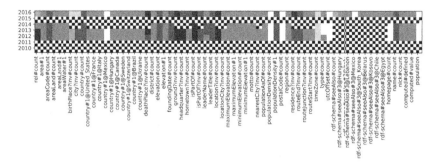

Figure 1.2 Historical features visualization using a feature heatmap (excerpt). The checkerboard patterns are missing values; the different shades of gray indicate different quantiles.

evaluation metrics, discussed in Section 1.2.1. To me, error analysis is all about the parochial, the anecdotal. Focusing on a few cases that capture your attention for important reasons then biting down on that problem and not letting it go, going deeper and deeper, trying to assemble a meaningful narrative behind the reasons why that error came to be. Of course, a great working understanding of the internals of the ML system helps quite a bit there, together with appropriate tooling, for example, mechanisms such as TensorBoard.[218] In general, to perform a reasonable error analysis, your ML algorithm will need to be instrumented so as to generate enough metadata to enable this type of drilling down. Looking at samples rather than aggregates and being skeptical are part of what has been referred as "responsible data analysis."[193]

For example, the first featurization shown in Chapter 6 has a few cities that contribute heavily to the overall error. For each of these "problematic" cities, Section 6.3.1.1 finds the feature that further contributes to the error by a process of feature elimination, reproduced in Table 1.2. From this analysis, the conclusion was to dampen the effect of the count features. See Chapter 6 for details.

From a successful error analysis, you might discover that certain features are hurting performance more than helping it (therefore deciding to incur in a session of feature selection, cf., Section 4.1, Chapter 4) or that certain features are really informative,[72] in which case you might want to further boost their signal engaging in some of the feature drill-down techniques discussed in Section 3.1 in Chapter 3. Single-feature visualization techniques might also prove useful.[352]†

---

† Chapter 2.

Table 1.2. *Ablation study. A 5% sample was retrained while removing one feature at a time. The highest contributor is listed here.*

City	Improvement	Feature to remove
Dublin	0.85 to 0.6 (29.41%)	city?inv#count
Mexico_City	−0.53 to −0.92 (−73.81%)	seeAlso#3@List_of_tallest_buildings
Edinburgh	0.17 to −0.19 (212.89%)	leaderTitle#count
Algiers	−1.0 to −1.2 (−15.33%)	name#count
Prague	−1.3 to −1.7 (−30.56%)	seeAlso#count
Milan	−0.84 to −1.1 (−30.81%)	seeAlso#count
Amsterdam	−0.74 to −0.96 (−29.86%)	homepage#count
Lisbon	−0.6 to −0.88 (−46.54%)	seeAlso#3@Belarus
Tabriz	−0.75 to −1.2 (−57.17%)	seeAlso#count
Nicosia	0.3 to −0.028 (109.40%)	country#count
OVERALL	−4.5 to −6.3 (−40.69%)	seeAlso#count

While you might use specific examples to generate hypothesis for improvement, whether to pursue those hypothesis should be informed by their potential impact on the whole dataset. Otherwise, you will encounter a situation akin to optimizing rarely used code.[267] Following Amdahl's law,[9] the code that takes the most time is the code that ought to be optimized the most. In the same vein, errors that account for more of the performance loss ought to be addressed first.

When drilling down on errors, use the contingency table (cf., Section 1.2.1), maybe even on a per-feature basis,[43] and remember your chosen metrics for this problem and domain: if type I errors are more important, drill down more on them, accordingly.

Also keep an eye out for spotting software errors. As ML produces results with intrinsic error, debugging ML systems can be very hard. Do not take behaviour that counters intuition lightly, as it might indicate software bugs that can be much more easily addressed than ML modelling issues.

Another interesting tool for error analysis is the use of random data and random models. If your trained model is doing something sensical, it ought to outperform a random model. If a feature is meaningful, its value from actual data ought to outperform replacing it with a random value.[72] The last approach might help you unveil errors in your data, which can be particularly difficult to appreciate when you are tunnel focused on your model errors.

1.5 Other Processes

I will conclude this introductory chapter with two highly related processes that wrap up the FE discussion: domain modelling, which in this book pertains to how to go from raw data to a first feature set, and featurization (Section 1.5.2), which deals with feature improvement and drill-down.

1.5.1 Domain Modelling

Domain modelling is separate from featurization to distinguish the more abstract from the more operational aspects. Representing a domain's raw data into features is an inherently creative approach, similar to modelling in any other area of mathematics and (software) engineering. Modelling and design in general are matters of decisions and approximations; as such, there is an inherent imperfection aspect to them. This discussion follows more abstract concepts while the next section covers more concrete terms, also related to how to generate follow-up featurizations, that is, featurization when certain features have already been identified. In the words of Max Kanter and colleagues from the Featuretools system:[175]

> Transforming raw data into features is often the part of the process that most heavily involves humans, because it is driven by intuition.

Let us see how to come up with features, and then discuss what makes particularly good features and list domains with a tradition of successful featurization. The process of coming up with features, **feature ideation,** is closely related to brainstorming, design, creativity and programming in general and thus benefits from general advice on brainstorming.[17,178] There are no hard truths here, just general guidelines and advice. A usual approach is to use anything remotely related to the target class as a feature (basically, all the raw data and variations), in what constitutes a **feature explosion.**[40] This rarely works in practice unless the raw data has very low dimensionality (5 or 6 attributes). You will be better off starting with features you believe will have predictive value.[49] But do not let the available raw data constrain you.

A very beneficial approach is also to think of the type of information *you* (as a human) would use to make a successful prediction.[127] Such "thought features"[72] can unveil a trove of ideas and lead to requests for expansions to be made to the original raw data. Of course, you do not need to reinvent the wheel; you can also build on the work of others[17] through published papers, blogs or source code. Post-mortem posts in online ML competition sites such as Kaggle.com can be very informative. Using features from existing work will most likely require some feature adaptation[21] but it might save you a world of trial and error. Do not feel constrained by the existing attributes in the raw data and look to propose features that are computed from existing attributes (cf., Section 3.1 in Chapter 3, for computable features).

A common oversight at this stage is to forget to reach out to domain experts for insights on what they would consider good features for this problem and domain. Here traditional techniques for knowledge acquisition in expert system can be helpful.[52,269]

Finally, once you start converging into a feature set, you might want to step back and start looking for rare new features that can explore other parts of the problem space.[17] The case studies provide an example of this approach: once a baseline has been established using structured data, we move to look at a textual description of each city. Another example is presented in Chapter 9, where we move from colour histograms to local textures expressed as the number of corners in the image (cf., Section 9.6). That might be particularly productive if your chosen ML model is one based on ensemble learning, like random forests.[48]

As you come up with the features, the next question is: **what makes for a good feature?** Which one of these potential features should you address in your first **featurizer**?[41] While any piece of information that is potentially useful for a prediction may do as a feature,[342] you want features with these three properties:[72]

(1) **Informative**, the feature describes something that makes sense to a human, which is particularly important when doing inference and seeking out interpretable models, but also for productive error analysis,
(2) **Available**, the feature is defined for as many instances as possible; otherwise you will need to deal with missing data (cf., Section 3.2 in Chapter 3), and
(3) **Discriminant**, the feature divides instances into the different target classes or correlates with the target value. Basically, you want to seek out characteristics of objects that are available, easily modelled and have a relation to the target being predicted.

In the words of Peter Norvig:

> Good features allow a simple model to beat a complex model.[250]

Moreover, you want them also to be as independent from each other and simple as possible,[127] as better features usually mean simpler models.[51] How many features to extract is also an open question, as ML can be very effective given a good feature vector.[202] In theory, the more features f you have, the more data you will need to give to your ML to achieve the same error ϵ, in the order of $O\left(\frac{1}{\epsilon^f}\right)$ amount of data.[206]

You can test your distilled features at this stage with statistical association tests (like the t-test, building an association table between the feature values and the target values),[23] and, in general, many of the feature utility metrics from Section 4.1.1.1 in Chapter 4 can be used. If needed, you can revisit this feature ideation process later on after a few cycles of FE and include more features. Brink, Richards, and Fetherolf propose[49] to start with the most predictive features first and stop there if they perform well; otherwise, try a feature explosion and if it does not work, prune the expanded feature set using feature selection (cf., Section 4.1).

Certain domains have standard representations by now. For new domains, studying the existing ones might give some ideas and guidance. Such domains include images, signals, time series, biological data, text data,[40] prognosis and health management,[337] speech recognition, business analytics and biomedical.[180] Part Two of this book includes seven domains.

Finally, in term of feature presentation, you want to make sure that related variables should be contiguous and that you use multiple levels of information (that is, you split features into sections), if needed.[324] This will not affect the ML but it will help you better visualize the feature vectors and ward off software errors.

1.5.2 Feature Construction

The last step in the process sketched in this chapter involves the actual execution of code (the featurizer) that assembles a feature vector from the raw data. The featurizer is algorithm dependent and it can change the types of features from the raw data. This process can be as simple as selecting columns from a DB but as the multiple cycles of FE start piling up, it can get quite complex. There are some software solutions for this problem (some of which I have built in the past[124]) but none that have attracted widespread use as of the writing of this book.

There seems to be some momentum within the academic community to express featurization as ETL (extract, transform and load) operations from data warehousing[167] or as SQL stored procedures[267] or UDFs (user-defined functions)[10] as a framework to standardize computable features. That seems like a good idea, as featurization is inherently a data manipulation activity, of which the DB community has a long and productive history to rely on. It is to expect that somewhat complex operations such as OOF estimation might become standard operations available in DB systems in the future.

I will now discuss a particular featurization operation, feature templates, which is usually employed early in the process and important enough to deserve its own section.

1.5.2.1 Feature Types

Features as defined in Section 1.1 are values of a certain type, as used by ML algorithms. We will review the following types, as they are accepted by many algorithms in widespread use: binary, categorical, discrete, continuous and complex features. Table 1.3 contains examples for each of these feature types. In this discussion and throughout the book, x_i refers to a feature within the feature vector $\vec{x}$ and y refers to the target class or target value.

Binary Features. These are the simplest possible features. They are features that can take one of two values: true or false, present or absent, 1 or 0, −1 or 1, A or B. They are also known as *indicator features*. Some ML models (such as some implementations of maximum entropy[164] and certain SVMs) can only take such features. Many ML models (including SVMs and logistic regression) can only predict binary targets.

Categorical Features. These are features that can take one among many values, known as *categories, categorical values*, or *levels*. The categories themselves are known beforehand. In general, there is no ordering among the different categories. Usually, the categories themselves receive a meaningful name from the domain. The number of categories tends to be small. That is, using the whole English dictionary (say, 20,000 categories) as a categorical feature is possible but models will seldom benefit from such a representation.

Discrete Features. These are features that represent values that can be mapped to integers (or a subset of them). Because integers have an absolute order, discrete features are also ordered. Representing large number of categorical features as discrete features is tempting (and many times done in practice), but leaves the model with a false sense of ordering if the categorical features do not posses an ordering. For example, what is the meaning of saying that Visa is less than Mastercard, which is less than American Express?[204]

Continuous Features. These are features that can be mapped to a real number (or a non-discrete subset of the real numbers). Ratios and percentages are special subtypes of these features. Due to physical restrictions of digital computers, all continuous values are actually discrete, represented as a set of bit values on a particular encoding. While this might sound like a theoretical point, the representational richness of the internal floating point implementation might be a key problem with sensor data. You must take care

Table 1.3. *Feature types and examples.*

Type	Description / *Note*	Example
Binary	One of two values	Did the customer leave a tip? Did the turbine make noise? Did the student turn in the exam before the end of the allocated time? Does the person like cats?
	simplest	Did the licence plate have a match in the DMV database?
Categorical	One among many values	Colour of the car, Brand of the car, Credit card type, Number of bedrooms (*also a number*)
	values known beforehand	Type of mattress (*also mattress surface area*)
Discrete	Can be mapped to the integers	Number of pizzas eaten, Times visited the gas pump, Times the turbine got serviced last year, Steps walked last week (*compare: distance walked, which is*
	order is important	*continuous*), Number of people living in the house.
Continuous	Can be mapped to a real number	Engine temperature, Latitude, Longitude, Speech length, Colour intensity at centre of image, Distance walked, Temperature
	representation issues	at centre of dish (*as measured by an IR camera*)
Complex	Records, lists, sets	Date (year, month, day; note that it can be expressed as number of days from a fixed date), Product name (*it might include brand, product type, colour, size and variant*), Location (latitude and longitude), Complaint (a sequence of characters),
	challenging	Countries visited (it is a set of categories)

to avoid extreme situations; either your values might underflow, with all values mapping to zero, or overflow, with all values mapping to the maximum possible value.

As a refresher, floating points are usually represented using the IEEE 754 format, which uses scientific notation, for example, the number 56332.53 is represented as 5.633253×10^4. The actual representation consists of a sign bit, a fraction and an exponent. Single precision uses 8-bit exponent and 23-bit fraction, double precision uses 11-bit exponent and 52-bit fraction. Due to the fraction and exponent behaviour, not all **segments of the real line are sampled at the same resolution.** These topics are studied in detail in **numerical analysis** courses. [123,248]

Complex Features. Some ML algorithms can process features in what can be called non-normal form in databases: records, sets, lists.[48,68] Most systems benefit from decomposing those, and we will see some simple techniques in Section 3.3 in Chapter 3 and advanced techniques in Section 5.1 in Chapter 5.

1.5.2.2 Feature Templates

Feature templates are small programs that transform raw data into multiple (simpler) features at once. They have two objectives: first, to present data in a way better suited for the ML model; and, second, to incorporate domain knowledge about the nature of the problem. Many of the feature expansion techniques in Chapter 3 involve feature templates.

For a simple example, consider a date attribute in the raw data. A feature template can transform it into three discrete features (year, month and day). If the month itself is meaningful, this transformation will make that information easily available to the ML. If the original date attribute is expressed as the number of days counting from a fixed date, the model will have to learn all the months by itself, which will require substantive amount of training data and it will seldom generalize.

For a more complex example, consider the keywords4bytecodes project,[92] where I seek to predict the name of a Java method based on its compiled bytecodes. In this task, we could start adding features of the likes of "there is an **iadd** operation in the method," but that is very tedious and labour intensive. Instead, we can use feature templates to extract features from the data. If we take a particular instruction (e.g., `getfield org.jpc.emulator.f.i`") and generate three features: the instruction (`getfield`"), instruction plus operand (`getfield_org.jpc.emulator.f.i`") and instruction plus abbreviated operand (`getfield_org.jpc.emulator`"), we can obtain a very large feature set as a first approximation. Further FE will be needed to reduce the set to a manageable size, if needed.

1.6 Discussion

In this otherwise very practical book, I would like to spend a paragraph on my opinions of the future of ML and FE. In a similar fashion that it is possible to trade time for space in many algorithmic problems, using more RAM to speed up the algorithm, it is my opinion that FE can trade domain knowledge for training data. Does that qualify for a learning machine? If you are helping the algorithm so earnestly, it is difficult to argue this is a reasonable direction for creating artificial minds (I think it is not). The interesting thing about the field of AI is that in many aspects, it defines the boundaries of the computer science field. In the 1950s, search was squarely part of AI. Finding a node in a tree was considered an AI problem. Nowadays, nobody will put the two problems together. In the same vein, empirical nonparametric statistical modelling using heavy doses of domain knowledge, for example, through FE, might soon be an accepted method to solve many real-world problems. There are many real-world problems, such as in medical research, where collecting more data or wasting data on uninformed models is unacceptable. Whether these techniques remain to be called ML or not it remains to be seen. This is my view on the topic, the convergence towards an engineering contribution of the techniques presented in this book.

Looking ahead to the case studies and Part Two, I would like to reflect on a few issues that can be distilled from the work presented in those five chapters. The first is the fact that FE does not always succeed in improving the performance of the ML process. Embarking on a FE process is prone to hit dead-ends and regressions, something I have tried to exemplify throughout the case studies. Omitting the dead-ends and regressions I encountered working on these datasets would have been straightforward, but it will paint FE in unrealistic terms. **The fact that a particular technique did not work on a particular problem should not discourage you from trying it in your problem. The techniques showcased are valuable tools with a long track of success in the field.**

Second, there is the intertwining of FE and ML algorithm optimization, where ML optimization includes choosing the algorithm and tuning its hyper-parameters. For the sake of covering more FE techniques, the case studies did not drill down into the ML algorithm optimization topic. Many applied ML books cover that topic quite well. The finer details of hyperparameter tuning jointly with FE are left cursorily discussed in the case studies. This issue is not only about obtaining better ML results. It does change the potential direction on which the FE process revolves around, as it changes the errors made by the ML. If the ML results change, it requires redoing error analysis. **Thus, error analysis for** FE **should be done at key points were the ML algorithm and its hyperparameters have been determined to have reached a local optimum.** And no technique can be expected *a priori* to consistenly outperform other techniques, what is called normally a "no free lunch" theorem.[332]

This brings us to the last topic I want to discuss: the human-in-the-loop nature of the FE process and experimental turnaround delays. When doing experiments for a publication or R&D for a production system, I would leave a hyperparameter search running for a week or use a cluster with hundreds of cores to speed it up. In a book format, my target has been to have all case studies for a chapter run in a day, two days tops. Given the number of featurizations explored per chapter, that has limited the exploration of hyperparameters, as mentioned. But there is another, deeper issue with experimental turnaround time.[†] It has to do with the mental focus of the practitioner. If the experimental turnaround time is in the order of minutes, then you can wait, see the results and proceed. Larger turnaround times will imply a context switch on your side. You will go work on something else for the period of time that the ML training and tuning takes place. The longer the turnaround, the harder it will be to reconnect with your own thoughts and ideas regarding the FE process at hand.

Luckily, many of the FE tasks can build on work from earlier versions. As hinted in Section 10.1 in Chapter 10, it is possible to reuse computation successfully in FE. Some recent work on this direction includes systems built by Anderson and Cafarella[10] that adapt DB technologies to detect the parts of the train set changed by a proposed FE operation. Their system then updates a trained ML model only over those values. This requires ML models that are updateable and will not work on techniques like dimensionality reduction that produce substantive changes to the training data but it is an exciting new development in the field.

I would like to close with the following advice: try simpler ideas first. In the case of FE, that means not doing any FE at all. If your problem is similar to problems successfully addressed by DL and you have comparable training data, start with DL. If you do not have enough training data but can adapt pretrained models, then also try DL. If DL fails for you or you do not expect it will work given your problem and data size, then try AutoML frameworks such as Featuretools (discussed in Chapter 5, Section 5.4.1.2). At that stage, you can start FE, maybe on top of DL pretrained feature extractors and/or AutoML features. And do not forget to reach out to domain experts. They can save you tons of time and training data. Good luck, and I look forward to hearing about your experiences with feature engineering!

1.7 Learning More

FE is not covered in depth in regular ML books. Luckily, new books are being published that focus primarily on FE, some of which we will talk about here.

[†] This discussion is informed by a debate I had with Dr. David Gondek in 2015. He was arguing the ideas I talk here. At that time I was arguing against them. It took me some time to come around. Thank you, David.

One of the earlier books is Alice Zheng's *Mastering Feature Engineering*,[351] which puts forward a mathematical formalism focusing in feature selection. It does a very good job explaining very complex mathematical concepts to a general public. The book has been expanded with the help of a coauthor, with more introductory chapters suitable for data science bootcamps (the book also has an emphasis on linear methods).[352] I highly recommend their appendix on linear algebra if you are missing that background, as the presentation is excellent and it is written from a FE perspective. The PCA chapter is also a great resource. Regarding the rest of the book, the emphasis on linear methods enables clear intutions but it concerns me that some of their intuitions only hold for linear methods and that might be lost to beginners. You might want to be extra careful and double-check their assumptions when reading it.

Dong and Liu[132] present a larger body of work than this current book, including 14 chapters authored by almost 40 different authors. It includes separate chapters on featurization for common data types (similar to the case studies in Part Two, but only focusing on featurization) and three case studies (without source code) on three novel domains (social bot detection, software analytics and extracting features from the Twitter API). Some of the chapters in the collection are quite introductory and others include advanced topics in active research. I have referenced the relevant chapters in this book, and I would advise an advanced and serious reader on FE to look at them in detail.

Regarding ML workflows and practical matters in ML, I recommend *Machine Learning for Hackers* by Drew Conway and John Myles White;[74] *Mahout in Action* by Owen, Anil, Dunning and Friedman;[249] *Real-World Machine Learning* by Brink, Richards and Fetherolf.[49] I am particularly fond of the last book and I have cited it quite a bit throughout this book. For a whole book on case studies, you might want to see *Fundamentals of Machine Learning for Predictive Data Analytics: Algorithms, Worked Examples, and Case Studies* by Kelleher, Mac Namee and D'arcy.[177]

In terms of EDA, I recommend *Doing Data Science: Straight Talk from the Frontline* by Schutt and O'Neil, as it includes EDA for many domains and problems in almost every chapter. The series of interviews with practitioners will prove valuable to anybody in the field, beginners and experts alike.

Finally, a great source of white papers related to practical ML lies in the KDD Cup series of ML competitions.[51]

2

Features, Combined: Normalization, Discretization and Outliers

This chapter discusses feature engineering (FE) techniques that look *holistically* at the feature set, that is, replacing or enhancing the features based on their relation to the whole set of instances and features. An ongoing issue in FE is how to provide more value to features by leveraging contextual information. In this chapter, we use the whole dataset to provide the context. The central question is how to consider all the features together. Note that humans, when faced with unfamiliar data, will usually look at the behaviour of a given feature value through all instances to gauge its impact. How does this value compare to others? Is it representative? Is it rather small? Rather large? The techniques described here seek to incorporate this type of intuition to the machine learning (ML) process.

The most common approach is to **scale** and **normalize** the feature values (Section 2.1), finding the maximum and minimum and changing the values to ensure they will lie in a given interval (e.g., $[0, 1]$ or $[-1, 1]$). The expectation is to let observed meaningful variabilities emerge without being drowned by the difference of behaviour for each different feature. Note that names such as "normalization" and "standardization" are very ambiguous, as they may mean different things for different communities and people. For example, calculating BMI (body mass index) is considered "standardization" by their community of users, when it is not a normalization technique in the sense used here (it is a great computable feature, though).[171] When in doubt, ask for the precise formula being used.

Another type of FE technique called **discretization** is discussed in Section 2.2 and involves dynamically finding thresholds to segment continuous features into intervals or categories: for example, to decide that all temperatures between -10 F and 50 F fall into a bin (which could be called "cold"), and between 80 F and 110 F fall into another bin (which could be called "hot") and so on. This way, you signal to the ML that differences between 15 and 45 degrees are not important for your task and domain.

Section 2.3 discusses **descriptive features**, that is, the use of compact summary statistics. This information has the advantage of always being defined (no missing values) and of producing dense feature vectors. We will look into using tables of counts (**histograms**) in Section 2.3.1 and general descriptive features such as maximum, minimum and averages in Section 2.3.2. Histograms are a tool of choice in computer vision and text length tends to be a very informative feature in natural language processing.

When looking at the feature values across many instances, some values might present themselves far from the rest, which is what constitutes **outliers** (Section 2.4). The chapter closes with advanced topics, including using feature differentials as features and inducing features from Random Forests.

Note that many of the techniques presented in this chapter (if not all) fall into the category of what has been called "model-based FE"[352] that is, after the FE process, the featurizer will contain trained models and parameters. To use the trained ML model over new data, you will need to preserve the featurizer model and make it available with the trained ML model.

2.1 Normalizing Features

Features in isolation can be difficult to compare with each other. Certain ML algorithms perform simple mathematical operations with them that assume their values are comparable. Other algorithms try to find ways to make them comparable using simple approaches. That means that if two features (say, flight length in kilometres and passenger weight in kilograms) are of widely different dimensions, the ML algorithm will require training data just to learn to scale them accordingly. That unnecessary burden can be alleviated by normalizing the features in various forms. Just remember that by changing the features you might lose information. Whether that information is important for the task depends on your understanding of the problem and domain. Thus, these decisions are also places to add domain knowledge. Nevertheless, there are times where the unnormalized value is relevant; in those cases, it is beneficial to maintain the original feature as a separate feature. Ultimately, these techniques drop information; if this information were important for the algorithm, it will make worse predictions.

The simplest approach is to scale the features so all the feature values have the same magnitude and are centred on zero. But there is also plenty of value in normalizing them according to their mean and standard deviation, so that they have a unit variance (**standardization**). Other approaches involve normalization according to a norm,[351] for example, L_2. We will also look into standardization and decorrelation techniques (Section 2.1.1), smoothing (Section 2.1.2) and feature weighting (Section 2.1.3).

Feature normalization is a great way of reducing the variations on feature values, that is, to have less **nuisance variations** and concentrate on variations that contain a signal to the target class. It also ensures that the feature values fall within a specific range during training. For example, to transform the features into floating-point numbers between 0 and 1 (or −1 and 1). This is crucial for support vector machines (SVMs) and neural networks (ANNs) that need input data scaled to certain specific intervals.[180] On the other hand, many ML algorithms are scale invariant (like decision trees) while others, like logistic regression, might have requirements of zero mean and unit variance if used with regularization. Care must be taken when working with sparse datasets. In the presence of a large number of zero entries, some of the techniques presented here, like centring, will change the zero entries to non-zero entries producing dense vectors that might be inefficient to use with many ML algorithms.[352]†

In general, when I talk about normalization, I am talking about normalizing against all instances in the training dataset. Normalizing against subsets is described as an *instance* engineering problem in Section 5.2 in Chapter 5. After the normalization parameters are computed over the training set, they are applied at runtime (and to the test set).[351] The parameters computed over the training set ought to be fixed, and may generate outputs on the test outside the desired range (for example, values over 1.0). It might be tempting to recompute the parameters on the test set, but doing so will give an incorrect portrayal of the behaviour of the algorithm in production. Normalizing the test set independently has been described as the most common amateur mistake in SVMs.[209] The normalized features could, however, be clipped to conform to the chosen interval (by taking the maximum or the minimum).

Scaling. The simplest normalization that can be done is to take the maximum and minimum values in the population, subtract the minimum to each value, then divide by range (maximum minus minimum):

$$x'_f = \frac{x_f - \min_{\hat{x}_f \in \text{trainset}}(\hat{x}_f)}{\max_{\hat{x}_f \in \text{trainset}}(\hat{x}_f) - \min_{\hat{x}_f \in \text{trainset}}(\hat{x}_f)}$$

† Chapter 2.

This will result in a value scaled to $(0,1)$. For example, for the feature values $\{5, 10, 2, 17, 6\}$, their maximum is 17 and their minimum is 2, with a range of $17 - 2 = 15$. The scaled values will be $\{(5-2)/15, (10-2)/15, (2-2)/15, (17-2)/15, (6-2)/15\} = \{0.2, 0.53, 0, 1, 0.27\}$.

This scaling is used with support vector regression in Chapter 6, Section 6.3. This approach has the problem that outliers might concentrate the values on a narrow segment, so when doing scaling it is recommended to perform outlier filtering first (Section 2.4). Alternatively, you can use standardization instead, as discussed later in this section.

Squashing functions, such as $\log(1+x)$ or the Box–Cox transformation, are sometimes called nonlinear scaling.[341] We will see these functions with other computable features in the next chapter (Section 3.1). While these functions squash the distribution of values, they do not take into account the whole distribution to perform the squashing, which is the focus of this chapter.

Centring. After scaling, it is also common to add or subtract a number to ensure a fixed value (e.g., 0) is the "centre" of the values. The centre might be the arithmetic mean, the median, the centre of mass, etc., depending on the nature of the data and problem. A reasonable new centre might be zero, one or e, depending on the nature of the ML algorithm. In general, you centre your data to align it with attractor points in the ML parameter space: if the origin is the default starting point for your ML parameters, it makes sense that your data has zero as the most representative value. Values scaled and centred to the (scaled) mean are called **mean normalized values**.[342]

For the previous example, as the scaled mean is 0.4, the mean normalized values will be $\{ -0.2, 0.13, -0.4, 0.6, -0.13 \}$. For a more comprehensive example, see Chapter 6, end of Section 6.2.

Scaling to Unit Length. This is a normalization method applied to multiple features at once. Given a norm definition, divide features by the result of calculating the said norm

$$\vec{x}' = \frac{\vec{x}}{\|\vec{x}\|} = \left\langle \frac{x_1}{\|\vec{x}\|}, \dots, \frac{x_n}{\|\vec{x}\|} \right\rangle$$

For example, given a feature vector $\langle 2, 1, 3 \rangle$, its Euclidean mean is $\sqrt{14}$, therefore, the unit-length scaled feature vector becomes $\langle 2/\sqrt{14}, 1/\sqrt{14}, 3/\sqrt{14} \rangle$. The type of norm to be used is dependent on the type of features. Usually the Euclidean or L_2 norms are employed but histograms sometimes use the L_1 norm (also known as **Manhattan distance**). We will see norms in detail as a regularization technique in Chapter 4, Section 4.2.

2.1.1 Standardization and Decorrelation

We will now look into operations over the whole dataset when seen as a matrix. For some of these transformations, you will need to estimate the **covariance matrix** of the training data. If you take the training data as a matrix M of size $n \times m$, for n instances and m features and centre it so that the mean of its columns is zero, you can then compute the covariance matrix as $C = M^T M / n$. This matrix can undergo a spectral decomposition into eigenvectors E and eigenvalues in diagonal D such that $C = EDE^T$. This is known as the principal components analysis (PCA) **decomposition** of the matrix M.

Standardization. This process transforms the features to have zero mean and unit variance. It is very useful for SVMs, logistic regression, and NNs, to the point that forgetting to normalize the data is considered one of the most common mistakes.[155]

Given the feature mean $\bar{x}_f$ and standard deviation σ_f, the standardized feature is defined as

$$x'_f = \frac{x_f - \bar{x}_f}{\sigma_f}$$

If you replace the denominator by the variance rather than the standard deviation, the normalization is called variance scaling[351] (not to be confused with the ANN initialization technique). Note that certain data will not play well with standardization, for example, latitude and longitude data.[171]

Decorrelation. For signals acquired from sensor data, it is common to have artifacts, like repetitions of the past data (or an echo in the case of acoustic data). Decorrelation is a technique to reduce such artifacts. If your understanding of the domain indicates that the relations of interest should *not* be of a linear nature, then linear influences between instances or features can be considered an artifact of the acquisition methodology (e.g., a voice from one speaker being captured from the microphone of another speaker, as discussed in the context of ICA in Section 4.3.6 in Chapter 4). Decorrelation is usually performed by discounting past versions of the data over the current data, which is a type of linear filter. We will see examples of such processes in the timestamped data case study, Section 7.6 in Chapter 7. Note that certain ML algorithms and techniques (like the dropout for ANN, discussed in Section 5.3, Chapter 5) need some redundancy to perform properly.

Mahalanobis Distance. A concept related to decorrelation is to scale the data using the inverse of the correlation matrix C:[217]

$$\text{Distance}_{\text{Mahalanobis}}(\vec{x}, \vec{y}) = \sqrt{(\vec{x} - \vec{y})^T \, C^{-1} \, (\vec{x} - \vec{y})}$$

If the instances are decorrelated, then C is the identity matrix and this distance is equivalent to the Euclidean distance. You can either decorrelate your instances or use the Mahalanobis distance in places you would normally use the Euclidean distance. A graphical interpretation of this distance has the intuition that the covariance is *stretching* the data in the direction of areas of higher covariance. By applying the inverse of the covariance matrix, the stretch is rectified.[45]

Whitening and ZCA. Standardization changes the data to have a unit variance; decorrelation removes correlation between the variables. Would it be possible to obtain both? That process is called **whitening**, as it transforms the data into white noise. Sphering transformation is another name for whitening, even though it is a linear transformation. Again, whitening destroys the linearities present in the data. You will only apply this process if you believe the signal in your domain is expressed through nonlinearities; otherwise, training on perfectly random data simply does not make sense.

Given the PCA decomposition discussed at the beginning of this section, the PCA whitening is $W_{PCA} = D^{-1/2} E^T$. The math is a little tedious but multiplying M by W_{PCA} obtains a matrix whose correlation matrix is a diagonal matrix (the cross-correlations are zero). Because the properties of a whitening transformation are invariant over rotation, there are infinite such transformations,[291] many of which are singled out for their special properties. This means that $W = R W_{PCA}$ with R orthonormal will equally be a whitening operation. Among them, **ZCA**[30] (also known as the Mahalanobis transformation) uses E, the eigenvector matrix, to be the R, then

$$W_{ZCA} = E W_{PCA} = E D^{-1/2} E^T = C^{-1/2}$$

ZCA has the property of obtaining a transformed data as close as possible to the original data. This is advantageous for computer vision as the transformed images will still resemble the sources images. For example, Figure 9.3, reproduced in Figure 2.1, shows a whitened version of satellite images. See Chapter 9 for details. Many ML problems, however, will benefit from whitening with any transformation. For those, the whitening based on PCA is a popular choice, as PCA is easily available in most statistical packages.

2.1.2 Smoothing

If your feature appears perturbed by errors unrelated to each other, then particular errors might push the observed value of the feature too far from

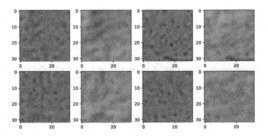

Figure 2.1 ZCA whitening results for eight settlements. The figure to the right is the whitened version of the figure to the left.

its true value and to the point of no longer being useful to the ML. To bring the value closer to its true value, you can compare it to other feature values in the *vicinity* of the instance and move it closer to other feature values in that vicinity. The intuition is that the aggregated independent errors will cancel each other out and the true signal will emerge. This process is called **smoothing**. Jeff Leek, in his data organization book, describes it as "one of the oldest ideas in statistics."[204]

What constitutes a "vicinity of the instance"? In the simplest case, if the instances contain a time or location, then the features could be smoothed taking a vicinity of instances, which are physically or temporally closer. This is succinctly put by Jeff Leek as "**smooth when you have data measured over space or time.**"[204]

Otherwise, you can consider the feature as a missing value, compute an imputed value per the techniques in Section 3.2 in Chapter 3 and average the imputed value with its existing value.

2.1.2.1 Probability Smoothing

A special type of normalization is used when dealing with sparse events where there are reasons to believe your training data constitute an imperfect sample, missing many naturally occurring combination of feature values. In those circumstances you want to discount your observed values and leave counts (probability mass) for unobserved events (feature value combinations). This smoothing is used with ML algorithms based on probabilistic methods, as the probability mass held aside needs to be included as input to the algorithm. It deals with unseen values at the sampling level, while in the next chapter (Section 3.2) we will see imputation, which is the problem of dealing with missing values explicitly marked in the training data.

The most common situation to smooth is dealing with one feature value that never appears together with a particular value of the target class. Without smoothing, certain algorithms like naive Bayes end up unable to produce any results as their core multiplication always results in a joint probability of zero.

However, how many unseen events are out there? How will you distribute the probability mass among them? If possible, you can use your understanding of the nature of the events (domain knowledge). For example, if the events are word pairs, you can estimate how likely an unseen pair will be, given how frequent the words are that make up the pair.[220]

Simple Smoothing. Different smoothing techniques are widely in use, including Lagrangian smoothing (every new unseen event is considered to have occurred at least once), ELE smoothing (add 0.5 to all counts) or Add-Tiny smoothing (add a very small number to all counts). These simple smoothing techniques are quite straightforward, although I have seen Lagrangian smoothing consistently outperform Add-Tiny over natural language processing (NLP) data and there are theoretical reasons to believe it should.[220]

Simple Good–Turing. The problem with simple smoothing techniques is that they overestimate the amount of probability mass to keep aside. The final systems are then timid, not trusting their observed data enough, due to the uncertainty of the unseen data. A more complex technique involves fitting a curve of frequency of frequencies to the observed data, and then using the curve to estimate unseen events. A probability distribution is said to be of Zipfian nature if it can be expressed as the following:[236]

$$p(f) = \alpha f^{-1-\frac{1}{s}}$$

where α and s are parameters that define the distribution. Such distributions explain many events of interest, such as distribution of words. If you believe that your probability distribution is Zipfian, then you can decide what amount of probability mass to set aside in a more informed manner.[117]

2.1.3 Feature Weighting

For the last technique of feature normalization, let us discuss using weights computed or adjudicated for features in all instances, basically, adding a statistical prior to the different features.[180] This is particularly advantageous if this prior is rich in domain knowledge and you do not expect the ML algorithm to be able to reconstruct it from the available data. Therefore, if you expect certain features to be more informative, you can weight them higher by multiplying them by a number. Alternatively, you can provide a feature-weighting vector directly to some ML algorithms.

While feature weighting can be used to add some meta-learning capabilities to a simpler ML (for example, by weighting up features highly correlated with the target class[55]), I find such techniques more related to ML algorithms than FE. An ideal feature weighting ought to bring information that exceeds the information available in the training data. You ought to be weighting a feature because of things you know about the domain, beyond the particular training data.

2.1.3.1 Inverse Document Frequency Weighting

One of the most popular feature-weighting schemes in the NLP world is known as **TF-IDF**, where in a Bag-of-Words representation of text (a word histogram, discussed in Section 2.3.1) the features (word counts) are scaled down by how popular the words are in a large collection of documents. A collection used to compute the IDF scores can exceed in many orders of magnitude the available training data, thus providing general knowledge about which words are too popular to be informative.

The weighting scheme has many flavours (aptly summarized on Wikipedia[329]); a popular one is

$$\text{idf}(t) = \log\left(\frac{N}{n_t + 1}\right)$$

where N is the total number of documents in the corpus and n_t is the number of documents where the term t appears (irrespective of how many times the term t appears in each document). When featurizing, if the term t appears $\text{freq}(t)$ times on the raw data (text) for a given instance, then setting the feature x_f (where f is the feature index associated with t in the feature vector) as $x_f = \text{freq}(t) \times \text{idf}(t)$ accomplishes this weighting scheme. For example, a word like "the" is very common; therefore, n_{the} will be very high and idf(the) will be very small. Compare that with a word like "scheme" that ought to appear rarely and will have a much higher IDF weight. Note that to use TF-IDF directly as a text-similarity metric you will need to penalize longer documents.[285] In the case study on textual data in Chapter 8, we use the IDF scores to combine the embedding representation for all the words in a Wikipedia page for a given city as extra features to calculate its population.

2.1.3.2 Camera Calibration

In computer vision, a common weighting scheme is camera calibration:[297] often optical elements and sensors exhibit variabilities in a predictable manner, measured by capturing data for a calibration image. The calibration data obtained can then be turned into a feature-weighting scheme. For example, a camera might produce lighter pixels on its upper-left corner. That might confuse the ML algorithm if lighter pixels are a good signal for a particular class elsewhere in the image. By reducing the luminescence of the pixels in the upper-left corner, the effect will be reduced.

2.2 Discretization and Binning

Instances in the training data and their features are models of events and entities from reality. The features are always a simplification of reality. That simplification often poses challenges to ML. However, there are times where there is value behind simplifying a representation even further. That is the type of processing performed in **feature discretization**: reducing the number of possible values a feature can take, usually from a real-value number to a discrete quantity such as an integer. It is a synonym of **quantizing**, different from the term in physics. In its most common form, it refers to changing a continuous feature into an (ordered) categorical feature. Other possibilities include transforming a real-valued feature into an integer-valued feature, or reducing the number of categories in a categorical feature (coalescing categories).

Every discretization incurs a **discretization error**, but you can expect that discretization will result in fewer parameters for some ML models, thus boosting the signal in the training data and improving generalization. Your number of parameters might increase, however, if your ML model of choice cannot accommodate categorical features directly and you resort to using one-hot encoding. Discretization is also useful for error analysis and understanding the behaviour of the system, enabling you, for example, to build summary tables. [239][†] It also enables you to squash differences on the actual numbers; a lower quantile in one feature is comparable to a lower quantile in another. [352][‡]

This operation can be done over the feature values alone, in isolation from the target class values, in what is known as **unsupervised discretization** or it can be done relative to the target class (**supervised discretization**). It usually involves finding thresholds on which to partition the data (univariate), but you can discretize on more than one feature at a time (multivariate).

In discretization, the intuition is to find quality boundaries on the data such that the number of feature values that fall between two boundaries is

[†] Chapter 4.
[‡] Chapter 2.

reasonably well distributed. You use this approach if you suspect that small differences between values in dense parts of the space should be taken more seriously than differences in sparse areas. Age is a great example: a difference of one year in age at age 5 is much more important than a difference at age 85. In discretization we want similar instances to discretize to the same value,[41] including, for example, to deduplicate multiple aliases for the same person.[49] The positive impact of discretization has long been established in the field:[191]

Many machine learning (ML) algorithms are known to produce better models by discretizing continuous attributes.

2.2.1 Unsupervised Discretization

Reducing the resolution of a set of numbers without referencing other data involves finding an underlying structure in them. This means realizing that, for example, the values are grouped around certain centres of mass or appear spaced regularly at a certain distance. Finding such a structure is the goal of unsupervised learning. We will see some simple yet popular techniques known as binning before discussing general clustering (Section 2.2.1.2). Note that unsupervised discretization is usually vulnerable to outliers[213] (Section 2.4). Also, these unsupervised discretization techniques lose classification information as they might merge many points with different values of the target class into the same discretized feature value.

2.2.1.1 Binning
Simple discretization techniques seeking to split the segment of observed feature values into equal segments either in size or length are called **binning** and have a long history in statistics. This is also known as discrete binning or bucketing. The original objective of binning was to reduce the error of observations by replacing them with a representative value (usually the centre) for the small interval (bin) on which the value is located. Intervals can be chosen so they have all the same size or they have the same number of observed values on each interval (quantiles). Alternatively, a bin size can be chosen and the full set of real numbers can be split into an integer number of intervals of the same size (rounding).

In the case study in Chapter 6, the target variable is binned using an equal frequency interval approach (Section 6.3.1.2). For 50,000 cities, their population range from 1,000 to 24,300,000. Splitting into 32 bins using a logarithmic scale, the first bin has boundaries (1,000; 1,126), and the last bin is (264,716; 24,300,000). The total discretization error incurred is 300 million (an average of 6.5% per city).

Equal Interval Width. This binning approach involves taking the range and dividing it into k equal regions. It is very sensitive to outliers, so either remove them first or do not use them if you have many outliers. It is one of the easier approaches but if you know anything about your data, you can do better.

Equal Frequency Intervals. In this approach, you take m instances and divide them into m/k values (possibly duplicated). It helps when you have different levels of data density in different regions of the possible values. This approach is useful when equal intervals will result in many empty bins due to clustering of points. [352][†] It operates by sorting the values (including duplicates) and picking the boundary items at the m/k-th position. Alternatively, the values can be recursively divided using the median element, which will be discussed in Chapter 6.

Rounding. A straightforward way to fully transform a real number into an integer is to multiply the real number by a fixed number, and then round it to a whole number on a given base (or just truncate it). For example, given the feature values $\{0.7, 0.9, 1.05, 0.25\}$ with multiplier 3 and flooring on base 10, we will obtain discretized features $\{2, 2, 3, 0\}$. The multiplier and base ought to be chosen based on domain knowledge. Otherwise, unsupervised learning can help, but in that case you will be better served using clustering, discussed in the next section.

Winsorising (Thresholding). A simple way to binarize or coalesce ordered feature values is to apply a threshold over them. Values below the threshold become an indicator feature with a value of false. Otherwise the feature value is true. [196] The threshold can be chosen in the middle of the range (maximum value minus minimum value), which is the mean, the median or such that the target class is evenly distributed (in a supervised variant of this approach). Winsorising is important for some ML algorithms that can only operate over binary features such as certain implementations of maximum entropy or certain types of SVMs. With an appropriate threshold, it is possible to boost the signal present in the data.

[†] Chapter 2.

Other Techniques. Maximal marginal entropy adjusts the boundaries so they decrease the entropy on each interval (this is a variation of equal frequency binning discussed earlier).[86] If the total number of different values in your data is small, you can bin by the exact number (e.g., observed value "27" becomes "observed-category-27") and use the resulting bins as categories.[55] Binning can also be applied to existing categorical values, basically coalescing categories,[171] a topic discussed in the next chapter (Section 3.1) in the context of computable features.

2.2.1.2 Clustering

The simple techniques already discussed reduce the feature space considerably and might enable the use of categorical-based ML algorithms over continuous data. Still, there are better ways to capture the underlying distribution of the input features: to apply unsupervised learning over the features. A common technique is to use k-means clustering (discussed next) and then use the number of the cluster ("Cluster-ID") as the feature category[41] (therefore, if you cluster using $k = 20$, you will end up with a feature with 20 categorical classes). Alternatively, it is possible to have the distance to each cluster (or the top clusters, to obtain sparse vectors) as a separate feature.[352] Chapter 7 uses this approach to build feature heatmaps, for example, Figure 7.3, reproduced here as Figure 2.2. The feature values for each feature are split into six clusters, visualized as different levels of gray. The feature heatmap allows for comparison of different historical versions of the same instance, or comparison across different instances. See Section 7.1.1 for the fully worked-out example.

The algorithm k-means[142] is based on the concept of synthetic instances: each cluster is represented by a centroid, a fictitious instance (the synthetic instance). Instead of computing the distances among all instances in the cluster, k-means computes just the distances to the centroids. It receives as parameters the number k of target clusters (which can be estimated using other

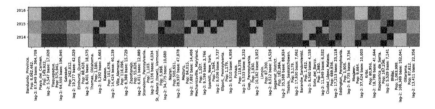

Figure 2.2 Historical features visualization using a feature heatmap. Different levels of gray indicate different feature clusters.

methods such as canopy clustering[226]), the distance function and a procedure to compute synthetic instances from a set of actual instances.

It starts by picking k instances at random as initial centroids (other initialization techniques are possible, for example, kmeans++[13]). In each iteration, it reclassifies each instance as belonging to the cluster that has its centroid closer to the instance. Then, for each cluster, it computes a new centroid based on the instances assigned to it.

This algorithm is an example of **expectation-maximization** (EM), a statistical estimation technique in which the algorithm switches between estimation and modelling steps.[80] Under certain circumstances, convergence is guaranteed, albeit quite slowly. Basically, you continue with the two steps until convergence, in one step you fix the model (assignment of each instance to a cluster), and estimate its parameters (the centroids) and in the other step you fix the parameters and estimate the model.

2.2.2 Supervised Discretization

Supervised discretization received plenty of attention in the 1990s and 2000s, most probably as the need to reduce parameter space was driven by memory bottlenecks. The different solutions proposed to the discretization problem can be organized around many facets and dimensions.[213] We will look into three algorithms of practical importance that are relatively easy to understand and implement and are also representative of many algorithms centred around similar ideas. These algorithms are ChiMerge, MDLP and CAIM. They all work on a single numeric feature, operating over its sorted distinct values.

What is the benefit of the added complexity of using supervised discretization? In the words of Alberto Bietti:[34]

> Unless you have good knowledge or intuition about the common values taken by the feature, hand-picked or equal-width intervals probably won't give good results.

Note that if you use the target class for discretization then you will need to find the boundaries over a held-out dataset that you will not be able to reuse in subsequent training. Otherwise, reusing the training data with the discretized features will result in a weak target leak: the ML will be misguided into trusting the discretized feature too much.

Discretization is a search problem where each algorithm is defined by (given candidate places to split into intervals) a criterion for determining how good a split is and a method to explore the space of partitions.[86]

Adaptive Quantizers. MDLP and CAIM, discussed next, both belong to the family of top-down **adaptive quantizers**, where the observed feature values are sorted and then split recursively, starting from an interval equal to the whole range. Each algorithm in the family has a different criteria to choose where to split an interval and whether to continue splitting. The candidate places (*cut points*) to split are the observed values or a "smart" subset of them. These are incremental algorithms and have the advantage that they do not require a number of internals provided beforehand. In its most computationally expensive version (and from which the name derives), you can train a full classifier on each partition and choose the cut point where the classifier performs better.[60]

2.2.2.1 ChiMerge

The ChiMerge discretizer[179] presents a bottom-up approach. Its starting point considers each observed feature value as a separate internal. At each step of the algorithm, it merges an interval with its neighbour depending on the χ^2 statistical test (discussed in the context of feature selection in Section 4.1.1 in Chapter 4) over the values of the target class associated with each interval. It merges an interval with its neighbour if the χ^2 test cannot reject the null hypothesis, that is, we cannot show the two sets to be statistically independent. Besides its simplicity and statistical justification, it can be applied to multiple features at once and can do joint discretization and feature selection.

2.2.2.2 MDLP

Fayyad and Irani[103] propose using the entropy of the target class to choose the optimal partition cut point. They define the entropy of the interval S as:

$$\tilde{H}(S) = -\sum_{i=1}^{k} \frac{\#(C_S = i)}{|S|} \log \frac{\#(C_S = i)}{|S|}$$

where k is the number of categorical values the target class can take and $\#(C_S = i)$ is the number of instances in S that have its target class equal to i. For a given cut point, we can define the split entropy defined as the weighted average (weighted on sizes) of the entropy for the two intervals obtained by splitting at the given cut point. If the splitting at a cut point is meaningful, the remaining intervals will have a more homogeneous class (which should facilitate learning and make the feature more informative). MDLP uses split entropy as the metric to score different cut points.

To speed up the algorithm, the authors prove a theorem that shows the only cut points that need to be considered are *class boundaries*. A class boundary is a feature value where the value of the target class has changed from its adjacent neighbour. The number of class boundaries will hopefully be much smaller than the total number of observed feature values. As a stopping criteria, the algorithm uses a minimum description length (MDL) criteria that stops splitting when the description (in bits) for the class labels without splitting is shorter than encoding the labels for the two resulting intervals.

While the algorithm seems very similar to decision trees,[48] it produces a different discretization: decision trees are local methods while the discretization technique discussed here is a global method. Local methods suffer from "data fragmentation" where intervals may be split unnecessarily, producing suboptimal results.[16] Global discretization algorithms have been shown to help decision trees and outperform their embedded discretization functionality.[213]

2.2.2.3 CAIM

The CAIM algorithm[197] uses the mutual information between the feature intervals and the target class. The authors claim that it generates very few intervals. CAIM seeks to minimize the loss of feature-target class interdependency. It uses the confusion table ("quanta matrix" in the paper, see Figure 2.3) between the intervals found so far (starting with a single interval covering the whole range of observed values) and the different categories of the target class. From the confusion table they derive CAIM scores by looking at the maximum counts for a class on a given interval ($\max_r$), versus the rest:

$$\mathrm{CAIM}(D) = \frac{\sum_{r=1}^{n} \frac{\max_r^2}{M_{\circ r}}}{n}$$

where the discretization D splits the feature into n intervals and $\max_r$ is the maximum value in the r-th column of the quanta matrix. The authors'

Class	Intervals					Class Total
	$[d_0, d_1]$	...	$(d_{r-1}, d_r]$	...	$(d_{n-1}, d_n]$	
C_1	q_{11}	...	q_{1r}	...	q_{1n}	$M_{1\circ}$
$\vdots$	$\vdots$	...	$\vdots$	...	$\vdots$	$\vdots$
C_i	q_{i1}	...	q_{ir}	...	q_{in}	$M_{i\circ}$
$\vdots$	$\vdots$	...	$\vdots$	...	$\vdots$	$\vdots$
C_S	q_{S1}	...	q_{Sr}	...	q_{Sn}	$M_{S\circ}$
Interval Total	$M_{\circ 1}$	...	$M_{\circ r}$	...	$M_{\circ n}$	M

Figure 2.3 CAIM quanta matrix, adapted from Kurgan et al.[197] It is a confusion matrix for a feature split into n intervals, for a target class with S categories.

expectation is that "the larger the value of CAIM the higher the interdependence between the class labels and the discrete intervals."

The cut point with the highest CAIM score is chosen at each iteration. If no segment produces a CAIM score higher than the larger CAIM encountered (after k steps, where k is the number of values the target class can take), it stops. In their evaluation of 30 discretizers,[118] García and colleagues conclude:

> CAIM is one of the simplest discretizers and its effectiveness has also been shown in this study.

2.3 Descriptive Features

Sometimes the ML does not need the actual data but only a compact statistical summary: the task can be solved knowing general characteristics about the shape of the data distribution. The general term to refer to such indicators is **descriptive statistics**. We will see histograms next, the most common descriptive features, and then present other descriptive features in Section 2.3.2. This approach is particularly important when an instance contains a large number of similar and low information features, like pixels or other sensor data.

Dense vs. Sparse Feature Values. Using descriptive features has the advantage of producing reliable, dense features. For example, if a user review is in a language different from the language used in the train set, a text-length feature might still be informative while any indicator feature for particular words will most probably be all zeroes. Dense feature vectors, however, might slow down considerably ML algorithms designed to operate over sparse feature vectors, like SVMs.

In their winning submission to the KDD cup (cf., Section 1.7 in the previous chapter), Yu and others[341] combined two systems with different approaches, one using binarization and discretization, which produced a very sparse feature set, while the second approach used simple descriptive statistics and thus produced a dense feature set. Their results show the value of the dense approach.

2.3.1 Histograms

Another way to obtain a holistic view of the features is to summarize their behaviour by means of a **histogram**. A histogram is a simple representation of the distribution of values for a set of features. It is amply used in image

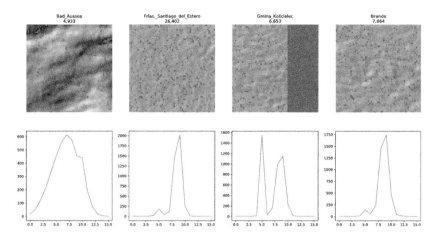

Figure 2.4 Four random settlements and histograms. The histograms show that
Bad Aussee is in the Alps, Gmina Kościelec downtown is next to a small pond
and the other two places are relatively flat.

processing. It transforms feature values to frequency values and can handle
continuous data by using bins to define each of the frequency columns.
The original feature vector then has multiple features of the same type. The
histogram feature vector has one feature per bin with its value equal to the
number of features in the original feature vector that fell into that bin.

This is a common technique when dealing with images. Chapter 9 uses
histograms for image classification, Figure 9.5, reproduced here as Figure 2.4,
shows how different images can have similar histograms (Frias and Brande in
the figure), which can help reduce the nuisance variations in the domain. See
Section 9.5 for the fully worked-out example. If you have a large number of
related but otherwise identical features, instead of (or in addition to) using the
features themselves, you can use the number of times a particular feature value
appears in that large collection of features. In the case of a 300×300 black-
and-white image, you can represent the whole image as two features: number
of white pixels and number of black pixels (the simplest possible histogram).
That reduces the number of features from 90,000 to 2 and it might contain
enough information to solve a variety of classification problems (e.g., indoors
vs. outdoors). Or, if you represent each pixel with 30 discernible shades of
gray (5 bits), that accounts for 566,250 bytes of input vector. A histogram then
contains 30 entries with a maximum value of 90,000 per entry (17 bits), for a
total of 64 bytes. Now, if the problem is solvable from the histogram that is a
reduction of almost 9,000 times.

It is interesting to note that, given enough training data, many ML algorithms will learn a decision function that internally computes the histogram or a close approximation to it. If you believe the histogram is related to the problem you are trying to solve, you can spare the ML algorithm that unnecessary burden.

Bag of Words. A theme of this book is to look at techniques used in different fields and abstract them with the hope that you can apply them to new fields of your own. In that vein, while histograms are usually associated with computer vision, it is worth noting that a popular representation in NLP, bag-of-words (**BoW**), is a histogram of words. In this representation, a piece of text is presented to the ML as a fixed vector of size equal to the whole vocabulary observed during training. The feature values indicate the number of times the given word appears in the text corresponding to a given instance. Chapter 8 uses the bag-of-words representation, which for the sentence

> Its population was 8,361,447 at the 2010 census whom 1,977,253 in the built-up (or "metro") area made of Zhanggong and Nankang, and Ganxian largely being urbanized.

would appear to the ML as the token counts:

> ['its': 1, 'population': 1, 'was': 1, 'TOKNUMSEG31':1, 'at':1, 'the':2, 'TOKNUMSEG6':1, 'census':1, 'whom':1, 'TOKNUMSEG31':1, 'in':1, 'built':1, 'up':1, 'or':1, 'metro':1, 'area':1, 'made':1, 'of':1, 'zhanggong':1, 'and':2, 'nankang':1, 'ganxian':1, 'largely':1, 'being':1, 'urbanized':1, . . . rest 0]

See Section 8.4 the fully worked-out example.

2.3.2 Other Descriptive Features

You can consider that the histogram is a particular type of summary for a set of data. More types of summaries are available, including the maximum, minimum, mean, median, mode, variance, length and sum.

Other descriptive features can be obtained by assuming a distribution of feature values. Then, for the values in the raw data for a particular instance, you can compute how close to the assumed distribution they are. By far the most popular distribution is the normal distribution, but other distributions are possible (good candidates include Poisson, bimodal distributions and distributions with "fat tails"). Assuming the data follows a normal distribution, the standard deviation captures a known percentage of the data as it measures the spread of the dataset from the mean. Other metrics related to the normal are possible, here, I discuss skewness and kurtosis.

Skewness. This statistic measures the lack of symmetry in the distribution:

$$s = \frac{\sqrt{N(N-1)}}{N-2} \frac{\sum_{i=1}^{N}(Y_i - \overline{Y})^3 / N}{\sigma^3}$$

This feature is to be applied similar to the histogram feature, given a large number of similar values in the raw data, the skewness value for them becomes the feature. A distribution with a high skewness will have the bulk of its elements to only one side of the mean.

Kurtosis. This statistic measures whether the data is heavy tailed compared to a normal distribution:

$$k = \frac{\sum_{i=1}^{N}(Y_i - \overline{Y})^4 / N}{\sigma^4} - 3$$

Heavy-tailed distributions are common in human data and when mismodelled with normal distributions produce a large number of outliers, which is discussed in the next section. This feature is applied similar to skewness.

Quantiles and Percentiles. These numbers summarize the distribution by indicating the boundaries over which the bulk of the points fall, dividing them into equal number of segments. Q2 is the mean, the segment (Q1, Q2) has the same number of elements as (Q2, Q3) and $(-\infty, Q1)$, $(Q3, +\infty)$. Percentiles are similarly defined over 10 segments.

Text Length in NLP. Descriptive features are not known by that name for all domains and problems. A very common (and successful) feature in natural language processing is text length. It predicts correctly many classes of interest. For example, is the customer happy or unhappy? Unhappy customers tend to leave much longer reviews, with plenty of details to justify their unhappiness. Note that text length is the L_1 norm of the bag-of-words (the word histogram) if there are no out-of-vocabulary words present. Otherwise, text length is more informative.

Other Descriptive Features. In the general case, you can compute the KL divergence (cf., Section 4.3.7 in Chapter 4) between all similar features in the instance (e.g., pixels) and the full probability distribution induced by all the instances. Such feature will tell the ML how "likely" the features are, as compared to the data seen during training.

2.4 Dealing with Outliers

In his book *The Analysis of Time Series,* Chris Chatfield[61]† mentions that

> The treatment of outliers is a complex subject in which common sense is as important as the theory.

Dealing with outliers might be the most domain knowledge–intensive task in FE. You can only drop outliers if you have a story behind them that can assure you they are invalid observations due to the idiosyncrasies of the domain. Indeed, the key issue in dealing with outliers is to differentiate errors from extreme observations. When analyzing the values for a feature, it is not unusual to find values (or small clumps of values) that clearly depart from the rest. The temptation is to remove these values, either the values themselves or to throw away the full instance, as there are few of them and the ML might work better if it focused itself on the more frequent "normal" cases. However, Dorian Pyle in his book *Data Preparation for Data Mining* exemplifies:[263] in insurance, most claims are small but a few are very large. Obviously removing the very large claims will completely invalidate an insurance model.

That is not to say that there is no value in realizing your data presents a large number of outliers; we will see outliers detection briefly at the end of this section. But if outliers are present, you might be restricted to ML algorithms that are robust in their presence. For instance, estimation for covariance matrices are very sensitive to outliers, and so is the mean (in the mean case, you can replace it with the median if there are many outliers).

For some examples of outliers, when working with sensor data, some equipment will produce rather large peaks on their signal when cables are being plugged in or the acquisition system is being switched on. Alternatively, you might know from domain knowledge that the encountered value is impossible (e.g., a patient of 999 years of age). Other examples include: a clerk making an error on entry, credit card fraud, unauthorized access, fault detection on engines, new features on satellite images and epilepsy seizures detection.[151]

From my perspective, outliers make it easier to identify potential data mistakes,[49] but you will have to do the legwork to find whether it is truly a mistake or not. Even though I am repeating myself, I will insist: do not throw out outliers unless you have definite evidence that these are erroneous observations. In his book *How to Lie with Statistics,* Darrell Huff[162] shows that even in normally distributed data, it is common to encounter "suspiciously extreme" values. Dropping them, however, will mislead you away from the true

---

† Chapter 1.

mean and standard deviation of the distribution. *That outlier you are about to throw might be one of your most informative instances.*

If you have determined that certain feature values are outliers, you can drop them and consider them to be **missing values**. Imputation techniques to deal with them are discussed in the next chapter, in Section 3.2. Unless you have a fully automatic method for identifying, removing and imputing outliers, leave them in the test set as-is, otherwise you will not have a correct appraisal of the behaviour of your ML model on production.

2.4.1 Outlier Detection

Outlier detection – also known as novelty detection, anomaly detection, noise detection, deviation detection or exception mining[151] – pertains to identifying outliers, either on a fully assembled dataset or on newly arriving data. Defining what is an outlier is a challenging task. Bannet and Lewis define them as:[27]

> An observation (or subset of observations), which appears to be inconsistent with the remainder of that set of data.

Identifying outliers is important beyond removing them, as data with many outliers might be indicative of a non-normal "fat tail" distribution. Also, the outliers you have received might be clipped or distorted data (what is known as **censored data**). You might want to train a separate model on the outliers, as sometimes they exhibit what is known as the **king effect**,[199] where the top representatives of the distribution behave very differently from the rest of the instances.

In the case of FE, outlier detection interests us for learning a model over the training data and using it to identify unusual instances and their feature values. In the general case, outlier detection techniques can be supervised or unsupervised. In the case of FE, spending extra effort labelling outliers is unlikely, so we will focus on unsupervised techniques. The main techniques are clustering, density estimation and one-class SVMs. When doing unsupervised outlier detection, there are diagnosis and accommodation techniques, where diagnosis just finds the outliers while accommodation seeks to make the ML robust in their presence.

Unsupervised discriminative techniques use a similarity function and clustering. These techniques define an **outlier score** as the distance to the closest centroid. Unsupervised parametric techniques only model the normal class, the new data is anomalous if its probability of being generated from the model is low.[133] Using k-means helps to distinguish sparseness from isolation (sparse means a cluster with a large distance overall, whereas isolated means a single item with large distance to others). Points in sparse areas are not outliers, while isolated points are. Large-scale clustering techniques like BIRCH[346] and DB-SCAN[101] handle outliers explicitly and can also be used but they do not provide a degree of outlier-ness. An intriguing method by Japkowicz and colleagues[168] is based on autoencoders (discussed in Chapter 5, Section 5.4.2). As autoencoders tend to behave poorly on novel data, their reconstruction error can be employed as an outlier score. Similarly, pruned nodes in a decision tree can be used as an outlier detector or, as kernel-based methods estimate the density of the distribution, they can detect outliers by identifying areas of low density.[170] Extreme values theory[272] models the outliers directly as a particular distribution and uses EM to estimate its parameters, including thresholds. If the data has spatio-temporal components, it is possible to leverage special outlier detection techniques.[133]

Finally, outlier detection over human data can have ethical implications that you need to factor into your decisions.[102]

2.5 Advanced Techniques

Many techniques in the following chapters also consider how the features behave when combined, particularly dimensionality reduction (Section 4.3 in Chapter 4) and certain computable features, particularly target rate encoding (Section 3.1 in Chapter 3). I have chosen to discuss them closer to other related techniques, such as feature selection.

There are two other techniques I would like to discuss here: using leaves from a Random Forest as features (discussed in the next section) and delta features, discussed next.

Delta Features. Also known as **correlation-based features**,[193] they involve building a model for the behaviour of the whole feature to produce a new feature that indicates how different the observed original feature in a given instance is from the model for the feature.

The simplest case is to take the average and to encode the difference to the average as the feature (the astute reader will realize that this achieves the same result as to centre the feature so its mean is zero). More interestingly, you can replace the feature with how likely are the feature values. For example, each feature value can be replaced with the percentile in the value distribution (is this feature value the top 10% more common values? the top 25%? etc.). You can see an example of this in the case study in Chapter 7, Section 7.1.1.

A similar concept are **z-scores**, the number of standard deviations that feature value is from the mean:[239]

$$z = \frac{f - \bar{f}}{\sigma}$$

As with other complex FE techniques, delta features will result in a complex featurizer that needs to be available together with the trained ML model for production deployment. That is, the means, histograms, etc., obtained from training data are then needed to compute these delta-features on test data and ought to be kept available together with the ML model.

Random Forests Feature Induction. Vens and Costa[315] present an exciting way of benefiting from the combined set of features: train a Random Forest and use the different paths as produced by the forest as features:

> Intuitively, two instances that are sorted into two nearby leaves share more similar features than two instances that are classified into leaves far apart.

The new feature vector is a concatenation of binary features obtained for each tree in the trained forest. For each internal node in the decision tree, a binary feature is generated, indicating whether the condition at the internal node holds or not over the instance. Notice how different trees intermix and combine different features, and how the Random Forest is normalizing, handling outliers and producing descriptive features automatically for us. In a way, it encapsulates all the techniques described in this chapter and more. If you train the random forest with many trees, you will achieve an expansion of your feature set. Or you can train a few shallow trees and obtain a reduction. You can combine the original features plus the tree features too.

2.6 Learning More

This chapter has described techniques usually considered part of a data preparation pipeline. General books on the topic such as Dorian Pyle's *Data Preparation for Data Mining*[263] or Jeff Leek's *The Elements of Data Analytic Style*[204] can be a good reference for this. In the same direction, the article *Tidy Data* by Hadley Wickham[324] can be of interest. For available tooling for binning and outlier detection, you might want to look into OpenRefine (formerly GoogleRefine).[22]

Discretization is a well-studied topic. I have referenced four surveys in this chapter,[86,213,191,118] and each of them is worth studying. I found the one by Dougherty and colleagues[86] to be the most succinct and easy to read.

Finally, outlier detection is a topic with many books written about it, from which *Outlier Analysis* by Charu Aggarawal[2] is a great resource. For a recent survey, see Hodge and Austin.[151]

3
Features, Expanded: Computable Features, Imputation and Kernels

While poor domain modelling may result in too many features being added to the model, there are times when plenty of value can be gained by looking into **generating** features from existing ones. The excess features can then be removed using feature selection techniques (discussed in the next chapter). This approach will be particularly useful if we know the underlying machine learning (ML) model is unable to do certain operations over the features, like multiplying them, for example, if the ML involves a simple, linear modelling. If you believe that the multiplication of the *height* by the *width* might be a better predictor to the target class than any of the features *height* or *width* alone, you might want to add an extra feature that contains the result of such an operation. This is the idea behind **computable features** (Section 3.1). As mentioned, whether that feature is needed or whether it renders the original two features redundant can be settled using feature selection, which is discussed in the next chapter.

Another type of feature expansion involves calculating a best-effort approximation of values missing in the data. That is known as **feature imputation** (Section 3.2). These values might be missing due to structural constraints from the domain or measuring errors. Trying to quantify their impact on the ML model is also paramount.

The most straightforward expansion for features happens when the raw data contains multiple items of information under a single column. That is the topic of **decomposing complex features** (Section 3.3) and it relates to ongoing efforts in the data analytics community to standardize tools and processes based on the meaning of the data. Sometimes this decomposition is as simple as splitting a string, but for truly complex fields, such as times and locations, you will have a number of decisions to make, which should be guided by your understanding of the domain and the ML algorithm being used.

The chapter concludes by borrowing ideas from a technique used in support vector machines (SVMs) called the *kernel trick* (Section 3.4): by projecting the instances onto a much larger dimension, in many cases a simpler classifier (for example, a linear classifier with a margin) can solve a problem that is much more complicated in a lower dimension. The type of projections that practitioners have found useful can be applied directly without the use of kernels.

All in all, any technique targeting feature expansion should be used when you have strong intuitions about their potential benefit. Given a few features, the space of all potential combinations of them explodes combinatorically. Trying them in a brute-force manner is infeasible in all but the simplest of problems. This is a topic of active research, as we will see in the automated feature engineering (AFE) section in Chapter 5, Section 5.4.

3.1 Computable Features

The simpler way of expanding features is by operating over them, that is, by doing a computation that takes existing features as input and produces new features as output. These small programs encode domain knowledge about the problem and dataset and are sometimes referred to as "interaction variables"[171] or "engineered features." For example, if you believe multiplying one feature by the other (say, *height* by *width*) might be a better predictor to the target class (for example, market price of a property) than any of the two features alone, you might want to add an extra feature that contains the result of that operation. This can be very advantageous if multiplying two features is not part of the representation used by the ML algorithm (e.g., naive Bayes). Indeed, computable features are better suited for linear models (e.g., logistic regression) as they do not handle interaction between features very well[25] and less suited for complex models such as neural networks that can model the interactions better.[295] That is not to say neural network models will not benefit from computable features, as we will see in Section 5.4.1, in Chapter 5. For example, trying to learn using neural networks (NNs), a function that is the result of dividing one variable by the other, encounters a much bigger error (mean error of 27 vs. 0.4) than trying to learn their difference (Table 3.1).

These features are intimately related to the concept of feature templates, which we saw in Section 1.5.2.2 in Chapter 1. I have chosen to discuss them in a different chapter because they are used in different parts of the ML process and with a different rationale: Feature templates are a technique from raw data

Table 3.1. *Example of computable features. Adapted from Jeff Heaton's thesis using an independent run of his publicly available algorithms.* [147] *The error columns relate to the complexity of learning such functions using neural networks.*

Name	Expression	Error			
		Std.Dev.	Min	Mean	Max
Difference	$x_1 - x_2$	0.788	0.013	0.410	0.814
Logarithm	$\log(x)$	0.721	0.052	0.517	0.779
Polynomial	$2 + 4x_1 x_2 + 5x_1^2 x_2^2$	0.810	0.299	0.770	1.142
Power	x^2	0.001	0.298	0.299	0.300
Ratio	x_1/x_2	0.044	27.432	27.471	27.485
Ratio Difference	$(x_1 - x_2)/(x_3 - x_4)$	0.120	22.980	23.009	23.117
Ratio Polynomial	$1/(5x_1^2 x_2^2 + 4x_1 x_2 + 2)$	0.092	0.076	0.150	0.203
Square Root	$\sqrt{x}$	0.231	0.012	0.107	0.233

to feature data. They focus on overgenerating features and they need a ML algorithm that can tolerate such overgeneration. It is used in the beginning of the ML process to go beyond raw data that is not structured in a way that can be attacked directly with ML techniques. The type of computable features discussed next requires more finesse and an understanding of the domain. It is to be employed later in the ML process, as part of a feature engineering (FE) drill-down on the data. Note that the meaning of a feature might change due to refinement. [24]

We will now see single-feature transformations, arithmetic combinations and different types of conceptual changes to the coordinate system on which the data is expressed. The discussions that follow are specific examples of a **feature drill-down**, the idea that if you have a feature that seems effective, you might want to consider providing variations of it. If it is binary, you might want to transform it on a probability based on how well it correlates with target classes (target rate encoding). If it is categorical, you can consider reducing the number of categories (by adding an "other" category). If it is discrete, you can threshold it or split it into bins (categories). If it is continuous, you can discretize it or apply a squashing function to it (discussed next).

Single-Feature Transformations. Operating over one feature is the simplest way to do a feature drill-down. Usual operations to consider (what is called the "operator palette" [99]) include e^x, $\log x, x^2, x^3$, $\tanh x, \sqrt{x}$ and a sigmoid operation discussed next. Unless you are using automatic FE methods (discussed in Section 5.4 in Chapter 5), you should have some intuition behind the chosen operation. For example, in the health domain, people being too heavy or too light will pose problems in the form of outliers, so you might want to take the square root.[72] Or, if you have proportional features, you might want to take the logarithm.[72] For an example of dampening features using a logarithm function, see Chapter 6, which concludes the need to use such a transformation from the error analysis in Section 6.3.1. Some single-feature transformations have strong mathematical intuition when considered as feature maps for kernel functions, a topic discussed in the last section of this chapter.

A sigmoid operation refers to a family of squashing functions given by s-shaped functions such as $\frac{1}{1+e^{-x}}$ and it is useful to maintain variations in the middle of the value range while collapsing the end points.[196]

Other squashing functions are also common. A popular one is the Box–Cox transformation that, given λ, is defined[61] as $y_t = \frac{(x_t^\lambda - 1)}{\lambda}$ if $\lambda \neq 0$ or $\log x_t$ if $\lambda = 0$. The value of λ can be approximated by trial and error or obtained via maximum likelihood. Note that the logarithmic and the square-root functions are special cases of the Box–Cox transformation. These transformations are appropriate if you believe the distribution of values has a long tail and you want to coalesce it to strengthen the signal.[196] Scaling and normalization (discussed in the previous chapter, Section 2.1) can also be considered as single-feature transformations. Other feature transformations include batting average (sports), EBITDA (finance) and partisan performance (politics).[99] If some of your values are negative and you need to apply functions to them that cannot be run over negative numbers, you can shift them to ensure all the values are above zero. The discussion from last chapter (Section 2.1) about transforming sparse feature vectors into dense ones applies here, too.

To see whether the transformation is useful, a quick way is to measure whether the correlation between the transformed feature and the target class is better than the correlation between the original feature and the target class.[295] Otherwise, use feature selection techniques described in the next chapter (Section 4.1).

Feature/Target Transformations. There are certain feature transformations, like applying the logarithmic function to the features, that are better performed in tandem with the target class (if numeric).[72] In general, you can apply any invertible function to a numeric target. That might help render the target space more amenable to learning. For an example of this approach in the case study, see Section 6.3 in Chapter 6.

Categorical feature "US State"
50 categories for one feature

$f_{\text{state}} \in \{\text{CA, NY, WA}, \ldots\}$

One-Hot Encoding
assign a separate feature for each state
total of 50 features, $f_{\text{CA}}, f_{\text{NY}}, f_{\text{WA}}, \ldots$

$f_{\text{state}} = \text{CA} \iff \langle f_{\text{CA}}, f_{\text{NY}}, f_{\text{WA}}, \ldots, f_{\text{FL}} \rangle = \langle 1, 0, 0, \ldots, 0 \rangle$
$f_{\text{state}} = \text{NY} \iff \langle f_{\text{CA}}, f_{\text{NY}}, f_{\text{WA}}, \ldots, f_{\text{FL}} \rangle = \langle 0, 1, 0, \ldots, 0 \rangle$

Figure 3.1 One-Hot encoding example.

Arithmetic Combinations. If a certain combination among features makes sense in the domain of the problem, it can be added explicitly.[99] For example, if there are features such as *height* and *width*, the area (*height* times *weight*) can be equally informative. There should be some intuition behind adding such a thing; adding all arithmetic combinations would be a mistake. For example, when the magnitude of the numbers differs too much, you might want to focus on ratios.[324] Because the combination space here is so large, you need to use as much domain information to guide you as possible, for example, hierarchical information within the feature space.[341] They are also called "polynomial features."[49][†] Certain feature combinations are harder to learn by different ML algorithms, see Figure 3.1. Chapter 6 trains a system to predict the population of a city. Error analysis shows the value of the features *city area* and *population density*. As the population of a city equals its area times its population, this insight enables a great computed feature, which in turn is available for a quarter of the instances; see Section 6.4 for details.

Winsorizing (Thresholding). A simple way to binarize or coalesce ordered-feature values discussed in the previous chapter is to apply a threshold over them. Any of the techniques discussed in the discretization section of Chapter 2 (Section 2.2) is applicable here to compute the threshold. A related approach is to use the difference to the threshold or its ratio to it rather than binarizing the feature.[196] An example of thresholding at zero is shown in Section 10.3 in Chapter 10.

Cartesian Product. If two features are to be taken together (for example, floor and apartment number), taking the Cartesian product of their values and using

[†] Chapter 9.

that as a single feature might help strengthen the signal available for the ML algorithm.[196] Please note that this is the opposite of decomposing a complex feature (Section 3.3). You will be strengthening the signal by indicating explicitly to the ML algorithm that these features are to be considered together. It can also help if certain segments of the product are impossible in practice. For example, if there are no apartments numbered 3 or 4 after the tenth floor, without using a Cartesian product the ML model will need to allocate parameters to cover such cases.

Changing the Coordinate System. Another type of transformation that can help a ML algorithm are changes to the coordinate system. For example, changing from Cartesian coordinates to polar coordinates (a list of common coordinate transformations is available on Wikipedia[326]). If you believe the angle between the two points might be meaningful, Cartesian coordinates will not be very helpful. It will be better to express x, y as a radius r and an angle θ:

$$r = \sqrt{x^2 + y^2} \qquad \theta = \text{atan2}\,(y, x)$$

Or, in the case of colours, to go from RGB (*red, green* and *blue*) to HSV (*hue, saturation* and *value*), again if you believe that the luminescence is meaningful, pure red, green and blue values will not be very helpful. Without these changes, the ML algorithm will just pick part of the signal (for example, high *red* values if there are many red images) but will fail to generalize. You can see an example in Chapter 10, Section 10.1.

One-Hot Encoding. When operating with categorical features, certain regularities in them might be lost with ML algorithms that have a hard time representing them. Also, some other ML algorithms might represent them as numbers, giving the false implication of them being ordered. One-hot encoding is a way to transform a categorical feature with n possible values into n indicator features such that only one of them is true at a given time.[72,341] It is very popular with neural networks, particularly with softmax layers[125] (also known as "dummy variables"[171] or "one radix notation."[45]) See Figure 3.1 for an example. While they are a requirement for certain algorithms, this change can help any algorithm, the intuition being that if one particular value is more impactful, this representation makes that information more easily available to the learning algorithm. By allowing multiple indicator features to be true at the same time, this is also a standard representation for sets, as discussed in Chapter 5, Section 5.1.1. For an example of one-hot encoding for categorical features in the case studies, see Section 6.3 in Chapter 6.

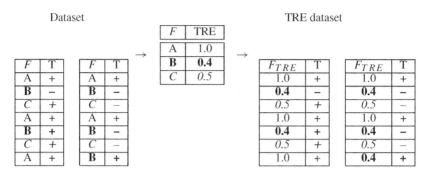

Figure 3.2 Example of target rate encoding. (The dataset is split into two tables to fit into the figure.) The categorical feature F has three categories, {A, B, C}. The category "A" always appears with the target class "+" so its target rate encoding is 1.0 (100%). This example is overfit; the target rates should be computed out-of-fold.

Target Rate Encoding. A binary feature is in some respect a very "blunt" feature. It is either at 100% or at 0%. To make it more informative, you can compute its rate of agreement with the target class. For example, let us say that 80% of the time the binary feature is true, then the binary target class is also true. Let us also say that 30% of the time the binary feature is false, then the binary target class is true. Then, instead of having the original feature as true or false, you can set it to 0.8 when it is true and 0.3 otherwise.[36] If there are multiple target categories, you can have a target rate for each of the categories. See Figure 3.2 for an example. It is better if you estimate these firing rates on a separate set from the training set, otherwise the ML will trust these features too much (i.e., it will overfit).

This idea of expanding and making a categorical/binary feature more informative allows many variations, some more complex than others. An alternative is to let go of the target altogether and just represent each categorical by its frequency counts.[196] The fact that a given category is rare or frequent might be more informative than the category itself. If the target is not categorical, you can estimate the mean of the target variable for each possible category and use that mean as the value of the new feature. Or you can also estimate the class ratios rather than the mean. Again, this has to be done on held-out data different from the training data (what is usually described as "out-of-fold" when doing cross-validation, see Section 1.3.2 in Chapter 1). Also known as categorical encoding,[196] CFAR (correct first attempt rate),[341] correct firing rate, "leave one out encoding"[99] or "bin counting."[352]†

---

† Chapter 5.

The interesting aspect of this approach is how it will conflate categories that may be indistinguishable when it comes to predicting the target class. This engineered feature might have a much stronger signal than the original feature, particularly if the number of categories was large.

This process can be applied to any variable but it is better suited for categorical variables for which we have a strong intuition that they will make a good predictor; however, feature importance analysis (described in the next chapter) indicates it is not the case so far. A fully worked-out example is presented in Chapter 6, where the target variable is the population of a city. For country-related categories, using target rate encoding (TRE) is akin to transforming the value into the average city population for that country, see Section 6.4 for details.

Coalescing Categories. For categorical features with many categories, not all categories might be needed. Dropping them might help amplify the signal available in the data. The coalesced categories then go to an *OTHER* category.[196] In general, you might want to coalesce infrequent categories or categories that will present a rather poor correct firing rate. For example, if a categorical feature, *colour*, has 10 possible values, of which three (*red, green* and *blue*) appear more than 20% of the time and the rest seldom appear, conflating the 10 values into four (*red, green, blue* and *other*) might help strengthen the signal. The feature with the coalesced categories might replace the original feature or be used alongside. See Section 6.3 in Chapter 6 for an example.

Expanding Features Using External Data. Many times there will be value to add external data from separate sources. This is equivalent to adding common-sense knowledge. For example, if the problem involves geographical data, say, when the target is to predict fuel consumption during a road trip, adding distance to major cities might help. This is very domain dependent. The important aspect to remember here is that you can go beyond the training data at hand. For an example, see Section 10.2 in Chapter 10. When the expansion happens at the instance level; that is, when it involves creation of new instances, it becomes an instance engineering problem, discussed in Section 5.2 in Chapter 5.

Ensemble Methods as Computable Features. Ensemble methods in ML involve training multiple ML models and combining them using a final model. It is conceptually possible to consider a simple ensemble as an engineered feature: a computable feature model is trained over a subset of the data and its predictions then used as a new feature. In this conceptual framing, you will be considering the computable feature model as a model that learns a computable feature, in line with supervised automated feature engineer (FE) discussed in Section 5.4.1 in Chapter 5. This idea is very productive. Deep learning (DL), as a way to obtain richer representations from raw data, fits into this criteria.

Aggregate Features. Pivot operations as described in Section 3.3 are not the only type of feature aggregation that can be accomplished. Other operations that can be performed are count operations, conditional count operations (count-if), and, in general, any database aggregate or spreadsheet operator.[18]

Advanced Techniques. Other advanced techniques for computable features are covered in other sections of this book, such as decorrelating variables, whitening the data and using trees from a random forest as features (Section 2.1 and Section 2.5 in Chapter 2) or handling numerical zeroes as missing data (see next section).

Domain-Specific Computable Features. In NLP, it is common to include features that speak of the "shape" of a word:

- Whether it is in all uppercase characters or not
- Whether it includes numbers
- Whether it includes accented characters

This approach can be used for features in other domains.

3.2 Imputation

Your training data may have instances where a particular feature value is unknown. This might be due to artifacts on the acquisition, due to merging from different data sources or due to limitations within the feature extractors. Some ML libraries (e.g., Weka) represent missing data explicitly, while others (e.g., scikit-learn) do not. Beware of their impact.

Most training data constitutes a partial sample of the population under study. The partial aspect might present itself as information explicitly missing during the data collection, due to sensor failure, database schema changes or loss of data during storage or transport. In this section we deal with missing data explicit in your training data. A separate topic is to deal with missing data implicit in the sampling process, to quantify and modify our observed values to accommodate for data you believe lies outside your current sampling. That process, probability distribution smoothing, takes the form of a special normalization of the values and requires looking at all the features at once, as already discussed in Section 2.1.2, Chapter 2.

There are different strategies to deal with missing data, ranging from simple approaches such as assigning a fixed value to those entries to techniques as sophisticated as involving training new classifiers just to deal with missing values. Each technique has its pros and cons and situations where they are appropriate to use but by far the worse thing you can do is to ignore the problem and assume your default ML toolkit will handle missing data in a reasonable manner. First, as mentioned, while some toolkits represent missing data explicitly (e.g., Weka), others might not (e.g., scikit-learn). If your missing data is conflated with zero (or empty or first category) your results will be severely compromised if you have missing values aplenty. Therefore, a good first step when dealing with missing values is to identify how many and what type of missing values you have. [204]

At this stage you can also try to identify structural missing values (e.g., number of pregnant male-born patients), as these numbers can be dropped or ignored. Structural missing values are also known as **censored values** and require different techniques to deal with them. [324] In the worse case you will need to train two models, one for the data with all features and another one for the data when certain features cannot possibly exist. As such, you need to know why your data may be missing. [204] At that stage you are presented with a number of alternatives to correct the missing values. I will discuss them in order of complexity and ease of deployment.

Dropping Instances with Missing Data. If your training set is large enough and there are just a few instances with missing data, you might as well drop those instances. [49] This can be very dangerous in the general case, as instances with missing data tend to be representative of particular phenomena in your data collection (for example, early data). But the numbers might show that the risk of the additional error is not worth the extra effort imputing the missing values.

Missing Data Indicator Feature. A first approach to handle missing data is to explicitly signal to the ML algorithm about the existence of the missing feature. The feature vector is thus expanded with an indicator feature for each feature that might contain missing values. [51] Those features will be true whenever the value was missing in the original data. This feature is independent of whether the value is replaced by a default (imputed) value as discussed next. See Section 6.4 in Chapter 6 for an example.

As mentioned before, sometimes the fact that the data is missing constitutes a strong signal on itself,[49] stronger than the original feature. For example, if a feature is *time-spent-reading-extended-product-description;* a missing value here may indicate that the visitor did not read the extended product description. That fact might be a stronger predictor for a target class capturing the final purchase decision.

Imputing Categorical Data. If the feature being imputed is categorical, you can extend the categories to include a *MISSING* category.[49] This imputation and others discussed next are best used concurrently with the missing data indicator feature.

Imputing Timestamped Data. Missing data due to sensor malfunction can be easily imputed with the last known value of the sensor, as close in time to the instance as possible.[49] Judgment should be used to pick a temporal threshold and avoid imputing values too far in time. If no domain knowledge about such a threshold is available, it can be computed from the data analyzing the variability of the feature over time. More complex approaches involving time series will fall into the custom ML approach discussed at the end of this section. Chapter 7 looks deeply into temporal imputation, comparing using the mean value over a sliding window versus a moving average with a memory with exponential decay. For the data available in that case study, the exponential decay was more performant. See Section 7.2.1 for the fully worked-out example.

Replacing with a Representative Value. When you do not have information about a value, that is, when it is missing, you do not want to complete it with a value that will be picked up as a strong signal by the ML algorithm. In the event of missing data, you want the ML algorithm to ignore this feature as much as possible. You can accomplish that by making it look as nondescript as possible, by replacing it with the average value (the mean or the median if there are strong outliers[49]) or the most common value (the mode). While this approach is very simple, it is still much better than leaving the values as zeroes as with many ML toolkits. In the same vein, if your data has many naturally occurring zeroes, you might want to look at them in detail to see whether the zeroes constitute a separate phenomena on themselves,[196] for example, by adding an indicator feature about whether the values are zero or not.

A way to check whether your imputation is misleading your ML is to separate data with missing values and check whether a model train on that data will behave very differently from a model train on that data plus the imputed data.[263] As the imputed data is statistically easier to tell apart, it might look like a strong and conclusive signal to the ML. Sometimes adding noise to the imputation mechanism can help, too.

Training a Separate ML Model for Imputation. By far, the most reliable way to impute data is to train a classifier or a regressor on the remaining (observed) features to predict the missing value.[49] Notice that picking a representative value is a special case of this technique (using a linear classifier with no features). A reliable choice and one that is relatively fast to operate is to use a k-NN algorithm. It also provides a strong intuition: instances similar to the current instance have this feature defined in a certain way. This process does not need to be done out-of-fold (discussed in Section 1.3.2 in Chapter 1), as the target class is not part of it (nor it should be). Irrespective of the technique employed, do not forget to include the missing data indicator features. Ultimately, that is the only reliable piece of information you are observing for that feature in that instance. The case study in Chapter 10 uses preference prediction algorithms to impute a training dataset with millions of missing items, see Section 10.3 for details.

Embedded Imputation. Certain ML algorithms can handle feature vectors with missing values directly. Particularly, CART trees as originally proposed by Breiman and colleagues[48] can train surrogate splits at every node of the tree. These surrogate nodes use a different feature to do the split, as a fallback mechanism in case the original feature chosen by the algorithm is missing. This capability is available to Random Forests in their OpenCV implementation.[45] Finally, when solving nonnegative matrix factorization (discussed in the next chapter, Section 4.3.6), it is possible to ignore missing values at the optimizer level.[345]

3.3 Decomposing Complex Features

ML algorithms expect their features to be low-level values, not unlike columns in a DB. Many times, raw data contains fields where multiple pieces of information have been aggregated, for example, through concatenation. In this section we will see approaches to decompose such features. While the idea seems to be simple and straightforward, at which level of granularity to decompose features depends, surprisingly, on the domain of the problem and the ML algorithm being used. The simplest case is to split a field where two data values have been joined together into a string. From there we will look into dates and times (the most common case) and drill down on a discussion about tidy data,[324] an ongoing effort to standardize tools and representations around the meaning of the data.

String Splitting. There are times that, for ease of typing while performing manual data entry, two or more pieces of information are encoded into a multi-character feature.[204] For example, age and gender might be joined together into a multi-digit, single-letter feature value such as "32m" or "56f." A simple string splitting (maybe with the help of regular expressions[111]) will suffice to expand these values. Beware of typing error or mistakes in your data (e.g., "56w" instead of "56f"). In some cases, realizing that information is encoded and can be split apart is key to modelling,[49] like in the case of using the *cabin* (e.g., "C123" where "C" indicates C-deck, the level of the deck is a great predictor of survivability) feature in the famous Titanic survival dataset.[173]

Dates and Times. By far the most common case of complex data values are date or time values.[51] While it is possible to have enough data to learn what ranges of seconds from January 1, 1970 constitute weekends, it is doubtful you will have such data available and your classifier will generalize poorly. Instead, if your feature is a timestamp, expand it as multiple features for day, day-of-the-week, etc. At this stage the issue of problem-dependent level of granularity arises. Whether you want to represent your dates as day-of-the-week, or day-of-the-year or week-of-the-year depends on your intuitions about the problem. The discussion about discretization in Section 2.2 in Chapter 2 is also very relevant to dealing with times: whether to use hours, minutes or quarter hours are valid discretization options. If you start drilling down into timestamps you might encounter cyclical behaviour and might want to encode the timestamps as positions within that cycle, a topic discussed in the case study in Chapter 7. For a simple example of expanding a date time string into separate features, refer to Chapter 10, Section 10.2 for a fully worked-out example in the geographical information systems (GIS) domain.

Imputing times also requires extra care as it does not render itself well to simple averages when timestamps cross midnight.[76] Finally, if your data is international, beware of the impact of time zones. If you convert all times and dates to a fixed time zone, do not forget to keep the time zone as a separate feature as it might be very informative on its own. The same goes for inverted seasons in the two hemispheres. If springtime is a meaningful feature, make sure to make it available explicitly and compute it correctly for your Australian users, too. Even in the same locality, daylight savings changes may pose challenges.

Locations. Similar to dates, locations represent a complex feature value that admits multiple decompositions.[127] Whether the location is represented as a string ("Boston, MA") or a pair of GPS coordinates (*latitude, longitude*), you have a choice of granularity in terms of including the city, province (state), country, region, etc. I cover geographical data in the GIS case study in Chapter 10, Section 10.2.

Pivoting and Its Inverse. Another technique to decompose complex features is to apply a pivot,[167] that is, to group multiple instances around the value of a given, usually categorical, feature. Different values of the chosen feature then become new features (or aggregates, like the average, if they appear in multiple rows). See Figure 3.3 for an example. This operation actually creates more complex features rather than decomposing them. It is also common to receive data that has been the result of a pivot operation and realize the ML will benefit from applying the opposite operation (which receives names such as "melting,"[324] "unstacking" or "de-pivot"). The realization here is that the training data rows are to be taken into an aggregated form as a larger, variable-size tuple.

Original Data   →   Data after Pivot

ID	Activity	Target
1	read	n
1	save	n
1	search	y
2	save	n
2	read	n
3	save	n
4	search	n
5	read	y
5	search	y

ID	Read?	Save?	Search?	Target
1	y	y	y	y
2	y	y	n	n
3	n	y	n	n
4	n	n	y	n
5	y	n	y	y

Figure 3.3 Example of the pivoting operation. The original data contains one row per activity, pivoting on session id, then generates binary features for whether the activity was present in that session or not. The target class for the pivot (in this example) is the logical OR of the target class as an aggregated feature.

Retracing the Data. Many times, there lies behind a complex feature aggregated data unavailable from the feature value itself. In such circumstances, going back to the original source might be needed. The takeaway here is to go beyond the available data to seek out source data if you believe it will be useful.[51] In general, you should try to get data as close to its source raw format and operate over that data in a well-documented way, in order to ensure reproducibility.[204] You might encounter this situation while trying to perform the inverse of pivoting when you realize the values are aggregates like the averages for all rows containing a particular value. In Figure 3.3, if you had received the second table, you might want to know after which activity the target becomes true. For example, for Session-ID equal to 1, it happens after the "search" activity. Because the second table contains the aggregated logical OR for the session, that information is not available and it is necessary to acquire and study the first table in the figure.

Tidy Data. The decomposition of complex features aligns itself with the goals of the tidy data concept, defined as "a standard way of mapping the meaning of a dataset to its structure."[324]

It is Codd's third normal form from relational algebra[67] expressed in statistical terms. The goal is for tidy datasets to express meaning through layout:

- Each feature should be in one column.
- Each instance should be in one row.
- There should be one table for each kind of feature.
- If there are multiple tables, they should have a column that allows them to be linked.

Having to transform the data for further processing (that is, having to undergo a data-tidying process) is frequent as many times the data will be in a bad format as tables are set up for human understanding or set up for easy data-entry. You should also watch out for common data problems such as column headers containing values, variables in both rows and columns or multiple observations in one table.[324]

3.4 Kernel-Induced Feature Expansion

Kernel methods operate on a higher-dimension *implicit* feature space. A complex problem in lower dimension might be solvable with a simpler representation (e.g., a hyperplane) in a higher dimension. Figure 3.4 shows some

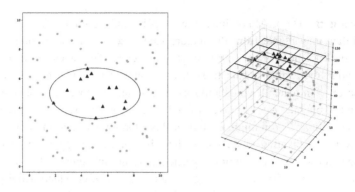

Figure 3.4 Kernel trick intuition.

graphical intuition. The data in the figure is expressed as two features a and b, with a complex, i.e., nonlinear, decision boundary (an ellipsoid). When transforming the original feature vector into three features, $f_1 = a, f_2 = b, f_3 = a^2b^2$, the decision boundary becomes a simple hyperplane, i.e., linear. Instead of explicitly representing the higher dimensions, the *kernel trick* operates on the inner product of the vectors in the higher-dimensional space. [180] Formally, a kernel over features $\vec{x}$ on a lower dimensionality space $\mathcal{X}$, is a function

$$K : \mathcal{X} \times \mathcal{X} \to \mathbb{R}$$

The kernel trick involves expressing K as an inner product in a different space $\mathcal{V}$: [153]

$$K(\vec{x}, \vec{x}') = \langle \varphi(\vec{x}), \varphi(\vec{x}') \rangle$$

where $\varphi: \mathcal{X} \to \mathcal{V}$ is the "feature map" function, which is the focus of this section.

Kernels define a distance between instances in the higher-dimensional space and are employed mainly in SVMs, but can be used in other methods such as kernel perceptron, ridge regression and Gaussian processes.

Using kernel methods lets you benefit from the higher dimensionality space without paying the extra computational costs associated with higher dimensions because operating over the inner products is cheaper than explicitly operating in the higher-dimensional space. [342] In this section, I will take a different view on the topic, looking explicitly at the mapping to the higher-dimensional space, as it can be useful to apply it over a subset of the feature vector for your task at hand. Back to Figure 3.4, if you only have a and b as features, you can use a SVM with a polynomial kernel (described next) and solve the ML problem without the need for additional dimensions. If a and b

are two features among many, replacing them with a^2, b^2, ab might help your chosen ML model to better solve the problem. This transformation allows you to add knowledge to the ML about the structure behind these two features. You can take advantage of the intuitions behind kernels without being restricted to kernelized ML algorithms, like SVMs.

Kernel methods have been around for decades and there are some established kernels with good intuitions on when to use them. Looking into their implicit dimensionality expansion might help you innovate targeted feature expansions. While this section is more mathematical than the rest of the book, you do not need to worry too much about these details, if you take advantage of the feature expansions presented in Table 3.2, unless you want to compute other feature expansions yourself.

If you want to let go of feature interpretability, you can also use recent techniques to generate random features from kernels.[88,265] Particularly, Rahimi and Retch show that picking random sinusoids from a Fourier decomposition of the kernel function is a valid feature-based approximation for it.[264]

The basis of kernel methods is a powerful theoretical result known as Mercer's theorem,[231] which says that for any given function K that defines a

Table 3.2. *Explicit feature maps.*

Kernel	Parameters	Dimension	Feature Map Size
Poly	$c, d = 2$	2	6
	$\left\langle c, \sqrt{2c}\, x_1, \sqrt{2c}\, x_2, \sqrt{2}\, x_1 x_2, x_1^2, x_2^2 \right\rangle$		
Poly	$c = 2, d = 2$	3	10
	$\left\langle c, \sqrt{2c}\, x_1, \sqrt{2c}\, x_2, \sqrt{2c}\, x_3, \sqrt{2}\, x_1 x_2, \sqrt{2}\, x_1 x_3, \sqrt{2}\, x_2 x_3, x_1^2, x_2^2, x_3^2 \right\rangle$		
Poly	$c, d = 3$	2	10
	$\left\langle c^{3/2}, \sqrt{3}\, x_1^2 x_2, \sqrt{3}\, x_1 x_2^2, \sqrt{3c}\, x_1^2, \sqrt{3c}\, x_2^2, c\sqrt{3}\, x_1, c\sqrt{3}\, x_2, x_1^3, x_2^3 \right\rangle$		
RBF	$\gamma = 1/2\sigma^2 > 0$ (approx. at 3)	1	3
	$\left\langle \exp\left(-\gamma x_1^2\right), \sqrt{2\gamma}\, \exp\left(-\gamma x_1^2\right) x_1, \gamma\sqrt{2}\, \exp\left(-\gamma x_1^2\right) x_1^2 \right\rangle$		
RBF	$\gamma = 1/2\sigma^2 > 0$ (approx. at 3)	2	6
	$\left\langle \exp\left(-\gamma\left(x_1^2 + y_1^2\right)\right), \sqrt{2\gamma}\, \exp\left(-\gamma\left(x_1^2 + y_1^2\right)\right) x_1, \sqrt{2\gamma}\, \exp\left(-\gamma\left(x_1^2 + y_1^2\right)\right) x_2, \right.$ $\left. \gamma\sqrt{2}\, \exp\left(-\gamma x_1^2\right) x_1^2, \gamma\sqrt{2}\, \exp\left(-\gamma x_1^2\right) x_2^2, 2\gamma\, \exp\left(-\gamma\left(x_1^2 + y_1^2\right)\right) x_1 x_2 \right\rangle$		

metric over the objects (i.e., symmetric and positive semi-definite), there exists a φ such that K can be expressed as an inner product of ϕ.

Many types of kernels have been proposed in the literature and are in widespread use, including linear kernels, polynomial kernels, the Fisher kernel, radial basis function (RBF) kernels, graph kernels and string kernels among many, many others. We will discuss the feature map (which in the context of this chapter are feature expansions) for two of the most commonly used kernels, the polynomial kernel and the RBF kernel. I will give some explicit formulas you can use in Table 3.2 and pointers for the general formulas. The general form for the features maps exceeds the mathematical complexity of this book.

Selecting a Kernel. Given their active use as part of SVMs, over the years some intuitions have evolved regarding the type of kernels that could be a good match for a given problem. For example, if the solution is expected to behave in a smooth manner, an RBF kernel is to be preferred; or if we believe we need to account for the covariance of the features, then a polynomial kernel has to be given preference.[196]

Polynomial Kernel. Given an integer d, the polynomial degree, and a real number c, the intercept, a polynomial kernel is defined by:

$$K_{\text{poly}}\left(\overrightarrow{x}, \overrightarrow{y}\right) = \left(\overrightarrow{x}^T \overrightarrow{y} + c\right)^d$$

The feature map is a function ϕ_{poly}, such that:

$$K_{\text{poly}}\left(\overrightarrow{x}, \overrightarrow{y}\right) = \langle\phi_{\text{poly}}\left(\overrightarrow{x}\right), \phi_{\text{poly}}\left(\overrightarrow{y}\right)\rangle = (x_1 y_1 + \cdots + x_n y_n + c)^d$$

This kernel needs all its data to be standardized (see Section 2.1 in Chapter 2). In two dimensions, with $d = 2$, its feature map will be[209]

$$\phi_{\text{poly}_2}(x_1, x_2) = (c, \sqrt{2c}\,x_1, \sqrt{2c}\,x_2, x_1^2, \sqrt{2}\,x_1 x_2, x_2^2)$$

which is a feature expansion from two features to six. You can verify that $(x_1 y_1 + x_2 y_2 + c)^2$ equals $\langle\phi_{\text{poly}_2}(x_1, x_2), \phi_{\text{poly}_2}(y_1, y_2)\rangle$. For instance, you will get a $x_1^2 y_1^2$ term, the product of the fourth component of $\phi_{\text{poly}_2}(x_1, x_2)$ with the fourth component of $\phi_{\text{poly}_2}(y_1, y_2)$ in the cross-product. The first feature (c) can be dropped as it constitutes a bias term that is unnecessary as it is often built into the ML algorithm itself, if needed. This might be all you need to give this approach a try; if you have two features, expand them into five features as above. I will now discuss the general case, which is more complex. Table 3.2

showcases two other examples, using three features with $d = 2$ and using two features with $d = 3$.

For the general case, the feature map can be computed using the multinomial theorem[327] (the extension to polynomials of the binomial theorem) and the total number of additive decompositions of the exponent d into $n + 1$ integers.[294]

RBF Kernel. Also known as the Gaussian kernel, it is defined as

$$K_{\text{rbf}}(\vec{x}, \vec{y}) = \exp\left(-\gamma \| \vec{x} - \vec{y} \|^2\right)$$

It ranges from 0 in the infinity to 1 for $\vec{x} = \vec{y}$. In general, γ is defined as $\frac{1}{2\sigma^2}$ and σ is a major tunable parameter: if σ is too big the kernel becomes linear, if σ is too small it will overfit. The feature map can be obtained[292] by the Taylor series decomposition of e^x:

$$\exp(x) = \sum_{i=0}^{\infty} \frac{x^i}{i!}$$

This translates to a feature map with an infinite dimensionality and needs to be approximated. For the simple case of a single feature,[209] this is

$$\phi_{\text{rbf}_1}(x) \mid_i = \exp\left(-\gamma x^2\right) \sqrt{\frac{(2\gamma)^{i-1}}{(i-1)!}} x^{(i-1)}$$

and then computing three or four features for a given feature using the first $i = 1, 2, 3, 4$ in the equation above for a suitable value of γ might help. This produces as many features as the number of values of "i" used. Table 3.2 includes for two dimensions, formulations approximated up to the first two terms. Notice the complex weighting over different exponents of the original feature, the term $\exp(-\gamma x^2)\sqrt{\ldots}$. The general case can be computed from the observation that[77]

$$\exp\left(-\gamma \| \vec{x} - \vec{y} \|^2\right) = \exp\left(-\gamma \| \vec{x} \|^2\right) \exp\left(-\gamma \| \vec{y} \|^2\right) \exp\left(2\gamma \langle \vec{x}, \vec{y} \rangle\right)$$

Here the first two factors do not involve $\vec{x}$ and $\vec{y}$ together so they are easy to separate. Then the third factor can be approximated by the Taylor series for e^x around zero. Table 3.2 includes for two dimensions, formulations approximated up to the first two terms.

3.5 Learning More

Computable features attract plenty of talk online and it is thus not surprising that the best available resources are not in traditional sources but in online forums. See, for example, Quora[72] or specific blogs.[51,196] Imputing missing data has a long history in medical research with very principled approaches and discussion.[298]

Kernels is a topic that has attracted considerable attention over the years and it is still an active research area. The discussion in this chapter is very different from the usual SVM approach as I stressed the implicit feature maps but you might want to look at the book by Scholkopf and Smola,[277] an at-length discussion of learning approaches with kernels. Currently, going from a data-defined K to a ϕ is an exciting topic of active research that might expand the feature maps with data-driven feature expansions.[153] Finally, automated FE handles a number of computable features as part of their search process. Therefore, as their operator palette is explicitly stated, it can provide new ideas, see Section 5.4.1 in Chapter 5. Most of the generated features are hard for humans to understand, but techniques using pattern induction can help in this case.[132]†

This chapter did not discuss automating the expansion of the raw data, as this is quite dependent on the raw data itself (and therefore, domain dependent), but I touch on the topic in the case study on textual data in Chapter 8, Section 8.9.1.

† Chapter 10.

4

Features, Reduced: Feature Selection, Dimensionality Reduction and Embeddings

Central to feature engineering (FE) are efforts to obtain fewer features, as uninformative features bloat the ML model with unnecessary parameters. In turn, too many parameters then either produce suboptimal results, as they are easy to overfit, or require large amounts of training data. These feature reduction efforts can be done either by explicitly dropping certain features (**feature selection**, Section 4.1) or mapping a feature vector, if it is sparse, into a lower, denser dimension (**dimensionality reduction**, Section 4.3). I will also cover how some algorithms perform feature selection as part of their inner computation (**embedded feature selection** or regularization) in Section 4.2, as you might want to try them on your data or modify your ML algorithm with a regularization penalty. Some embedded feature selection algorithms allow feature importance scores to be read out from their models, too.

How many features to use? How many dimensions to further reduce the data? These questions are usually settled through a grid search as part of a hyperparameter search. Otherwise, you can set these numbers to conservative estimates, as done in the case study in Chapter 8.

Due to the poor modelling of ML problems, plenty of the FE discussion in the literature focuses on feature selection to the point that it can become an interchangeable synonym with FE. Of course, feature selection is part of FE. But FE is not *only* about feature selection. I hope this book helps to widen the scope of the term by showing other aspects of FE that are available to practitioners, including the normalization techniques discussed in Chapter 2 and the feature expansion techniques discussed in Chapter 3.

A reason behind feature selection taking the spotlight within FE might lie behind its intrinsic utility for error analysis. Some techniques, such as feature ablation using wrapper methods (cf., Section 4.1.1.4), are used as the starting step before a feature drill-down. Therefore, the utility of these techniques go beyond just feature selection. I exemplify such uses in the case study in Chapter 6 (Section 6.3.1.1). Moreover, the fact that feature selection helps build understandable models intertwines with error analysis as the analysis benefits from such understandable ML models. Still, I believe calling FE simply feature selection misleads users about the whole picture.

4.1 Feature Selection

It is common to approach an ML problem from instances derived from databases or other structured data sources. These instances contain spurious columns (in the sense that they are unrelated to the target) such as National ID numbers, unrelated IDs, etc.[40,41,250] Dropping such features, in what constitutes the **feature selection** process, brings ample value to increasing the signal over the noise, as the ML algorithm would have to sort through large amounts of data to learn that these columns are irrelevant.[180] Worse yet, some algorithms (like naive Bayes) use all the features, irrespective of whether they are relevant or not. In such cases, there is plenty of value in prefiltering the features. Similarly, sometimes the features are not necessarily unrelated but redundant (e.g., weight in kilograms and weight in pounds). Redundant features increase the parameter search space of the ML optimizer unnecessarily,[127] even though they are helpful for building robust models.

Feature selection can also be performed to obtain not necessarily a more accurate model but a model that is easier to understand and interpret by humans, who have an innate difficulty in handling more than a dozen variables.[41] Interpretability is particularly important for domains like bioinformatics where you can encounter millions of features per patient.[281]

These two goals (improved accuracy and interpretability) have been the traditional objective of feature selection. In recent years with the Big Data movement,[225] I have seen an increased interest in feature selection to reduce the *memory footprint* necessary for storing and executing the models and, to a lesser degree, for storing the raw data. Similarly, to reduce the *running time*, both during training and prediction.[134] For the goals of interpretability and footprint reduction, the practitioners are willing to undergo a modest drop in classifier accuracy. In the spirit of Guyon and Elisseeff,[134] I consider feature selection as the opportunity to "focus mainly on constructing and selecting subsets of features that are useful to build a good predictor." Finding all relevant features is not as important, as many redundant features can help produce more robust models.

As personal sidenote, my focus using feature selection had been in reducing memory footprint and algorithmic training time. As such, I have never achieved improved performance using feature selection. My experience in that regard is not unusual.[281] But improved model performance examples are abundant, for example, Brink and others[49] show an example in classifying real from false galaxies in which feature selection netted a 5% improvement in model performance. Feature selection is demonstrated in the case studies in Part Two, particularly in graph data (Section 6.3.1.1 in Chapter 6) and textual data (Section 8.4.1 in Chapter 8).

The usual approach to discuss feature selection involves looking at three approaches: the filter approach, the wrapper approach and embedded methods.[250] Instead, I decided to focus on feature selection as a search process over different feature subsets and divide this problem into the evaluation metrics for feature subsets (Section 4.1.1) and the search process (Section 4.1.2). I keep the distinction of embedded methods, which are ML algorithms that perform feature selection, as part of the internals, and I will discuss them in Section 4.2. Should you use feature selection in your solution? If you feel you have too many features, it is definitely worth trying, as feature selection is one of the FE techniques most widely available in ML toolkits. Besides removing less useful features, the feature metrics discussed next are a great tool to better understand your features, whether you are considering dropping them or not.

I conclude with a quote from a blog post by Saurav Kaushik, on his analysis on online competitions:

> Over time, I realized that there are 2 things which distinguish winners from others in most of the cases: feature creation and feature selection.[176]

4.1.1 Metrics

As feature selection can be understood as searching for a good feature or subset of features, the question is how to automatically ponder how good a feature or subset of features is. You can capture this goodness-of-fit into one number taking into account the target class. You can consider the feature alone, as using feature utility metrics, discussed in the next section, or you can also take into account interactions. The more informed your metric, the more accurate are your results, so you might take into account as well the target ML algorithm (wrapper methods, Section 4.1.1.4) or just the available data.

Once a metric is defined, you can let go of a full search process and use it directly through ranking to provide a reasonable subset of features, however, more complicated search strategies are possible.

The simple feature utility metrics discussed next are fast, as they do not take into account interactions between features, and in the general case, many features operate jointly to predict a class.[25] Still, some of the simple metrics discussed next can function as heuristics to guide a search process.

4.1.1.1 Feature Utility Metrics

I will now discuss single-feature utility metrics. These are metrics that operate over only one feature and their value distribution, together with the target class. They are independent of other features and the ML algorithm employed. While they have limitations, they tend to overfit less as a result, which is always a welcomed characteristic given the harsh nature of the feature selection process (remember, you are about to *throw away information*). All these metrics apply to categorical features (some after mapping them to continuous data), but some also apply to continuous features and targets. I have explicitly marked each as possible. The different metrics build on different assumptions over the data. Which metric should you use? I have offered some thoughts on the topic after presenting the metrics.

We will refer to the feature-target pairs as $\{(f_t, t_t)\}$. In this discussion, I have included the formula for many of these metrics as a fallback if you need to implement it (in the unlikely case it is missing in your toolkit) but, more importantly, to highlight the computation involved, as it is useful to decide when to use each of them. Also, there seems to be a little bit of inconsistency in naming techniques when it comes to toolkits. When in doubt, check their code against the formulas. In the discussion of their implementation, I simplify the math by assuming all features are to be binary. Likewise, I assume the target class to be binary. This is an explanatory simplification. You can use the metrics with multiple classes directly. Metrics that can be applied to numeric features are also distinguished.

Given these assumptions, we will be using the **confusion table**, which is composed of *true positives* (O_{11}), *false positives* (O_{12}), *false negatives* (O_{21}) and *true negatives* (O_{22}). The sum of all observations equals the size of the dataset over which the feature selection process is being executed. For consistency with the nomenclature, we will refer to this as O_{oo}. For some of the metrics we will see next, it is useful to distinguish also the feature positive ($O_{1o} = O_{11} + O_{12}$), feature negative ($O_{2o} = O_{21} + O_{22}$), target positive ($O_{o1} = O_{11} + O_{21}$) and target negative counts ($O_{o2} = O_{12} + O_{22}$). These are all observed counts (thus the "O" name for the variable), and the different metrics will use these counts to estimate different probabilities and combine them into metrics.

We will now see a number of feature utility metrics described in the literature and used in practice. Two single-feature metrics are discussed in other sections: Fisher's criterion (as a single-feature Fisher score, in Section 4.1.1.2) and maximum likelihood estimator (as single-feature classifier, in Section 4.1.1.3). Let us start with simple metrics based on counts.

TPR, FPR. These are ratios between true positives or false positives generated by one feature against the target class, namely O_{11}/O_{oo} and O_{12}/O_{oo}. As you will use these numbers for ranking, you do not need to compute ratios and just sort the features by O_{11} or O_{12}.

Firing Rate. For features with missing values, simply to know how many times that feature is defined can be a powerful metric. Dense features tend to be more useful, although they tax the parameter search more heavily, as some algorithms efficiently focus on instances with a given feature defined when searching for models.

Now let us take a look at metrics based on statistical tests.

Chi-Square. The χ^2 correlation between one feature and the target class[41] is a statistic computed from the confusion table of counts. The χ^2 statistic[237] is used to reject the null hypothesis that the feature chosen and the target class happen at random.[†] Chi-square is a very popular metric but requires all entries in the confusion table to be of a certain size (I recommend more than 30). χ^2 is the difference between the observed values and expected values:

$$\chi^2 = \sum_{i,j} \frac{\left(O_{ij} - E_{ij}\right)^2}{E_{ij}}$$

The expected values can be computed from the row totals. For the binary case, it reduces to

$$\chi^2 = O_{oo} \frac{(O_{11}O_{22} - O_{21}O_{12})^2}{(O_{11} + O_{12})(O_{11} + O_{21})(O_{12} + O_{22})(O_{21} + O_{22})}$$

Pearson Correlation Coefficient. Similar to χ^2, using this statistical metric or mutual information (MI) (discussed next) are among the most popular choices due to their speed.[250] This is a ranking criterion for **regression**, and it captures a goodness of linear fit on individual features. The coefficient is defined as

---

[†] It was developed as an early approximation of MI using the Taylor series and lookup tables.[279] Thanks to Professor Brown for sharing this historical tidbit.

$$R_i = \frac{\text{cov}(X_i, Y)}{\sqrt{\text{var}(X_i)\text{var}(Y_i)}}$$

and estimated as

$$R_i = \frac{\sum_{k=1}^{m}(f_{k,i} - \overline{f_i})(t_k - \overline{t})}{\sqrt{\sum_{k=1}^{m}(f - \overline{f_i})^2 \sum_{k=1}^{m}(t_k - \overline{t})^2}}$$

The coefficient ranges from 1.0 (perfect correlation) to -1.0 (perfect anticorrelation). Values closer to zero indicate no relation. As anticorrelation is equally useful as correlation, feature selection uses the square of the coefficient as metric, R_i^2. It is related to Fisher's criterion and t-test.[134]

The following metric is based on information theory.

Mutual Information. It is the number of bits of information that is known about a second random variable if we know a first random variable. It is related to information theory's **entropy** of a random variable, the amount of information held by the variable. For m categories, it is

$$H(F) = \sum_{v \in \text{values of } F}^{m} -P(f = v) \log_2 P(f = v)$$

MI is the entropy of one of the variables minus the conditional entropy of one variable given the other:

$$I(T; F) = H(T) - H(T|F) = \sum_{f \in F} \sum_{t \in T} P(t, f) \log\left(\frac{P(t, f)}{P(t)P(f)}\right)$$

This metric is related to KL divergence (discussed in Section 4.3.7) as $I(I; Y) = D(P_{x,y} \| P_x P_y)$. For values absent in the universe (i.e., $P(f = f_v) = 0$ or $P(t = t_v) = 0$), the joint probability is zero, and they are ignored by this metric unless you do some smoothing (see Section 2.1.2 in Chapter 2).

To use MI as a feature utility metric, we seek to compute the MI between the feature being evaluated and the target class. The probabilities in the formula can be estimated using counts on the training data:

$$I(X; Y) = \sum_{y \in \{1,2\}} \sum_{x \in \{1,2\}} \frac{O_{xy}}{O_{\circ\circ}} \ln\left(\frac{O_{xy}}{O_{x\circ} O_{\circ y}}\right)$$

Note that MI generalizes well to multiclass classification, as with more classes there is less chance that a random subset will work well on the data.[134] If a joint mutual information can be estimated beyond one feature, this metric can be employed as a multi-feature metric. Estimating the conditional entropy, however, is NP-hard (see Brown and others for details[50]). As the metric indicates the number of information bits gained about the target by knowing the feature, sometimes it is referred as **information gain**, but that term is very ambiguous and refers to a variety of metrics, among those, the Gini impurity, discussed next.[73,110] When in doubt, look at the implementation source code.

Chapter 8 uses the text in a Wikipedia page for a given city to predict its population. Due to the large vocabulary, relevant words are distilled using MI Therefore, a sentence such as

> Its population was 8,361,447 at the 2010 census whom 1,977,253 in the built-up (or "metro") area made of Zhanggong and Nankang, and Ganxian largely being urbanized.

Appears to the ML as

> ['its', 'population', 'was', 'at', 'the', 'TOKNUMSEG6', 'the', 'built', 'metro', 'area', 'of', 'and', 'and', 'largely', 'being']

Table 8.3, reproduced here as Table 4.1, shows the top MI words, many of which make clear semantic sense for the population prediction task. See Section 8.4 for the fully worked-out example.

This next metric is based on a probabilistic interpretation.

Gini Impurity. An alternative view of a feature (or a particular feature value) is whether it splits the instances into easier to solve sub-problems. This criteria is shared with decision-tree building, and this metric is thus also used with them.[48] Given the split induced in the instances by a feature, we can compute how clean the subset is, based on computing how well a random instance

Table 4.1. *Top 20 tokens by MI on the second featurization in Chapter 8; see Section 8.4 for details.*

Position	Token	Utility	Position	Token	Utility
1	city	0.110	11	than	0.0499
2	capital	0.0679	12	most	0.0497
3	cities	0.0676	13	urban	0.0491
4	largest	0.0606	14	government	0.0487
5	also	0.0596	15	are	0.0476
6	major	0.0593	16	during	0.0464
7	airport	0.0581	17	into	0.0457
8	international	0.0546	18	headquarters	0.0448
9	its	0.0512	19	such	0.0447
10	one	0.0502	20	important	0.0447

will be reclassified if all instances were reclassified using the probability distribution induced by their categories.

$$\text{Gini-Impurity}(f) = \sum_v^{feature} impurity(f = v)$$

$$= \sum_v^{feature} count_{f=v} \left(1 - \sum_c^{target} \left(\frac{count_{f=v,t=c}}{count_{f=v}} \right)^2 \right)$$

and for the case of binary target and feature, it becomes:

$$\text{Gini-Impurity}(f) = \frac{2O_{1\circ}^2 - O_{11}^2 - O_{12}^2}{O_{1\circ}} + \frac{2O_{2\circ}^2 - O_{21}^2 - O_{22}^2}{O_{2\circ}}$$

ANOVA. For a categorical feature and a continuous target, the analysis of variance (ANOVA) test can be used. It tests whether there is a difference between groups, by comparing their means and their variances.[239†] In your case, the mean and variances are from values of the target, as produced by grouping the different values of the categorical feature. The expectation is that a feature where the target value is different for different categorical values will be an useful regressor. For example, if the target is "price" and the feature "size" has three categories ("large," "medium" and "small"), the prices of instances with sizes equal to large form a group, but whether that group is independent from the groups formed by instances with sizes equal to medium and small can be determined by ANOVA. This metric returns an F-statistic that indicates whether the groups are similar or different, which can be used for feature selection.[261] This is a generalization of the t-test beyond binary categories.

Picking a Metric. If your data distribution is roughly normally distributed and categorical, the predominant advice is to use chi-square. I have seen chi-square overselect extremely rare features, however, and its underlying statistic is unreliable if any count in the confusion table is less than 30. Therefore, I prefer mutual information, but Gini impurity is also a reasonable choice. Pearson's R^2 works well for continuous features and a continuous target and ANOVA for categorical features and a continuous target. Irrespective of the metric employed, be prepared to analyze the results with as much domain expertise as possible: do the top-ranked features make sense? Is there a particular feature you believe to be particularly explicative? Where did it end

---

[†] Chapter 4.

up ranked? Compare the different algorithms based on these intuitions. Finally, if you are happy with the results provided by a particular metric, double-check for stability by running on different subsets and checking whether the result seems similar or compatible enough. An unstable output means your model will change massively if your training data expands and you were to want to train a follow-up model.

4.1.1.2 Multiple-Feature Metrics

Plenty of attention has been given to metrics that evaluate a single feature in isolation. Evaluating multiple features based on their data behaviour with respect to the target class, however, is seemingly not popular, with the wrapper method discussed in Section 4.1.1.4 being the main exception. The reason may lie in the need to undertake a full search process when you decide to look at feature interactions. At that stage, the feature selection will become an onerous task, and you might as well run the full wrapper algorithm. However, I believe there is plenty of value in using the full search with data-only metrics, as they are fast to compute and will be less tuned (read: overfit) to the chosen ML machinery. Also, there is plenty of value in analyzing feature interactions. As mentioned, single-feature metrics will fail to select two features that need to be together to approximate the target. Moreover, good redundant features will always be picked together as the single-feature score will be high for both of them.[131]

We will show two valid metrics, Fisher score and multifactor ANOVA.

Fisher Score. Extra, irrelevant features will make instances with different target classes seem closer, as they might overlap on these irrelevant features. A good feature subset will then be one where the instances for a given target class are very close to each other and very far from the instances of other classes. This metric is known as the **Fisher score**,[131] defined as the ratio between class variance and the within class variance.[134] It is also related to quality metrics for clustering algorithms – for example, the Dunn index.[137] The full formula for the Fisher score is defined for a subset Z of features, $f_{Z_1}, \ldots, f_{Z_{|Z|}}$,

$$F(Z) = tr(\bar{S}_b)(\bar{S}_t + \gamma I)^{-1}$$

where γ is a regularization parameter to ensure the inversion is computable. S_b is the between-class scatter matrix and S_t is the total scatter matrix,

$$S_b = n_+(\bar{\mu}_+ - \bar{\mu})(\bar{\mu}_+ - \bar{\mu})^T + n_-(\bar{\mu}_- - \bar{\mu})(\bar{\mu}_- - \bar{\mu})^T$$

$$S_t = \sum_{i=1}^{|Z|}(f_{Z_i} - \bar{\mu})(f_{Z_i} - \bar{\mu})^T$$

where $\bar{\mu}_+ = \frac{1}{n_+} \sum \vec{f}_i$ is the mean vector for the positive class and $n_+ = |\{i/t_i = +\}|$ is the number of elements in the positive class and likewise for $\bar{\mu}_-$ and n_-. The mean vector over all classes is $\bar{\mu}$. Instantiating this formula for a singleton Z produces the single-feature utility metric **Fisher's criterion**, defined as

$$F(f_j) = \frac{n_+(\mu_+^j - \mu^j)^2 + n_-(\mu_-^j - \mu^j)^2}{(\sigma^j)^2}$$

where μ_+^j is the mean of the feature when the class is positive (likewise for μ_-^j) and σ^j is the standard deviation for the feature.

Multifactor ANOVA. For multiple categorical features and a continuous target, a multifactor ANOVA[119] (also known as two-factor ANOVA for the case of two features) can be employed. It will allow the user to find subsets of features that work better together with respect to the target value.

4.1.1.3 Single-Feature Classifiers

Another way to evaluate a single feature against the target is to train a single-feature classifier (or regressor). This can be done using the target ML algorithm or a different, simpler one. Of special mention is the **maximum likelihood estimator**, the best possible predictor, probabilistically speaking. It falls in between wrapper methods (which evaluate feature subsets) and single-feature utility metrics.

Strictly speaking, single-feature classifiers are wrapper methods. As with wrapper methods, it is possible to evaluate the feature over the full set (resulting in an overoptimistic metric) or using a held-out set or cross-validation. Also, any metric for ML assessment as discussed in Chapter 1 (Section 1.2.1) can be employed, including custom ones that better fit the problem and domain. Some recommended metrics include ROC curves, TPR, break-even point or the area under the curve as metrics.[134]

4.1.1.4 Wrapper

Instead of analyzing the statistical similarities between the target variable and a feature or a set of features, it is possible to retrain the whole target ML model and analyze its performance on unseen data (via a held-out set or through cross-validation). This process is called a **wrapper method** for feature selection,[189,274] and it is computationally expensive. Evaluating all possible subsets, for the most part, is out of the question for all but the smallest feature sets.

As this technique uses the performance on unseen data to compare different features or feature subsets, to be fully specified it needs the actual evaluation metric to use (F_1 is a good alternative) and the held-out set to use. A note of caution: if the training data is small and the ML algorithm is prone to overfitting (e.g., unpruned decision trees), the performance numbers might vary more due to changes on the train plus test set than changes in the feature set. Therefore, for the wrapper method to be of any practical use, you will need to fix the train plus test sets or the cross-validation folds (the latter can be achieved by passing a fixed seed to the cross-validation algorithm if that option is available in your ML package).

Using the whole ML algorithm might overfit rather boisterously. In the vein that FE is a race against overfitting, you might end up with a higher-performing feature subset if you can use a simpler, less prone to overfitting model in the wrapper. Common alternatives include linear models and naive Bayes. Using a simpler model can also shorten the running time. [134] Some algorithms, like neural networks, allow reusing information from one run to the other.

The advantage of using the whole ML is that wrapper methods do not make any assumptions with respect to the underlining ML algorithm and can be applied to any algorithm. The obvious disadvantage is the computational cost, which might be prohibitive for large feature sets. In the general case, it requires training and testing the system $O(2^{|F|})$ times where F is the original feature set. To reduce its computational cost, individual feature utility metrics can be used to shortlist the features to be investigated at each step, but this becomes a search strategy issue, discussed next.

Feature Importance. Related to wrapper methods, it is possible to take advantage of some of the algorithms that do embedded feature selection (as discussed in Section 4.2) to obtain a feature importance value, as measured by the ML algorithm. For example, random forests produce an out-of-tree feature importance score for each feature as part of their training process. These values can also be used as metrics for explicit feature selection.

4.1.2 Assembling the Feature Set: Search and Filter

Given a quality metric for a feature set, you can then proceed to search for the feature set that optimizes the metric. This search can be done exhaustively but that involves enumerating every subset of features and evaluating the metric on them, what is known as the **SUBSET** algorithm, which is expensive even for the fastest metrics, due to the exponential number of subsets. In general, finding such a subset is NP-hard. [8,40]

A simpler alternative to search for the most relevant feature subset is to use individual feature utility metrics, sort the features and either get the top *k* features or the features above a given threshold. This is known as the **filter approach to feature selection**. It can be combined with the random feature method (described in Section 4.1.2.2) to find a meaningful thresholding value. Besides their speed, filter methods are robust against overfitting. They are limited to single-feature metrics, though, so they are prone to produce suboptimal results. For instance, two good redundant features will score both highly and be both selected. [176]

A **greedy approach to feature selection** (cf., Section 4.1.2.1) is to start with the whole set of features and evaluate the set without one feature at a time, removing the feature that hurts performance the least and then repeat. Or start with only one feature, and add one at a time while it keeps improving the metric. The greedy approach can be executed multiple times over random subsets of the features: this allows the user to then rank the features based on how common they are selected at top or bottom (random selection). [250]

Other search strategies are possible, including stochastic search, simulated annealing and full-fledged gradient descent. In the nested subset method, it is even possible to optimize the goodness function $J(subset)$ using finite differences, quadratic approximation and sensitivity analysis. For certain ML methods, it is not necessary to rerun the full wrapper. [134] If the goodness function $J(subset)$ is monotonic, so that the value of J is less for a proper subset than for a target set, then a Branch and Bound search can be applied.

Finally, certain domains have available lists of taboo features that ought to be avoided in the general case (Section 4.1.3.2).

4.1.2.1 Greedy

As finding the best feature subset is NP-hard, you can instead pursue an iterative process using heuristics. You can start from an empty set and add one feature at a time (**forward feature selection**), or you can start from the full set and drop one feature at a time (**backward feature selection**).

Forward feature selection involves evaluating each individual feature, starting from the feature with a higher score and then adding one feature at a time so that the extended subset improves on the selected metric. This involves evaluating all the remaining features plus the selected feature at each step. If the remaining features are still too many, it is possible to shortlist them using single-feature utility metrics. It is also called **incremental construction** of the feature subset.

Backward feature selection, on the other hand, involves starting from the full set and evaluates the metric for the set without each feature. If there are too many features to evaluate, again, it is possible to shortlist them using the inverse of a single-feature utility metric. Backward feature selection is also called an **ablation study** of the feature set. At each stage, the set is shrunk by the feature that produces the smallest reduction to the target metric. This approach is preferred if the ML performs very poorly with few parameters.[49] It is also called **recursive feature elimination** (RFE).[136] Under the RFE moniker, the name is extended to signify the metric employed. For example, RFE with random forest feature importance is referred to as RF-RFE.[128]

A greedy approach is usually combined with wrapper methods but can also be used with any multi-feature metric discussed in Section 4.1.1.2. With wrapper methods, it is most efficient against overfitting when trained using a different, simpler ML – for example, a linear predictor over an expanded feature set using some added nonlinearities (computable features, cf., Section 3.1 in Chapter 3). Also, note that in practice forward feature selection is faster than backward feature selection, but backward tends to produce better subsets.[134] This method can be accelerated by adding or dropping multiple features at once.

4.1.2.2 Stopping Criteria
Once the search process is defined, you need to specify a stopping criteria (without it, you will end up with all the features you originally have, just ranked). For backward feature selection, you can keep dropping features as long as the performance improves or stays the same. That is, stop when it gets worse. For forward feature selection, you can keep adding features as long as the selected set of features keeps improving the selected metric. However, most utility metrics will be nonzero, and using this technique will render the whole feature set. A better approach is to threshold the value of the metric, but you will need a way to estimate the threshold. We will next see a great technique to estimate a threshold (using a random feature). Alternatively, evaluation over held-out data can also be employed.

Random Feature as Cutoff. Once the feature utility metric has been defined, it is possible to use a **random feature** as a cutoff value[299] (also known as *fake variables, shadow features*[176] or *probe features*[134]), as sometimes it is necessary to define a *minimum utility value* to help drop features and stop greedy methods. For this, you can incorporate a random feature to the set and evaluate it together with the other features.

The random feature could be obtained in a non-parametric way by shuffling actual features values[309] in what constitutes a permutation test. Alternatively, you can use a pseudo-random number (i.e., numbers obtained from a random number generator) sampled from an uniform distribution in the interval $[\min_{feature}, \max_{feature}]$. The utility values obtained for this artificial feature can be used as a cutoff value. It thus provides an empirical model of a random feature's behaviour within this dataset and ML machinery. Real features worse than a random feature can be dropped.

Alternatively, the random features can be used as a stopping criteria. The addition of features to the feature set stops after one or more random features has been selected.

Chapter 6 uses 10 random features and drops all features that appear after three of the random features have been selected. It uses an MI as the utility metric, for a total reduction of about 70 features over a total of 400. See Section 6.3.1.3 for the fully worked-out example.

4.1.3 Advanced Techniques

We will now see a few advanced techniques for feature selection. A related technique in instance engineering is that of **instance selection**. We will touch on that briefly when we go over instance engineering in the next chapter (Section 5.2).

Class conflation techniques – for example, mapping features to a representative value – can be considered feature selection, such as mapping a word to a root form.[341]

For large datasets, the predominant advice[49,†,206] is to use LASSO, discussed in the next section. In terms of automation, there is new exciting technology being developed from the databases community.[10,250,344]

Streaming. When data is arriving continuously and new instances are added in large numbers, the importance of different features might change. It is also possible that new data for existing instances is also being added, resulting in a stream of features. Both situations require special feature selection algorithms.[132‡] The intention is to divide the features into four categories – (1) irrevelvant, (2) redundant, (3) weakly relevant and (4) strongly redundant – and then operate over the data in two phases, first an online relevance filtering and then a redudancy analysis.[334]

---

† Chapter 9.
‡ Chapter 5.

Relief. The Relief algorithm [185] encompasses many new ideas. It samples the training data. As it samples, it keeps a list of positive (I^+) and negative (I^-) instances seen so far. For a newly sample instance, it finds the closest instance in I^+ and I^- using a given distance, such as Euclidean distance. The closest instance with the same class is the closest hit, and the one with the different class is the closest miss. The ratio of closest hit over closest miss for all features is the importance ratio for the feature, which Relief updates as more instances are sampled. The intuition is that irrelevant features will not have any bias on their appearance in I^+ and I^-; therefore, the ratios will be close to 1. The advantages of Relief include taking into account feature interaction, a probabilistic interpretation to choose a termination criteria and the fact that it might converge without seeing all data. [281]

AIC. Instead of selecting features, we can consider that each feature subset defines a different **model** of the data and compare the models using a model metric. [41] One such metric is the Akaike information criterion (AIC), [58] a non-interpretable measure that can be used to compare different models over the same data. It is defined as AIC $= 2k - 2\ln(L)$, where k is the number of parameters in the model and L is the maximum value of the likelihood function for the model – that is, the best possible parametrization of the model given the training data. For ordinary linear regression, leave-one-out cross-validation is asymptotically equivalent to AIC. [325] A similar concept is BIC, the Bayesian information criterion (BIC). [59] BIC is much harsh on the number of parameters. [325]

4.1.3.1 Stability

The optimal subset of features can be quite unstable, meaning small variations in the data will result in very different subsets. If you have two redundant features, a good feature selection algorithm will pick only one of them; which one might depend on very small variations or even the output of a random number generator. To check whether a given algorithm is stable, you can run it over different bootstraps (subsets of your original data) and then apply a stability metric over the feature selection results (i.e., which features got selected and which did not) from the bootstrap runs.

A recent metric by Nogueira and others [246] is a well-justified method to estimate stability. The proposed metric is based on the unbiased sample variance for the selection of each feature, and it is equivalent to Fleiss kappa over two categories (see Section 1.2.1 in Chapter 1). The authors also provide an open-source implementation.[†]

[†] www.cs.man.ac.uk/~gbrown/stability/.

4.1.3.2 Blacklisting Features

A simpler approach to feature selection involves having a list of features known to be bad in a particular domain and always exclude them (for example, Social Security numbers). The most popular such approach in NLP and IR is to use lists of **stop words**,[180] function words that contain little to no semantic information content for theme assignment of full documents.[219] For example, terms such as "for," "a," "to," "in," "them," "the," "of," "that," "be," "not," "or," "and," "but." Of course, function words are very important for human understanding of documents and there are expressions only composed of such stop words ("to be or not to be") so whether the system will improve by removing them is task dependent. Stop words are discussed in the case study on textual data in Chapter 8. For an example sentence

> Its population was 8,361,447 at the 2010 census whom 1,977,253 in the built-up (or "metro") area made of Zhanggong and Nankang, and Ganxian largely being urbanized.

the removal of stop words will render it as

> ['population', 'TOKNUMSEG31', 'TOKNUMSEG6', 'census', 'TOKNUMSEG31', 'built', 'metro', 'area', 'made', 'zhanggong', 'nankang', 'ganxian', 'largely', 'urbanized']

Note how semantically dense the output becomes. See Section 8.5.1 for the fully worked-out example.

4.2 Regularization and Embedded Feature Selection

If overabundance of features is such a pervasive problem in the field, it makes sense that algorithm designers will have worked from early years (as early as 1984[48]) to address them automatically as part of their algorithm. This makes sense; if something presents itself as a problem that hinders the deployment of ML solutions, researchers will work on addressing it. A similar situation has happened with FE and DL as we will see in the next chapter. Therefore, some ML algorithms can perform feature selection as part of their inner workings in what has been called **embedded feature selection** (the name is prone to cause confusion with feature embeddings, discussed later in this chapter), also known as implicit feature selection. Embedded feature selection methods accomplish the reduction of features employed by the model, not by removing them from the training data but by discouraging the model from using too many features. If you suspect your training data is suffering from too many poor features, trying an ML algorithm that performs embedded feature selection and observing its behaviour can quickly help you assess whether this is the case or not. Many contain explicit parameters (like regularization parameters) to control their preference for a larger or smaller number of features. But their use for FE does not stop there. In many cases, you can read back from the final models the most important features as determined by the model. You can then disregard the model and train a different ML only on those features. A typical case will be to use LASSO on a large feature set and then keep the reduced feature set to train a SVM. LASSO is recommended for its ability to deal with large amounts of features. If the number of features is truly immense, use Winnow, described at the end of this section. Performing feature selection is crucial for algorithms like SVM that suffer from performance degradation in the presence of excessive irrelevant features.

The most common manner to achieve this is by **regularization techniques**, where you constrain the search space of parameters for the model – for example, requiring the sum of the square of all parameters to fall below a certain regularization parameter. If the training data is properly standardized and zero-centred and the error function used in the search process is well behaved, it is even possible to include the regularization constraint as a penalty score based on the complexity of the model. Different penalties produce different regularization approaches (compare features being used versus the sum of the weights for all the features). These techniques are not applicable to all ML models, but certain algorithms regularize with ease. In general, any ML algorithm where the objective function is explicit (and, therefore, it can be directly extended), and the model representation has a fixed size of parameters (so different penalties can be computed) can be regularized in a straightforward way (if the search methodology works over the extended objective function). Moreover, some algorithms can only operate under strong regularization as they are mathematically ill-defined (for example, logistic regression). Regularization parameters are usually set using cross-validation. The interesting aspect is that you do not need to specify the number of features to select, just the regularization parameter. This is desirable, as you might have no intuition of how many features to select and are needed for your problem.

To reiterate, regularization techniques are a particular case of ML algorithms that perform an **implicit feature selection**. Other examples of embedded feature selection include the weights assigned to features in linear and logistic regression and the feature importance in decision trees.[49] I have an overview of ML algorithms that perform embedded feature selection in Section 4.2.3. Embedded feature selection is also known as applying a minimum description length (MDL) term to the objective function.[167]

Regularization is a method for capacity control, the same as feature selection. Other forms, such as early stopping, fall into this category.[40] Keep this in mind if you find it useful in your problem. You might want to explore other capacity control methods. On the other hand, regularization is much more than feature selection, as it impacts the ML algorithm directly. It helps with overfitting and ill-posed problems.[†]

We will now see two popular regularization techniques based on norms, L_1 and L_2 regularization, popularized by the Ridge regression and LASSO algorithms. The following discussion refers to L_p norms and quasi-norms, built on the less-known Schatten norm, defined as follows, for $\alpha_1, \ldots, \alpha_n$ parameters of the ML algorithm:

$$\|\alpha\|_p = \left(\sum_{i=1}^{n} |\alpha_p|^p \right)^{-1/p}$$

For $0 < p < 1$, it is not a norm, as the triangular inequality does not hold, but it is still used in practice. L_0 is defined by taking the limit as p goes to 0 and it equals the number of nonzero elements. If there is a correspondence of features to nonzero parameters, as in linear regression, then L_0 is the number of selected features.

4.2.1 L_2 Regularization: Ridge Regression

The most popular way of regularizing is by computing the L_2 norm (also known as the Euclidean norm) of the parameter vector (L_2 **regularization**).[167] This approach will dampen bad features but never fully remove them. When applied to least squares regression it is called **Ridge regression**.[152] Ridge regression requires its features to be zero-centred and standardized. Other regularized algorithms might pose similar requirements. Check the documentation of your ML package as these requirements are implementation specific.

L_2 regularization is popular because the search space induced by such regularization is easy to explore. Certain SVM kernels such as linear kernels induce a search space that is L_2 regularized. This is why SVMs have a hard time dealing with irregular features, which always influence the result and impact negatively in running times.[40]

4.2.2 L_1 Regularization: LASSO

Instead of computing the L_2 norm, you can compute the L_1 norm (summing the absolute value of the parameters, L_1 **regularization**). Regularizing using

[†] Thanks to Dr. Brochu for stressing this difference.

this norm will force some features to zero, which in turn means that from a model trained using L_1 regularization, it is possible to infer features to drop. This induces an explicitly selected feature subset *post hoc*. However, the search space induced is not as well behaved as L_2, and, therefore, it might take longer to explore and might not converge. While MDL names a heuristic and it is not precisely defined, it is most similar to L_1 regularization in practice. [147]

LASSO. When L_1 regularization is applied to least squares regression, it is known as LASSO, [41,167] for "least absolute shrinkage and selection operator" where shrinkage refers to reducing the coefficients from regression in an absolute manner (making them zero) in comparison to Ridge regression that just dampens them. While originally developed for least squares, it can also be applied to other techniques, including generalized linear models, proportional hazards models and others, on which it is also referred to as LASSO.

As with Ridge regression, most LASSO *implementations* need their data to be centred and standardized. What makes the coefficients exactly equal to zero is the introduction of a soft threshold operator in the search process. It explicitly multiplies the weight by $max(0, 1 - \frac{N\lambda}{|weight|})$. For this to hold the features need to be orthonormal. Comparatively, Ridge regression will push the coefficients down by $(1 + N\lambda)^{-1}$. To solve LASSO problems, there exists multiple techniques, but gradient descent cannot be applied as the penalty is not differentiable.

While LASSO is preferred for large feature sets, it will only be able to select as many features as the number of instances in the training data. Also, if two features are correlated, the minimization is not unique and LASSO will fail to drop one of the features. ElasticNet, described next, addresses this problem. Other variants include the group LASSO, which uses groups of features as a pack, and the fused LASSO, which allows for added constraints for structured domains like time and space. [305]

4.2.2.1 ElasticNet

ElasticNet[353] is a one-parameter weighted sum of the L_1 and L_2 norms. In the extremes, the parameter selects L1 or L2. Curiously, it is mathematically equivalent to LASSO and it does not require a new regressor algorithm, but it exhibits a different behaviour with a number of advantages. First, ElasticNet helps when the number of features is larger than the number of instances. In such circumstances, LASSO will only be able to select features up to the number of instances. Second, if there are strongly correlated features, Ridge tends to perform better than LASSO, whereas in ElasticNet, highly correlated features will end up with the same coefficient, which is called "a grouping effect." This allows to control the redundancy better than in LASSO.

Other Norms. Bridge regression uses the other norms L_p and quasi-norms $0 < p < 1$. It is claimed that quasi-norms produce better results, but as they are non-convex they require approximate solutions, such as EM. A hybrid L_1, $L_{1/2}$ approach is claimed to work better in practice. [40]

4.2.3 Other Algorithms Featuring Embedded Feature Selection

A particular regularization technique in DL, drop out, is discussed in Section 5.3 in Chapter 5. Other algorithms that perform embedded feature selection include random forests, MARS and Winnow, discussed next. Other examples of embedded methods include gradient boosting machines, [241] regularized trees, the memetic algorithm and multinomial logit. [176]

Random Forests. Decision trees in general compute feature importance by a variety of means, including Gini impurity discussed earlier in this chapter in Section 4.1.1.1 (a factor exploited for error analysis in Chapter 6, Section 6.3.1.4). Random forests [46] go a step further, allowing feature importance to be measured on instances outside the set that was used to create each tree, providing out-of-bag estimates, which are more reliable. These feature importance metrics are usually returned back as part of the model and can be used as feature selection techniques on their own, for example, in RF-RFE. [128]

MARS. Multivariate adaptive regression splines (MARS) [112] is a regressor where a linear combination of nonlinearities is fit on the data. The nonlinearities *hinge functions* (also known as *ramp*, *hockey stick* or *rectifier functions*) of the form max(0, *feature − constant*) or max(0, *constant − feature*). The MARS models are built using a forward and backward pass, similar to CART trees. [48] The embedded feature selection happens at the forward pass when features are chosen to extend the model (based on the parameters supplied to the algorithm) but most importantly as part of the generalized cross-validated (GCV) score that it is used to select nonlinearities to prune.

$$GCV = \frac{error\ on\ unseen\ data}{N \times penalized\ number\ of\ parameters}$$

GCV is so named as it "approximates the error that would be determined by leave-one-out validation." [328] Due to this regularization, MARS does embedded feature selection.

Winnow. Winnow [212] learns a linear classifier from labelled examples. It is very similar to perceptron but uses a multiplicative scheme that handles many irrelevant dimensions. It is a simple algorithm that scales well to high-dimensional data. The feature selection is embedded into the algorithm, during its update step. It is an embedded feature selection that does *not* use regularization.

4.3 Dimensionality Reduction

To reduce the feature space and escape the curse of dimensionality, another technique to shrink the number of features is to find a related representation for the input features into a lower dimensional space. This is called **dimensionality reduction**. This process ought to be able to accommodate unseen data at testing (execution) time and to generalize properly from there. If your features are sparse, you might suspect that only a fraction of the possible feature vectors are likely to occur. That means your data normally falls into a smaller, more regular subspace of the feature space.[†] The key is to find that subspace and to operate inside of it. Finding this underlining structure within the data is also the primary objective of unsupervised learning and many dimensionality reduction techniques fall squarely within it.[49] Note, however, that turning sparse vectors into dense representations might result in significant computational cost increase.[351] You might want to revisit your decision of which ML algorithm to use if you decide to try the dimensionality reduction route.

Dimensionality reduction is the ultimate way of looking at the features as a whole,[180] which is the subject of Chapter 2. I have decided to discuss the topic in this chapter as it is usually considered closely related to feature selection.

In terms of approaches, less-informed (but not less-effective) ways to deal with a large number of features is to aggressively reduce their dimensionality either by (1) projecting them to a lower dimension in a smart way (using singular vector decomposition, for example, Section 4.3.3, or (2) a generative probabilistic model of the data; see Section 4.3.4) or (3) in a random way (just trusting that the space is so sparse that collisions within the mapping will be infrequent in very sparse datasets see feature hashing, Section 4.3.1 and random projections, Section 4.3.2). In general, any unsupervised learning technique in the form of clustering can be applied (Section 4.3.5). This is a topic of active research and many other techniques have been proposed, including low rank approximation, nonnegative matrix factorization and ICA

[†] What mathematicians call a manifold but as I promised to write this book without talking about manifolds; this footnote should not be considered part of this book.

(Section 4.3.6). This section concludes with a general discussion of the dimensionality reduction within the embeddings conceptual framework.

A note of caution: once you decide to go the dimensionality reduction route, your error analysis capabilities (and explainable models in general) will be severely diminished. This is why certain techniques (like low rank approximation or NMF) focus on obtaining reduced representations that are "similar" to the input data, in the sense that visualization approaches to the original data will also be applicable to the reduced data. I have only seen that done for images, though. I further discuss the complexities of error analysis on data that has undergone dimensionality reduction in the case study on textual data in Chapter 8, Section 8.7.

4.3.1 Hashing Features

The simplest dimensionality reduction technique possible is just to apply a **hashing function**, that is, any function that maps data of arbitrary size to a fixed size. You use either the type of hashing functions employed in data structures, such as murmur hash,[12] or a more complex one from cryptography, for example, SHA1.[96] As a refresher, nonidentical input data that maps to the same hash are called **collisions**, with good hashing functions intended to minimize collisions for the type of data over which it is normally employed. The intuition is that collisions will be rare and that, when a collision happens, other hashed features will inform the ML system which of the original features is being observed. It is quite impressive that it works as effectively as it does. This approach is a key component of the fastText ML system.

Note that hashing features is different from performing a random projection (discussed in the next section) as hashing is a computationally cheaper operation. Good hashing functions can also be learned. A hash that produces no collisions on a given set is called a **perfect hash**, a topic of continuous interest in computer science, with recent techniques being able to construct perfect hashes over large datasets.[303] We will now see a type of hash that learns functions with specific type of collisions.

Chapter 8 uses feature hashing to deal with the feature explosion resulting from considering pairs of words at a certain distance as features (skip bigrams, cf., Section 5.1.2). Dimensionality reduction is needed as using regular bigrams (with no extra words in between) results in half a million features. Skip-bigrams will be several orders of magnitude more. The interpretability of the model, however, suffers. See Section 8.7 for the fully worked-out example.

Locality-Sensitive Hash. LSH differs from regular hashing in that it targets for collisions to happen for inputs close to each other in the source space. It is similar to clustering or nearest neighbour search and it is indeed a technique used to speed up this type of algorithms. When trained over data, it is called locality-preserving hashing (LPH),[347] which minimizes both the average projection distance and the quantization loss. Other algorithms include random sampling of bits and using random hyperplanes and producing a hash bit of whether the input is above or below each hyperplane. When used in dimensionality reduction for FE, it will achieve similar behaviour as, for example, stemming (discussed in Section 8.5.2 in Chapter 8).

Hashing Features as Polysemy. When using bag-of-words approaches to NLP (discussed at length in Chapter 8), the operation of hashing features is equivalent to artificially increasing the polysemy of words; if *door* and *banana* map to the same hash code, for the ML, it behaves as if the English language now has a *bananadoor* word and it has to distinguish between the two senses on a given instance.[†] This in turn is not unlike if the word was *bank* (that conflates many meanings, for example, *river bank* vs. *money bank*). A good ML algorithm that can handle polysemous words as signals should also be able to handle hashed features well.

4.3.2 Random Projection

Also in the category of "simple methods that can curiously work well sometimes," you can use a **random explicit projection** matrix from the original feature space to a reduced space. Such matrix is a sparse matrix with values in the set $\{-1, 0, 1\}$ with probabilities of the order of $1/\sqrt{D}$, where D is the number of dimensions.[208] The methods shown next compute such matrices based on a number of desiderata. However, oftentimes the value is in executing a projection, *any projection*. Moreover, if the number of dimensions and the amount of training data is big, computing a "good" projection might be prohibitively expensive from a computational point of view. Note that a random projection is an actual projection while hashing is much more random: a random projection is expected to preserve distances between the instances.

[†] The use of pseudo-words so constructed is a traditional technique to evaluate word sense disambiguation algorithms.[220]

4.3.3 SVD

A more meaningful projection can be found using the "direction" of the dataset and keeping only the directions that are stronger, where the directions are the eigenvectors of the singular value decomposition (SVD) and their strength is given by their eigenvalues. This is also discussed in terms of PCA (principal component analysis) with the stronger directions being the principal components. This direction of projection is given by linear algebra, not domain knowledge, both a blessing (you do not need to have strong domain intuitions to use it) and a curse (the SVD direction might not make sense in the domain and there are no real reasons why it should). As with other techniques, it is usually the case that performance (i.e., accuracy) will not improve (it might take a small hit) but training time after SVD will be significantly reduced (see for example, over the CIFAR-10 dataset[206]).

As a refresher, SVD is a factorization of a matrix M of dimensions $m \times n$ into the multiplication of three matrices $U \Sigma V^T$ where U is a $m \times m$ unitary matrix, Σ is $m \times n$ matrix with nonnegative real numbers in the diagonal, and V is a $n \times n$ matrix.[293] The diagonal values σ_i of Σ are the singular values of M (usually listed in order).

In our case, the matrix has one row per instance and one column per feature. If the matrix M is centred (the mean of each column has been subtracted) then its covariance matrix $C = M^T M /(m-1)$ of size $n \times n$ is symmetric and can be diagonalized $C = V L V^T$ where V is the eigenvector matrix (eigenvectors are the columns of V, also known as **principal axes or directions**). Note that M has to be centred for this technique to be applied.

Computing the eigenvectors of the covariance matrix and their eigenvalues can be done with a numerical package. The projection matrix is V and the dimensionality reduction is achieved by truncating V to the larger eigenvalues. If the truncation only keeps the top r eigenvalues, then $\tilde{V}$ is a matrix of size $r \times r$ and we are reducing the number of features from n to r. The projected representation of an instance i (row i of M) is the i row of $M\tilde{V}$. New data can be encoded by multiplying with $\tilde{V}$.

One of the advantages of SVD is that you can plot the eigenvalues and pick the percentage to keep visually. Alternatively, you can specify it as a percentage of the larger eigenvalue (σ_1). Other techniques different from SVD will require you to define the reduced dimensionality by trial and error.

SVD and PCA are memory-intensive as the whole training data has to be kept in RAM to invert the associated matrix. A distributed implementation using map-reduce has been proposed[336] and there exists PCA approximations[207] and hybrid PCA plus random projection alternatives.[138]

Finally, the prevalent advice[351] is not to use PCA on raw counts, as correlation and variance are very sensitive to outliers. You will want to squash your features (through logarithmic transformation or frequency-based filtering) before applying it.

4.3.4 Latent Dirichlet Allocation

In practice, the singular value decomposition becomes a computational bottleneck for large datasets. Moreover, SVD does not allow adding domain knowledge as it is based on a linear algebra identity. A different framing of the problem is one based on a probabilistic story for generating the data. From that story (model), its parameters can be estimated from the available data. The model can be further expanded based on our understanding of or assumptions on the data. That is the case for latent Dirichlet allocation but we will start looking into an earlier (and simpler) related technique, probabilistic latent semantic analysis (pLSA).

pLSA: Probabilistic Latent Semantic Analysis (or Indexing). We want to estimate $P(f, v)$ where f is a feature ("word" in pLSA terms) and v is an instance (the full feature vector or "document"). The pLSA algorithm[154] assumes there are unseen "topics" c that generate the features, and that the instances themselves generate (or contain) topics rather than the feature themselves. Therefore, the probability of a feature appearing in an instance is given by the sum over all topics of the probability of the topic, the probability of the instance given the topic and the probability of the feature given the topic.

$$P(f, v) = \sum_c P(c) P(v|c) P(f|c) = P(v) \sum_c P(c|d) P(f|c)$$

This is the generative story, with the first expression being its symmetric formulation (everything is generated from the topics) while the second expression is its asymmetric formulation (first pick an instance, then generate topics, then features). The number of topics is a hyperparameter and it is similar to the number of eigenvectors to use in SVD, although in SVD we can compute the dimensionality reduction based on the ratio of the most dominant eigenvalue, here you will be operating more blindly. The total number of parameters is then $|c||v| + |f||c|$ (number of topics times number of instances plus number of features times number of topics) and can be estimated using the EM (estimation-maximization algorithm), discussed in Section 2.2.1.2, Chapter 2. Dimensionality reduction is achieved by moving away from feature space into topic space.

LDA: Latent Dirichlet Allocation. An improvement over pLSA is using a given prior over the topic distribution. Particularly, **LDA** uses a sparse Dirichlet prior, hence the name.[38] Such a prior is a multivariate generalization of the beta distribution. It encodes the intuition that instances have few topics and topics generate few features. This intuition holds for NLP tasks. Other priors could be used for other tasks with different intuitions.

Both pLSA and LDA model the training data using a generative process. The test data becomes a problem (there is no instance v associated with the test documents). To use them at runtime, it would need to continue the EM process on the training data plus test data (which in practice is too expensive and not stable). Instead, a few steps of EM are used, maintaining the training data fixed and only adjusting parameters over the new data. This is better done one instance at a time. Using all the test data in one batch is tempting as it will be faster, but that is not representative of the behaviour of the algorithm in production.[296] All in all, PCA optimizes for representation while LDA optimizes for discrimination.[167] These issues ought to be considered when deciding to use one versus the other for dimensionality reduction.

4.3.5 Clustering

Another dimensionality reduction technique (unrelated to the rest) is to cluster the data and use the number of the cluster, e.g., its cluster ID, as the feature itself.[351] For new data, that is, to use it at test time, we need a way to assign clusters to unseen data. For example, in k-means you can pick the cluster with closer distance to its centroid. The amount of dimensionality reduction achieved is equivalent to the number of clusters used, assuming one-hot encoding of the cluster number. Clustering techniques that assign overlapping clusters (e.g., canopy clustering[249]) can be used to provide dense representations. Alternatively, the distance to the centres of nonoverlapping clusters can be used to produce dense feature vectors. In NLP, using word synonyms (e.g., using WordNet[105]) is a way of using clusters for dimensionality reduction.

4.3.6 Other Dimensionality Reduction Techniques

Dimensionality reduction is a topic of active research. We will now see four advanced techniques that expand the space of solutions: ICA, low-rank approximation, nonnegative matrix factorization and linear discriminant analysis. Another dimensionality reduction technique, autoencoders, is discussed in the next chapter; see Section 5.4.2.

ICA. ICA [163] goes beyond separating correlated features into "independence" in the mutual information sense. Also known as *blind source separation* and a solution to the *cocktail party problem*, it separates normal signals from abnormal ones. The classic example is two mics that both receive signals from two speakers but one is stronger in each mic than the other. If we assume the merging is linear, then ICA will separate the two speakers. [251] If we know the mixing matrix, separating is trivial (just inverting the matrix). ICA estimates the matrix from outputs, assuming the mixing is linear, the sources are independent and do **not** follow a Gaussian. It builds on the central limit theorem that says the sum will be more Gaussian than the sources (only if they are not Gaussians themselves), so we can remove it and obtain the sources. The caveats are that it only covers linear mixings and does not order the sources.

Low Rank Approximation. It is a minimization technique that seeks to find a lower rank matrix as close as possible to some input matrix, where proximity is defined given a matricial norm. [221] Usual norms include the **Frobenious norm** [320] (the square root of the sum of the squares of all its elements, a generalization of the Euclidean vector norm) and the **spectral norm** [159] (the maximum singular value of a matrix, the maximum "scale" a matrix can stretch a vector). Sometimes the sought matrix has also other properties besides lower rank. It is used in recommender systems to infer missing values, and also for completing distance matrices. In the unrestricted case, it is the same as performing SVD and keeping the top eigenvalues. When the instances are not weighted equally (i.e., when extended with a weight vector), the solution no longer has a closed form and requires a numerical solution involving local optimization methods. This technique is significant as it was used in the winner submission to the Netflix competition, one of the most important competitions in ML. [306]

Nonnegative Matrix Factorization. NMF, also known as *nonnegative matrix approximation*, *self-modelling curve resolution* and *positive matrix factorization*, involves, given a matrix M with no negative values, finding matrices W and H such that $M = W \times H$, also without negative values. [203] It has no closed solution, and needs to be approximated using a distance metric for approximation. Two common ones are Frobenious and an extension of KL divergence to matrices. Its main appeal is that W and H can be much smaller in size. With L_1, regularization is called **nonnegative sparse coding**. While SVD/PCA is also a factorization technique, NMF contains different constraints and therefore produces different results. NMF results can be more interpretable as the results are additive, which in the case of images, produce matrices that look like the source images.[276]

Linear Discriminant Analysis. A supervised dimensionality reduction technique, LDA shares the acronym with latent Dirichlet allocation but is unrelated. LDA finds computable features in the form of linear combinations of the original features that better separate a categorical target. It helps find a new feature space that discriminates between the different classes as efficiently as possible, using inter-class and intra-class distances and a generalized eigenvalue decomposition. LDA works with more than two classes, and the dimension of the resulting subspace equals the number of classes.[132†]

4.3.7 Embeddings

Embeddings are a function that map a set of discrete objects, usually large, into vectors of a given dimension. Such functions therefore perform dimensionality reduction. The relationship between the vectors are expected to follow some relationship between the discrete objects themselves. For example, for words, you ought to expect that related words (in the semantic sense) will have close vectors in the Euclidean sense. These are also known as **distributed representations** as the semantic information is distributed within the vector, compared with other vector representation techniques using specific columns to encode specific information such as microfeatures.[282]

Embeddings are related to the **distributional hypothesis** that says that the meaning of a word lies not in the word itself but in the places where the word is used. For example: "the meaning of a ☐ lies not in the ☐ itself but in the places where the ☐ is used." Large collections of texts (**corpora**) can be used to obtain representations for words or other sequential artifacts based on this hypothesis. Therefore, if two words are used in similar contexts, then they might have a representation that is close to each other. In the case of word embeddings, a representation is a fixed-size vector of floating point numbers (**vector space model**). The vector for *dog* might be close to the vector for *cat* (using Euclidean distance). If this seems quite similar to SVD or pLSA, it is, with a key difference: context in the case of embeddings is taken to be a window of words around the term. In SVD or LDA, context is taken to be the whole document. Therefore, SVD and LDA produce vectors that are related semantically (e.g., chicken – farm) while embeddings are expected to be semantically similar (chicken – rooster).[275]

---

† Chapter 5.

Throughout this section, the discussion uses "words" to refer to "features" but these models apply equally to any domains where the raw data includes large numbers of sequential data. For example, it is possible to represent nodes in semantic graphs by encoding random paths starting on each node, in what has been called the Rdf2Vec approach.[271] Once the vector representation for each element of the sequence has been obtained, it needs to be combined to obtain a fixed-size feature vector (if needed, using recurrent neural networks discussed in the next chapter alleviates this need). The techniques discussed in the next chapter for variable-length raw data are useful for that (Section 5.1). For example, in the textual domain you can do a weighted sum of the embeddings, as exemplified in the case study in Chapter 8, Section 8.8, where the embeddings are also weighted by the inverse of the term frequency on the corpus.

We will now see an embedding technique amply used in visualization (t-SNE) to introduce the overall concept of embeddings. Then we will look at the associated task the embedding learning is trying to solve and how it is very onerous, computationally speaking (Section 4.3.7.1). We will then switch to local embeddings as popularized by the Word2Vec tool (Section 4.3.7.2). This section concludes with other embedding techniques.

t-SNE. A popular visualization technique is t-distributed stochastic neighbour embedding (t-SNE).[311] The t-SNE algorithm is based on the realization that you can define how "close" two objects in a dataset are by looking at how likely it would be to pick one as a random "neighbour" of the other. The random neighbour concept is formalized as a radial Gaussian centred on the point. If you have a dense set of points near a point, then the points are not necessarily that close: by chance, plenty of points can be picked as neighbours. Similarly, two points far apart, in an Euclidean sense, can be very close using this probabilistic distance if the dataset is sparse in that region. The beauty of the concept is that it is dimension-independent. A value of one minus this probability is used as a distance definition over 100 dimensions or just two. Therefore, computing a t-SNE projection is accomplished by searching a lower-dimensional placement of points so the two probability distributions are the same, using KL-divergence (discussed next) to determine whether they are the same distribution or not. The algorithm finds the projected points using a gradient descent method, and while quite useful, it is not intended to be used on unseen data. Chapter 8 uses embeddings to predict the population of a given city. For the t-SNE projection of the embeddings (Figure 8.2, reproduced here as Figure 4.1), it was possible to conclude that all the numeric tokens were

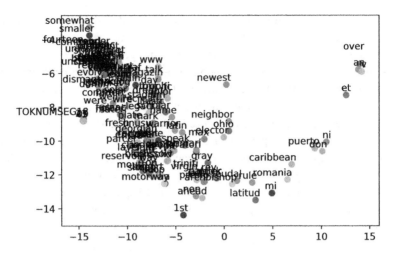

Figure 4.1 Two-dimensional rendering using the t-SNE algorithm on a sample of the 50-dimensional embeddings computed over the training set; see Chapter 8 for details.

clustered together. This leads to the inclusion of the original terms as features, as the numeric tokens were among the most informative features. See Section 8.8.1 for the fully worked-out example.

KL Divergence. Kullback–Leibler divergence is one of the most useful metrics in ML. It measures how well a new probability distribution can be explained given a previous one. In that way, it defines a nonsymmetric metric over distributions, telling you how close one distribution is to another:

$$D_{\mathrm{KL}}(P \,\|\, Q) = \sum_i \log_2 \left(\frac{P(i)}{Q(i)} \right) P(i)$$

For the cases $Q(i) = 0$, it is defined as zero.

4.3.7.1 Global Embeddings

The concept of embeddings has been around for decades [107] but they had the problem of poor scalability for large object sets, [125] which rendered them not particularly useful in practice. In this technique, an embedding is defined by solving a related problem in the object space. Finding embeddings can then proceed as an optimization over the related problem. For words, we use the prediction of surrounding words using a given word as the related problem (skip-gram model; see Section 5.1.2 in the next chapter for a definition of

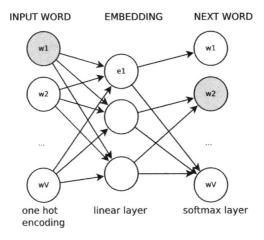

INPUT WORD   EMBEDDING   NEXT WORD

one hot   linear layer   softmax layer
encoding

Figure 4.2 Global embeddings.

the term) or predicting the central word given its context (continuous-bag-of-words model). We will use the skip-gram model for this discussion.

We then have a network (Figure 4.2) where the input is a one-hot encoding (cf., Section 3.1 in Chapter 3) of all the vocabulary, representing the chosen word. There is a hidden layer, with no activation function (linear unit) and a softmax output layer (see Section 5.3 in the next chapter if you are unfamiliar with these concepts) of size equal to the vocabulary. The embedding is the activation in the hidden layer (similar to an autoencoder; see Section 5.4.2 in the next chapter). This is not much of a neural network, as the one-hot encoding just selects one row from the weight matrix. The key ingredient is the softmax layer, and this is an application of softmax learning. The expectation is that, if two words appear in similar contexts, then their hidden layers (embeddings) will be similar.

Global embeddings require that a system is able to predict the correct word probabilities over all the words in the vocabulary, which is very time-consuming, as you do that in every step of the search for optimal embeddings. For a 200-component embedding over a 50,000-word vocabulary results in a 10-million-parameter network with a very slow gradient descent and will require billions of words of training data. This hindered their application to real data until the arrival of local embeddings, discussed next.

4.3.7.2 Local Embeddings: Word2Vec
Instead of computing global embeddings, Word2Vec[233] trains a discrimination objective to tell apart the target word from noise words (Figure 4.3). This

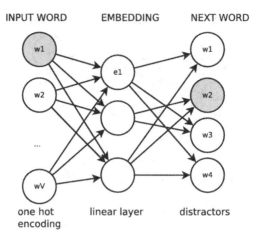

Figure 4.3 Local embeddings.

transforms the problem from global learning to local learning. The idea is called negative sampling, instead of training each word-pair to produce 1 for target and 0 on the rest, they train it to produce 1 for target and 0 on 5 sampled *negative* words (selecting 5 to 20 words for small datasets and 2 to 5 for big datasets). Then Word2Vec only updates the weights for the positive and the negatives; all the other weights stay the same. The negatives are sampled based on their frequency, the likelihood given by $f_i^{3/4}$.[228] See Section 8.8 for an example of the use of embeddings in the case study over textual data in Chapter 8.

4.3.7.3 Other Embeddings: GloVe and ULMFiT

In recent years, two models deserve mentioning: GloVe and ULMFiT. GloVe[255] manages to revisit global embedding learning by creating a co-occurrence matrix using a window around each term instead of full documents to define co-occurrence. Takurita describes GloVe's main assumption as[302]

> The co-occurrence ratios between two words in a context are strongly connected to meaning.

where co-occurrence ratios indicate how likely are words to appear in similar contexts. Interestingly, while starting from very different assumptions and methods, both Word2Vec and GloVe produce similar results, with GloVe training faster than Word2Vec.[302]

Finally, universal language models (ULMFiT)[157] have recently revolutionized the way we think about NLP by allowing pretrained models over large datasets to transfer to specific problems. They achieve this by using a triangular scheduling on the momentum parameter fed to the neural network, plus other improvements.

Current research focuses in hierarchical representations that look at the data at different levels of abstraction (words, sentences, paragraphs, etc.) and disentangled representations, which produce more interpretable representations.[132][†] Using the transformer framework, BERT models are also increasing in popularity.[82]

4.4 Learning More

The topics discussed in this chapter are by far the most popular FE topics covered in ML books. Many great ML books in print also include excellent chapters on feature selection and dimensionality reduction.[7,219,220,331] I particularly recommend the book by Manning and others, *Introduction to Information Retrieval*,[219] for specific formulas to implement single-feature utility metrics. Being an area of active research, the field has also spanned full books on the topic.[135,214] See Guyon and Elisseeff[134] for a feature selection survey. For recent research topics, including streaming feature selection, unsupervised feature selection, privacy preserving and adversarial feature selection, see chapters 5 and 8 of *Feature Engineering*, the book with contributed chapters edited by Dong and Liu.[132]

Coverage on embedded feature selection is more scattered, as it relates to multiple disciplines. It is possible to drill down on each technique separately, for which I have tried to provide meaningful references, on any of the topics presented in this chapter, of which by far has LASSO as the most popular one. A good study of the feature selection capabilities in LASSO has been done by Tibshirani.[305]

Dimensionality reduction is a problem studied by multiple disciplines, with very different sets of interests and requiring different skills from the reader. Some approach the problem from a linear algebra perspective and others from an optimization background, while others rely on probabilistic modelling. For classic approaches, the dimensionality reduction chapter in Manning and Schütze's *Foundations of Statistical Natural Language Processing*[220] book describes the techniques at length. For newer techniques, you will need to resort to research papers, cited in the respective sections.

[†] Chapter 11.

5

Advanced Topics: Variable-Length Data and Automated Feature Engineering

To conclude Part One, let us cover a few advanced topics, some in areas of active research. Section 5.1 discusses variable-length raw data, which have been a challenge for traditional machine learning (ML), as it requires fixed-size feature vectors. We will see techniques involving truncation, computing the most general tree, local representations and projections into simpler representations. While this book focuses on *feature* representations, the related problem of changing *instances* by dropping, grouping or synthesizing them is discussed in Section 5.2 as instance engineering. Feature engineering (FE) is a problem that ML researchers have been actively working on. They have made substantive progress in reducing the need for FE with deep learning (DL) at the cost of requiring massive datasets. I will briefly delve into some DL concepts and what they entail for FE in Section 5.3. Particularly, how the use of recurrent neural networks allows encoding sequential data in new ways that might be useful for other approaches beyond DL (Section 5.3.1). As FE is such a labour- and time-intensive task, it makes sense that there is plenty of interest in automating it (Section 5.4). We will see techniques that take into account the target class (automated feature engineering or AFE; see Section 5.4.1) versus techniques that do not need the target class (unsupervised feature engineering; see Section 5.4.2). For AFE, I will discuss convolutions, genetic programming and one of the most popular FE tool called Featuretools. For unsupervised FE, we will briefly discuss autoenconders. This chapter will give you a taste of current research in FE.

5.1 Variable-Length Feature Vectors

Many problems involve raw data of variable length that in turn is difficult to feed to ML algorithms with fixed-size vectors as inputs. We will now see techniques to deal with raw data easily expressed as sets (Section 5.1.1), lists (Section 5.1.2), trees (Section 5.1.3) and graphs (Section 5.1.4). Note that time series and streams are special cases of variable-length raw data.

5.1.1 Sets

The simplest type of variable-length raw data are sets, that is, raw data that takes the form of multiple elements without ordering. The possible elements themselves are known *a priori* but the number of elements present for a given instance is unknown. We will see the following techniques: list of indicator features, addition and multiplication, sort then lists. You can also use a ML algorithm that takes set-valued features as inputs, such as RIPPER.[68]

List of Indicator Features. The most popular way of encoding sets is to transform them into a list of indicator features for each of the potential elements in the set. The indicator feature is true if the set contains that element. This is not feasible for sets of discrete features, only for sets of categorical features. In a way, this is equivalent to a logical OR of the one-hot encodings (cf., Section 3.1 in Chapter 2) of the original categories. For example, for a set of categories Red, Green, Blue, Yellow, it could be encoded as four features ⟨HasRed, HasGreen, HasBlue, HasYellow⟩. An instance with raw data {Red, Yellow} will be encoded as ⟨**true, false, true, false**⟩, while {Red, Blue, Yellow} as ⟨**true, true, true, false**⟩.

Addition and Multiplication. Another way to deal with set features is to combine them using associative operations, and then leave it to the ML model to sort out the aggregated signal. Operations such as additions, logical ORs and multiplications can be used. This is a common way to represent a set of word embeddings by adding the vectors, but your mileage might vary. See Section 8.8 in the textual data case study in Chapter 8 for an example.

Sort, then Lists. Another option is to order the elements in the set, for example, based on popularity or lexicographically, and obtain a list. Then, use some of the techniques described in the next section, for example, explicit position and truncation. The ordering criteria used at train time has to be used at test time and a method to order unseen data is required. This approach was used to sort relation values in the semantic graphs case study in Chapter 6. The values were sorted based on how frequent a value was in the overall graph, using the intuition that elements that are more popular might be more informative to the ML. See Section 6.3 for a fully worked-out example.

5.1.2 Lists

Lists are ordered sequences of elements. Representing them encounters two issues: first, the sequences can have variable length. The second issue concerns with how lists with slight differences in content might result in very different representations due to poor positional encoding. This is known as **nuisance variations** in terms of the exact position. However, while an exact position might not be important, position itself carries information for the task. How important is the exact position depends on the task, choosing the right encoding is a way for you to signal to the ML the type of positional differences that make sense in your domain. [132†]

We will see some techniques (like truncation) that address the variable-length problem and others (like histograms and n-grams) that address the nuisance variations issue. You can also use recurrent neural networks, discussed in Section 5.3.1 or convolutional neural networks, discussed in Section 5.4.1.1.

Truncation. This is a simple approach of truncating the list to a fixed size, chosen so that most of the instances' lengths fall within that size and pad lists with less than the fixed size with a newly introduced, "NULL" value. This will work if the position of the elements has an exact meaning. It is difficult to make it work for language: compare "cancel my account," which becomes $f_1 =$ cancel, $f_2 =$ my, $f_3 =$ account, $f_4 = \ldots = f_9 =$ NULL, with "please I would like you to cancel my account," which becomes $f_1 =$ please, $f_2 = $ I, $f_3 =$ would, $\ldots$, $f_7 =$ cancel, $f_8 =$ my, $f_9 =$ account. The important signal ("cancel") is available to the ML through features f_1 and f_7, diminishing its impact. Convolutional neural networks manage to make this representation work, however, by using shared neural connections (Section 5.4.1.1). You can truncate at the beginning, at the end or starting from a designated marker (e.g., "first non-stop word," cf., Section 8.5.1 in Chapter 8).

Fixed Regions Histogram. You can compute a histogram of the data (cf., Section 2.3.1 in Chapter 2) but you will lose ordering information. However, you can keep some ordering information if you split the list into a fixed number of regions (potentially overlapping, if needed) and compute histograms on each region. That way, the ML will know that certain elements appear in the beginning of the list versus in the middle or at the end. That approach can be combined with a full histogram. The idea of summaries for ordered representative sections of the list can be expanded to other type of data

---

† Chapter 6.

summaries beyond histograms, such as averages or standard deviation (see Section 2.3 in Chapter 2).

_n_-Grams. While global ordering may be difficult to encode, it might not be necessary for the ML. Instead, local ordering relations can be encoded as n-tuples of consecutive elements, called n-grams.[180] For example, pairs of consecutive items are called bigrams (n-gram of order 2). The n-gram is a tuple that represents a fixed-size (of size n) window over the list. The n-grams can be padded with special values (e.g., NULL) to include n-grams in the beginning and in the end of the list. The number of distinct features explode with this approach. For an n-gram for order beyond 3, 4, it becomes prohibitively large if the number of elements and the data is large, like in natural language processing (NLP). The method is manageable using hashing techniques (cf., Section 4.3.1 in Chapter 4). See the second row of Table 5.1 for an example. The resulting set of n-grams can then be fed into the ML algorithm using any of the techniques for encoding sets. The n-gram technique can work outside text domains as long as the items in the raw data sequence are discrete or categorical. The n-grams are also called "windows," "motifs," "sliding windows," "fingerprints," "pattern fragments" and "detectors" depending on the community.[133] The case study in Chapter 8 showcases a full ML system using bigrams, together with a suitable error analysis (Section 8.6).

Skip _n_-Grams. Fixed-size n-grams are also prone to nuisance variations in the form of interspersed irrelevant items (like adverbs or adjectives in text). Compare "cancel the account" with "cancel that awful account." A solution to alleviate these nuisance variations is to generate n-grams skipping items. Skip bigrams are also known as "k-gapped-pairs."[132][†] This will of course produce a number of skip n-grams larger than the number of words in the original list. See Table 5.1 for an example. This technique can be combined with feature hashing (cf., Section 4.3.1 in Chapter 4) to bound the number of generated

Table 5.1. *Example with bigrams and skip bigrams up to three tokens.*

Original sentence	The dog eats the bone.
Bigrams	the-dog, dog-eats, eats-the, the-bone
Skip bigrams at length 3:	the-dog, the-eats, the-the, dog-eats, dog-the, dog-bone, eats-the, eats-bone, the-bone

[†] Chapter 6.

features or aggressive feature selection (cf., Section 4.1 in the same chapter) to reduce their number to a manageable size. For a fully worked-out example of this technique, see the case study in Chapter 8, Section 8.7.

For an example combining multiple techniques, in the Keywords4Bytecodes project, I seek to identify the name of Java methods from their compiled code.[92] For learning, I combine a histogram of bytecodes found on the method (250 features) plus a truncated list of the first 30 opcodes (where 30 opcodes is the median length of a method). In this way, the ML has access to the specific ordering information, if needed, or the full distribution of values.

General Patterns. Skip n-grams are a particular case of a pattern over the list. Generalizing the concept, it is possible to use existing algorithms for pattern induction over the raw data list and represent it as histograms of pattern matches or as positions where the pattern matches. A combination of both approaches by splitting the list into segments and having histograms per segment is also possible, including using a sliding window. There are many efficient methods to mine "maximal" patterns (i.e., patterns that do not contain other meaningful subpatterns) in the literature.[4,270] Meaningful patterns are such that appear in a minimum number of sequences (the *support* of the pattern) or allow to meaningfully distinguish between classes of the target variable (also known as contrastive patterns or *shapelets*). Note that the concept of patterns over raw data can be extended beyond variable-length raw data and applied to arbitrary featue vectors.[132]†

5.1.3 Trees

Representing trees is even more complicated than lists as trees contain parent-node relations. When the tree has explicit ordering among siblings, you can linearize the tree, for example, using a depth-first traversal, and encode the resulting list using the techniques discussed before for lists. When your representation does not lend to a natural linear ordering, you can resort to two types of techniques: (1) techniques that encode the specific parent-node relations and (2) you can resort to structural SVMs.[340]

Computing a Most General Tree. You can take all trees in the training data and unify them (Figure 5.1). Therefore, if a tree contains 10 edges labelled RELATIVE and an AGE edge and no NAME edge, when unified against a most

---

† Chapters 4, 6 and 10.

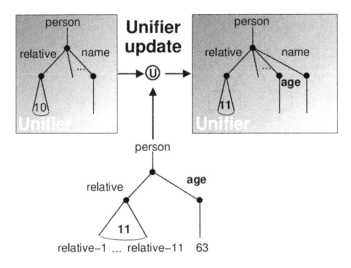

Figure 5.1 Most general tree. It contain all possible relations encountered with the maximum number of edges found for each relation.

general tree containing nine RELATIVES, a NAME and no AGE, it will produce a new most general tree with 10 RELATIVES, one NAME and one AGE. Doing a breadth-first traversal of the most general tree produces a fixed position encoding of the tree. That produces a positional model for your training data. You can then encode each position as a fixed coordinate within the instance vector. Trees with unknown edges or too many edges for a given edge name will be truncated. It will be insensitive to some nuisance variations but will generalize poorly. For example, a given property, say, whether they are in high school, of the elder child will be a completely different feature from whether the second child is in high school. If the signal that is important to the ML lies in that there is a child (any child) in high school, the signal will be severely fragmented to the ML. I used this as a baseline in my doctoral dissertation[89] versus custom techniques targeted for knowledge graphs.

Parent-Node Pairs. To avoid the nuisance variation issue with the most general tree approach, it is possible to follow a path similar to the use of n-grams, encoding all parent-node relations as pairs (Figure 5.2). The resulting set of pairs can then be fed into the ML algorithm using any of the techniques for encoding sets. Longer relations can also be encoded, but that is more unusual. This technique is popular with textual domains (Chapter 8), particularly to encode syntactic parsing features.[35]

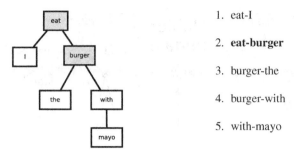

1. eat-I

2. **eat-burger**

3. burger-the

4. burger-with

5. with-mayo

Figure 5.2 Parent-node pairs example for the sentence "I eat the burger with mayo." The highlighted pair eat-burger is the main action being carried out.

In the general case, it is possible to transform the tree by running it through a set of feature detectors that signal the presence of specific subtrees. This is useful, for example, for text classification within an information extraction system (e.g., sentences with a certain structure might be worth further analysis) or in genomics, where DNA structure has been successfully analyzed with tree adjoining grammars[64]). Note that in the general case, the nodes might contain a variety of information (word, lemma, part-of-speech, etc.). As such, the parent-node pairs might be pairs of feature-of-parent or feature-of-node. Plenty of domain knowledge and intuition go into deciding which information from the nodes to use. Otherwise, the feature space will explode in size rather quickly.

Shift-Reduce Operations. Another possibility is to encode the tree as a list of shift-reduce operations to parse (or generate) the tree.[182,282,304,333] Shift-reduce refers to a parsing technique using a stack (also known as LALR(1) parsing[5]). The nodes being constructed are placed into the stack (shift) or taken out of the stack and used to build a subtree (reduce). See Figure 5.3 for an example. From a FE perspective, the shift-reduce encoding transforms the tree into a sequence over a very reduced vocabulary and you can use sequence modelling approaches to deal with them. It is particularly advantageous to use sequence-to-sequence approaches over trees, as popularized with DL approaches (see the next section).

5.1.4 Graphs

The most general case of raw data of variable length are graphs: sets of objects with arbitrary relationships between them. Graphs are usually hard to encode and process. Local relations can be encoded similarly to trees and lists: encoding a set of pairs of nodes or a set of triples (source node, relation, target node).

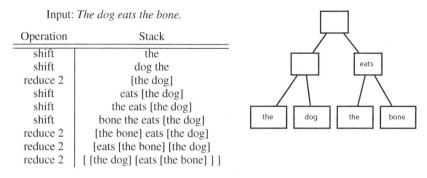

Input: *The dog eats the bone.*

Operation	Stack
shift	the
shift	dog the
reduce 2	[the dog]
shift	eats [the dog]
shift	the eats [the dog]
shift	bone the eats [the dog]
reduce 2	[the bone] eats [the dog]
reduce 2	[eats [the bone]] [the dog]
reduce 2	[[the dog] [eats [the bone]]]

Figure 5.3 Parent-node pairs example.

Alternatively, special ML techniques, e.g., graph kernels can be used.[190,318] The case study in Chapter 6 encodes graphs as paths relative to a selected node.

MST, then Tree. If there is a distinguished element that can be considered the "root" of graph and the graph has only one connected component, you can then run a spanning tree for the graph centred on such a root using a depth or breadth-first search. From there, you use the techniques to process trees described before. Otherwise, you can obtain a tree for each connected component and join the trees for connected components by some criteria (for example, size).

As a refresher, a spanning tree is a tree built using the edges of a connected graph. By virtue of being a tree, if there are n nodes in the tree, the spanning tree will pick $n - 1$ edges over those nodes such that all the nodes are reachable and there are no cycles. If the edges have a cost associated with them, it is possible to find a tree whose cost is minimum (what is called a minimum spanning tree or MST). A distinguished element will become the root of the tree. Efficient algorithms based on dynamic programming exist to build MSTs from graphs.[75]

Embeddings. The same way it was possible to use a linear context to produce representations for elements (words) in the previous chapter (Section 4.3.7), it is possible to use random walks on a graph.[130] Interestingly, this type of representation is equivalent to a specific factorization of a matrix view of the graph.[132†] This relationship is similar to the Word2Vec and GloVe embeddings discussed in the previous chapter. The factorization view has the advantage that is easier to incorporate additional information.

---

† Chapter 7.

5.1.5 Time Series

Bridging ML and statistical techniques, here and in the second half of Chapter 7, we will look into time series. Many information regarding FE is available through the work of statisticians and it is worth to learn their language, although their way of seeing ML problems is quite different.[47]

Time series analysis (abbreviated TSA in this discussion) is different from other statistical analysis because of the explicit recognition of the *order* of the observations.[29] These problems have been tackled with mathematical modelling for centuries. This means that the mathematics can be a little tortuous, but many of the final algorithms are simple enough to be performed manually.

They are used to describe, forecast, test hypothesis and assess effect of events. Describing a time series refers to capturing the main properties of the series, e.g., seasonal effect with sales high in winter and low in summer or an upward trend.[61] Forecasting refers to predicting the output in the future and it is important in sales, economic and industrial TSA. Testing a hypothesis is usually done on the relationship between inputs and output. Finally, assessing the effect of an event involves understanding a historical effect, that is, explaining the past or predicting the effect of a similar event in the future.

TSA is one of the oldest topics in statistics, as they were originally invented to track the position of celestial bodies. A time series is defined as "a collection of observations made sequentially in time."[61†] Normal statistics are concerned about random samples of independent observations. What is special about TS is that the successive observations are not independent and the time order of the observations has to be taken into account. As such, future values can be predicted from past values.[61] Because their invention predates computers, many models are amenable to mathematical handling (also know as "tons of theory applied to tiny amounts of data") with a preponderance of linear models. Looking into TSA helps us with FE not only for timestamped data but with series in general. The theory is about a series with an implicit index variable that is taken to be time, but applies to other index variables as well, like displacement on a plane.

The simpler models are called **error models**, which model the data as a simple, deterministic signal (represented by a low degree polynomial) plus white noise.[29] These models were used in astronomy to account for the position of a planet over time: $X_t = f(t) + Z_t$. The measurement errors Z_t (due to poor equipment, weather, human error, etc.) are well modelled by independent identically distributed random variables with zero mean,

---

† Chapter 1.

constant variance and zero autocorrelation (Section 5.1.5.1). These single-equation models lead to inconsistent estimates and different subsets of the data producing different estimates when there is a feedback from outputs to inputs.

We will see a few key concepts and models in the next sections, including stationarity, autocorrelation, trend and cycle, and finally the ARIMA and related models.

5.1.5.1 Autocorrelation

Let us remember that **covariance** is a measure of the linear association of two random variables and it is defined as

$$Cov(X, Y) = E[(X - \mu_X)(Y - \mu_Y)]$$

If the variables are independent, then the covariance is zero. If they are not independent, then the covariance tells you whether when one increases the other variable increases along with it, but its magnitude is unstable (it depends on the actual values of the random variable). Instead, you can divide it by their standard deviation and obtain the **correlation coefficient**.

For TSA, the two variables are the same variable but time lagged. The autocorrelation coefficient, therefore, measures the correlation between observations at different temporal distances apart (**lags**). It provides insights into the probabilistic model that generated the data.[61] Its shape can be said to capture the essence of the time series.[49]

It is important to note that many processes have the same autocorrelation function,[61] which means that there are many misleading correlations: if the parameters in the autocorrelation of two unrelated Y_t and X_t are very similar, ordinary regression can show a strong relationship even when X_t has no explanatory power. If both X_t and Y_t tend to wander away from a fixed overall level, then regression will show a strong relationship by mistake.[29] From a FE perspective, an unrelated feature that grows over itself with a similar growth process as the target will score a very high feature utility, even though the two variables are unrelated, and therefore, it will not help the ML algorithm.

5.1.5.2 Trend, Cycle and Seasonal Components

In TSA, the data is assumed to be a combination of four types of subprocesses:

(1) **Trend**: a variation persisting over time (period is long compared to the cycle). These are long-run movements. A very long cycle and a trend are indistinguishable if your observations are shorter than the cycle.[61†]

---

† Chapter 2.

(2) **Cycle**: quasi-periodic oscillation (alternation of expansion and contraction); tends to be combined with trend, for analysis. Not to be confused with the sines and cosines basis of Fourier analysis.
(3) **Seasonal component**: regular weekly, monthly or quarterly variations caused by climate or institutional practices.
(4) **Irregular component**: unforeseeable events, with stable random appearance; assumed purely random, non-autocorrelated process.

Trend, cycle and seasonal are assumed to follow systematic patterns (they are the signals of the process).[29] After trend and seasonal components have been removed, the residuals might not be purely random and are thus modelled with the TSA models described in Section 5.1.5.[61]

5.1.5.3 Stationarity

To apply TSA methods, there are strict requirements for the time series to satisfy certain statistical assumptions. In ML, it is common practice to leave these assumptions to be empirically tested over the available data.[47] That will not work with TSA methods, as they only apply to stationary data (defined below). You need to test for stationarity and transform your data to ensure stationarity.

What Is Stationarity. A stationary TS is one that has no systematic change in the mean (no trend) and no systematic change in variance (no strictly periodic variations).[61] The stationarity means the distribution is stable over say, n-samples, irrespective of which sequence of n-samples is used. *It is not that all the values are the same, just that their distribution is the same.* This is too strict, so, in general, is defined as "stationary in the wide sense" or "second order stationary" when the differences are stationary.[29] Why do you need to care about stationarity? Without it, you have a process with a trend, for example, increasing continuously. That increase will be the stronger signal and will dominate the results, as well as its indicative statistics, like mean and variance. As the methods for fitting the data assume stationarity, they will consistently underestimate a nonstationary time series with an increasing trend. The original time series must be transformed to a stationary one by removing its trend.

Testing for Stationarity. There are two approaches to check for stationarity. The first approach, a visual inspection technique, is to plot the moving average or the moving variance and see if it varies over time. Alternatively, statistical tests can be used, for example, the augmented Dickey Fuller (ADF) test of stationarity, in which rejecting the null hypothesis means the TSA is stationary and can be modelled using the models in Section 5.1.5. It is a regression of the first difference of the variable on its lagged version plus additional lags of the first difference picked by minimizing the AIC across a range of lag lengths (see Section 4.1.3 in Chapter 4 for a discussion on AIC).

Achieving Stationarity. Estimating and eliminating the trend is as straightforward as training a regressor on the data, subtracting its predictions and leaving the residuals as the signal to be modelled by the TS. Of course, if the regressor is too expressive, it will cut out some of the TS signal you want to model. Therefore, a simple linear or polynomial fitting is preferred. By far the most common expression that captures trends is a power law of exponential nature. As such, to filter the trend, you can take the logarithm of the signal (or cube root if you have negative numbers). Irrespective of the regressor employed, remember to have available its inverse at prediction time, as you are most certainly interested in a predicted value for the signal, not its residuals.

Other techniques involve aggregation (taking an average for a time period), and differencing (taking the differences with a given lag until the TS becomes stationary). Differencing uses cumulative sums at prediction time. Finally, there are decomposition techniques that will model trend and seasonality but I will not discuss them here as they are hard to use for prediction. A warning worth stressing is that detrending something without trend will destroy it. [263†] Graphical inspection is the best way to reveal a trend.

5.1.5.4 Time Series Models: ARIMA

We will look into AR and MA, the two that give rise to ARIMA, which is showcased in the case study in Chapter 7. All these models are parametric, as a few parameters describe them. These parameters are important for us as we can use them as features.

Autoregressive. Autoregressive processes were introduced in 1921, and are used when you believe the time series depends on its immediate past plus random error. [61] Formally, an $AR(p)$ of order p has X_t expressed as a linear combination of p past values of X_t plus a purely random Z_t: $X_t = \alpha_1 X_{t-1} + \ldots + \alpha_p X_{t-p} + Z_t$.

Autoregressive processes capture "organic growth" processes. For example, if your product is of good quality and current customers bring new customers, your sales will behave as an AR process. The Fibonacci series, familiar to any

---

[†] Chapter 9.

computer scientist, is an AR(2) process. Fibonacci's stationarity can be seen from the fact that it does not matter where you find yourself in the sequence, you can take two contiguous values as $F(0)$ and $F(1)$ and it holds that $F(2) = F(0) + F(1)$. Fibonacci describes many processes in nature, but what if your signal is Fibonacci and *something more* (called **residuals**)? Then you can use ML to model the residuals. Using the available data to learn Fibonacci itself would be a waste of data, which is a reason to eliminate the trend. Note that an AR model is a single-layer linear predictor, as compared to a RNN (cf., Section 5.3.1) that is nonlinear.[133]

Moving Average. If the AR process models organic growth, the MA process models the ripple effect of errors, events that change the temporal locality around them but do not have a lasting effect. Formally, a $MA(q)$ of order q equals to $X_t = \beta_0 Z_t + \beta_1 Z_{t-1} + \cdots + \beta_q Z_{t-q}$. Note that the correlation between X_{t_1} and X_{t_2} when $|t_1 - t_2| > q$ is zero. This has important implications to identify them visually, as autocorrelations beyond a lag q will be zero. If your product is of bad quality and you launch an advertisement campaign, your sales will increase and stay up for a little bit, before the effect of the advertisement will die out completely over time.

ARIMA. ARMA(p,q) is the combination of AR and MA: $X_t = \alpha_1 X_{t-1} + \ldots + \alpha_p X_{t-p} + Z_t + \beta_1 Z_{t-1} + \ldots + \beta_q Z_{t-q}$. It is the sum of the AR plus a MA, a linear combination of the last q errors. If we add also a difference of order d, we get an ARIMA(p,d,q).

5.2 Instance-Based Engineering

Throughout this book, we have looked into techniques that apply to individual feature or sets of features. However, in the same search for improved representations incorporating domain knowledge to the input to the ML system, it is possible to modify the **instances** over which the ML operates. These advanced techniques involve special normalization approaches where clusters of instances are represented as single instances, instance weighting techniques and, more intriguingly, transforming a problem into a different, related problem from which you can read an answer to the original problem. Finally, techniques targeting the generation of synthetic data loosely fall into this category. We will briefly look at them in turn.

Instance Selection. In the same way you do feature selection, you can choose to trim your available instances based on a certain criteria, for example, if you feel a certain group of instances is overrepresented. This is another way of adding domain knowledge to the problem. A technique involving upsampling the rare class and downsampling the other classes can be used to deal with a rare class. [167] Even if you do not have intuitions about the domain, you can conclude that the data is too biased and decide to have a system that operates with uninformed priors. A way to achieve this is to cluster the data and replace each cluster of instances by representative elements in equal number (other ways involve manipulating the internals of the ML, for example, resetting the priors in naive Bayes to a uniform distribution). [49]†

Instance Weighting. A less drastic approach to unbias the data is to weight different instances according to some criteria. [204] If you have clustered the data, you can weight each instance so all the clusters have the same total weight, achieving a soft unbiasing of the data. Alternatively, you can weigh the data based on the errors made by a classifier trained on a different dataset: instances that are misclassified ought to receive special attention. This approach has been popularized by boosting meta-learning techniques. [241] Finally, it is not unusual to have data sourced and annotated in different ways. If you know certain instances are less error-prone or have better quality labels (e.g., labels annotated multiple times or where human annotators disagreements have been adjudicated by an expert), you might want to put more weight on these high-quality instances. Irrespective of your weighting scheme, many algorithms take an explicit instance weighting input parameter. Otherwise, you can resort to repeat instances that are heavily weighted, although that might destroy the underlying statistical expectations of the ML algorithm. An example of the negative effect of repeating instances is discussed in Chapter 9, Section 9.4.

Normalizing Against a Subset of the Data. The techniques from Chapter 2 can be applied to subsets of the instances instead of all the instances at once, for example, all instances with the same value or the same value range for a given feature (e.g., date of purchase, customer). This is particularly advantageous when the instances are topically related or they are derived from an underlying object outside the instance data. For example, in a task where the hope is that customer behaviour will predict a purchase decision, many instances may be generated from the same session. Normalizing per session might smooth session specific idiosyncrasies, improving the quality of the data. Note that

† Chapter 9.

session ID will make a very uninformative feature so you might need to go back to the source raw data to obtain it.

For a more involved example, in the DeepQA question answering system,[124] we had: (1) the original question (e.g., "What U.S. city has its largest airport named for a World War II hero?"); (2) a potential answer (e.g., "Toronto"); (3) a supporting passage from where the answer is found (e.g., "largest airports in North America: New York, Boston, Toronto, Los Angeles") (4) the target class is whether the answer is correct or not (e.g., "false"). The feature is the weighted word overlap between the supporting passage and the question but longer questions will have higher overlap, as they have more words to match. In this case, normalizing the scores against the original question scores allows the overlap feature to be used in a meaningful fashion.

Synthetic Data. If your domain allows for a certain level of inference, you can transmit that domain knowledge by providing synthetic instances, modifying your instances based on variations that ought not to change the target class. For example, you can assume a customer that made a purchase could have seen an extra random item before without losing interest in purchasing. Or you can use crowd workers to write paraphrases of text labelled for classification.[308] This is standard practice in computer vision (CV), as an upside-down giraffe is still a giraffe, albeit quite an uncomfortable one. Using CV techniques, Chapter 9 uses satellite images to predict the population of a city and finds a base model too brittle in the event of rotations and scaling. Enriching the dataset with variations from affine transformations results in an improvement over a baseline (but the baseline is dominated by instance weighting issues). See Section 9.4 for the fully worked-out example.

Alternatively, you can train a base ML system, generate random synthetic instances and label them with the base classifier, as done by the DECORATE algorithm.[229]

Derived Instances. At the end of the spectrum in instance engineering you can use your instances to solve a different problem and read from the output of the second classifier the answer to your original problem. For example, a common solution in a learning-to-rank problem is to replace N instances with $\frac{N(N-1)}{2}$ differential instances, assembling a full tournament among them. The target class in this case is whether the first instance in the difference ought to be ranked higher than the second one. Basically, replace all the instances with pairs of instances and to transform the problem as "instance one is better than instance two." This allows normalizing values of the features better, particularly if not all original instances can be compared in pairs.

5.3 Deep Learning and Feature Engineering

Neural networks (NNs) are biologically inspired models of computation started in the early 1940s, preceding the von Neumann architecture used in all current CPUs by two years. In NNs, the computation is divided into "neurons," computational units where each neuron computes the same function: it receives the output of the neurons in the previous layers, adds it and applies an **activation function** to it. The activation function adds a nonlinearity. The output is then passed to the next layers. Architectures with loops are also possible.

The main advantage of NNs is that there exists an efficient algorithm to train them called **backpropagation of errors**. Given a train set of inputs and expected outputs, an error metric and a given configuration of weights, the network can be evaluated and its gradients with respect to the errors computed. The gradients can then be employed to change the weights. This technique, **gradient descent**, trains the network. In reality, not only fully connected feed-forward networks can be trained by this technique. If the neuronal graph is derivable or near-derivable, its weights can also be trained.

Deep learning (DL) is a series of techniques enabling the training of deep (multiple hidden layers) neural networks with backpropagation. Since its introduction in the mid-2000s, I think DL has redefined the meaning of the term ML, in a similar way that ML redefined the meaning of the term AI.

Among the improvements we have – better activation functions (rectified linear units, ReLUs, $relu(x) = max(x, 0)$, a linear unit with a nonlinearity at zero); better initialization of weights[122] (traditional weight initialization exhibits higher variability than the data variability, and the initialization procedure dominated the training results); better training scheduling (mini-batches, which perform the weight updates over small number of training instances); better objective functions (softmax layers, a differentiable layer that can learn a pattern of activation where only one neuron is active, the maximum, and the rest are as close to zero as possible; a differentiable, "soft," version of the max function).

Aside from its substantive successes in the research world[62] and products backed from state-of-the-art research groups,[222] plenty of problems of interest remain beyond what is practical for DL techniques. As Mirella Lapata said in her keynote speech at the Association of Computational Linguistics in 2017,[200] there are plenty of interesting problems that will never accumulate the amount of training data needed for current DL algorithms. To support her case, she used movie plot summarization from subtitles as an example and pointed out there will never be enough movies made to train a quality sequence-to-sequence system. A similar point could be made about the number of human settlements in the planet, as used in the case studies in Part Two.

DL offers the possibility to eliminate FE by trading large amounts of training data for the painstaking process of feature improvement. It presently brings together many new and exciting ideas to FE that we will explore in this section. I am taking the perspective that DL makes available precomputed feature extractors that can be shared and fine-tuned on data (transfer learning). The features you get from available, pretrained networks will be very opaque, not unlike the ones you can obtain from other opaque techniques, such as dimensionality reduction (cf., Section 4.3.3 in Chapter 4). And not all problems and networks work well with fine-tuning, e.g., networks trained on regular images have difficulty dealing with medical images.[314] The algorithms that can benefit from them are also more limited, as you will then have very dense features. NNs will be an obvious choice for this type of featurization.

A particular subtype of network that poses a substantive leap forward in terms of modelling variable-feature length raw data is the use of DL recurrent neural nets such as the long short-term memories and the gated recurrent units, so we will look at them also in detail in Section 5.3.1.

The key concept behind DL is representation learning (although not all representation learning methods are DL,[337] as we saw in Chapter 4 with GloVe; see Section 4.3.7.3). From the raw data, DL seeks to train feature extractors in the form of neural network layers. These models can be learned in a layer-by-layer basis (e.g., "stacked"[99]). Earlier layers can be trained over large datasets on related tasks and then shared for reuse by the community (e.g., AlexNet, VGG, Word2Vec embeddings[206]). In a way, these pretrained layers beg the question: are they features or models?[289]

What about FE for DL? While many techniques in DL perform FE, some FE techniques are also useful for DL, for instance, computable features, particularly ratios, as we saw in Chapter 3, Figure 3.1. Normalizing features is also important, as representing them in ways the neural network can operate upon (for example, one-hot-encoding or embeddings). Neural networks are also amenable to embedded feature selection, neural networks in DL now are trained with **dropout**, a technique where a percentage of the connections are hardwired to zero[†] in each training step so that different connections are active at each step, which is a form of regularization.

Finally, the injection of domain knowledge that FE enables is also present in DL, but in this case by carefully crafting a neural architecture that reflects beliefs about the domain (see, for example, the introduction of dialog

---

[†] This is an oversimplification, see Goodfellow, Bengio and Courville [125] for details.

acts cells[321]). How to effectively architecture deep neural networks to reflect domain knowledge is an area of active research.[98] Comparatively, FE has a longer tradition in the field.

5.3.1 RNNs

A recurrent neural network (RNN) is a neural network where you feed back the output into the network, it incorporates a concept of time. RNNs can be trained by "unrolling" the network in a process known as backpropagation through time (BPTT). In BPTT, the network at time $t - 1$ is considered a separate network executing before the one at time t. During weight update, care is taken to ensure all the weights are updated the same, as they are all weights of the same network (what is called **tied weights**). Traditionally, they had the problem of **vanishing gradients**, where inputs too far away in time from the output will impact the learning process too little.

Deep Learning RNNs. To mitigate the problem of the vanishing gradients, it is possible to confine the recurrence to a complex set of neurons that hold a small local memory. This memory is thus passed as output to be reused next time. The set of neurons can operate in this memory by accessing parts of it (by multiplication with a soft bit mask); by deleting it (by subtracting after applying a soft bit mask); by updating it (by addition after applying a soft bit mask). Based on this idea, two such units are in use: gated recurrent units (GRU), which are simpler and long short-term memory (LSTM), which are more complex. We will briefly look into GRUs as they are simpler to explain.

GRU. A GRU unit (Figure 5.4) receives the input at time t via the x_t parameter and the memory from the previous iteration as h_{t-1}. The output at time t, h_t will be a weighted average between h_{t-1} and an updated version $\tilde{h}_t$ (hh_t in the figure). The weighted average is controlled by z_t, the zeroing mask, trained from h_{t-1} and x_t with weights W_z. The updated version $\tilde{h}_t$ is obtained from a reset mask r_t, trained from h_{t-1} and x_t with weights W_r. Finally, $\tilde{h}_t$ is trained from r_t, h_{t-1} and x_t with weights W. The beauty of the process is that the weight matrices W_z, W_r and W are all learned from data using BPTT. In terms of FE, LSTMs and GRUs bring the possibility of obtaining an encoding of a sequence that is more informed than just an associative operation on top of representations for individual items (like the average of embeddings or the logical OR of one-hot-encodings). The true value of DL RNNs is when training the whole ML end-to-end from raw data to labels

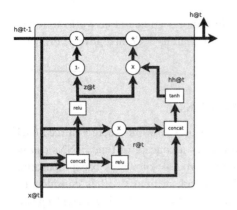

$$z_t = \mathrm{relu}\left(W_z \cdot [h_{t-1}, x_t]\right)$$
$$r_t = \mathrm{relu}\left(W_r \cdot [h_{t-1}, x_t]\right)$$
$$hh_t = \tanh\left(W \cdot [r_t * h_{t-1}, x_t]\right)$$
$$h_t = (1 - z_t) * h_{t-1} + z_t * hh_t$$

Figure 5.4 GRU.

(or even to a second sequence, when doing sequence-to-sequence models). However, it is also possible to introduce an auxiliary task and train the DL RNN to solve that task, run the sequence through it and use the final memory (the h_t in the GRU) as a feature vector representation for the sequence. This feature vector representation can be combined with other features, separate from the sequential raw data.

Computing Paradigm. Training in backpropagation-through-time computes an update for the weights and applies it only once, usually as the average of the updates. All these updates are tied to the same weight. Gradient descent, weight-tying and loosely differentiable updates define a computing paradigm. Any graph of units can thus be trained if the path from input to output is loosely differentiable. This graph is sometimes made explicit in some NN frameworks, like TensorFlow.[1] Programming in this new paradigm takes the form of master equations or flow diagrams. While this enables a new age of computing, in the immediate case of FE, frameworks like TensorFlow present themselves as a great opportunity to be used as a domain specific language for FE (independent of DL), which is an idea worth further investigation.

5.4 Automated Feature Engineering

In this section, we will see techniques that seek to automate the FE process based in what is called automated feature engineering (AFE) on training data (next section) or assumptions about the data (Section 5.4.2).

5.4.1 Feature Learning

Using enough training material, it is possible to analyze large amounts of raw data and synthesize computable features to use by the rest of the system. In a way, you have skeletal computable features and can leave the data to flesh out the details. We will study three examples of this approach, one using convolutions (next section), the Featuretools/data science machine system as an AutoML approach (Section 5.4.1.2) and another approach using genetic programming (Section 5.4.1.2). Note that DL in general can be considered feature learning. I have chosen to discuss it separately to cover other topics beyond feature learning itself.

5.4.1.1 Convolutional Neural Networks

Convolution involves applying a filter (called a **convolution kernel**) to a region of the feature space (for example, a segment of an image). The filter is of fixed size and maps the features (pixels) to a smaller dimension, for example, by multiplying the pixel values and applying a nonlinear function such as a ReLU. Kernels used this way are a traditional feature extraction method in image processing. They are very popular these days with text data, too, based on the Transformer model.[313] For example, a kernel could be written to detect a vertical red line followed by a horizontal blue line. Kernels perform feature extraction, going from input features to kernel outputs as the kernel slides over the input raw data.

Using convolutional neural networks, such kernels can be trained, realizing them as neural networks with tied weights, which in turn results in fewer parameters. Figure 5.5 shows a one-dimensional convolution where the first four elements of the sequence are fed into two convolutions of a kernel of size 3×2. The weights going into the second convolutional unit are shown in a lighter tone. You can see that s_2 is connected to c_{21} using the same black solid links as s_1 uses with c_{11}: the first convolution has s_1 as its first element, while the second shifts the sequence one element and it has s_2 as its first element.

5.4.1.2 Featuretools

The Featuretools effort is lead by James Max Kanter, which in his own words:[174]

> The key piece of advice I'd give someone new to machine learning is not to get caught up in the different machine learning techniques. Instead (1) spend more time on translating your problem into terms a machine can understand and (2) how do you perform feature engineering so the right variables are available for machine learning to use.

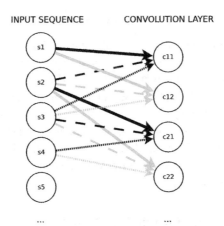

Figure 5.5 One-dimensional convolution with a 3×2 kernel. Three elements in the input sequence result in two neurons in the convolutional layer. The weights indicated by the same colour and line style are the same (shared weights).

They have developed the data science machine (DSM) that derives models from raw data[175] in a two-step process: (1) deep feature synthesis: feature generation from relational data, following relations to base database row, then applying mathematical operations from there and (2) generalizable learning pipeline tuned with a Gaussian copula.[266]

Their DSM reads like a summary to the present book – it does data preprocessing (removes null values, cf., Section 3.2, one-hot-encoding, cf., Section 3.1, normalization, cf., Section 2.1), feature selection plus dimensionality reduction (truncated SVD, cf., Section 4.3.3, and then feature selection using F1-score against a target, cf., Section 4.1.1.3), and modelling (random forests, cf., Section 4.2.3, and clustering plus random forest, where they first cluster using k-means, cf., Section 2.2.1.2, then train a random forest on each cluster and use a cluster-classifier on top).

They focus on relational data that captures human interaction with a system and where the said data is used to predict human behaviour. From their perspective, domains involving text, images and signals have their FE problem fully automated, while data involving human behaviour do not. I share that perspective and I believe human behavioural data and many other domains still need custom FE. There are case studies for these better-understood domains in Part Two of this book, so you can learn from them for new domains. Another insight is that common data questions, such as "when was the last time this customer ordered an expensive product?" actually result in queries against the data that produce features. Their algorithm seeks to approximate this.

Their input is in the form of SQL database. Their depth-based feature synthesis uses depth from the base field and it is unrelated to DL. It involves three types of operations: entity-level (*efeat*), direct level (*dfeat*) and relation-level (*rfeat*). The *efeat* operations are computable features over a single row in a table. Their *dfeat* operations are applied to forward (one-to-many) relation between two rows, where the source (unique) produces features to transfer to the linked. The name direct is because the efeat in the source is copied directly to the target. Finally, their *rfeat* operations are applied to backward (many-to-one) relation between one row and many rows. The feature obtained in this way is the result of an aggregate over the other rows (e.g., min, max, count).

Their algorithm runs over one table and uses the other tables to enrich the features. It performs the operations rfeat and dfeat on the other tables first (recursing until the end or until a maximum depth), then combines the results and expands them using the operation efeat. This explodes in the number of features very quickly. It automatically produces SQL queries with appropriate join and where clauses.

The second innovation of the DSM is how they tune the parameters of the full process using the Gaussian copula process,[287] where they sample parameters, evaluate the model end-to-end and adjust. All in all, a data scientist can start with the data science machine's solution and then apply their expert knowledge to refine it as it produces human-understandable features. Note that Featuretools now has a company behind it and is gaining new functionality at a rapid pace. This description follows their published work, however, visit their documentation[†] for up-to-date information regarding new functionality and capabilities.

5.4.1.3 Genetic Programming

Another approach for feature learning is to search the space of potential small programs over the features, that is, to automatically generate computable features. Of course, the search space is massive but that is the goal of automatic programming techniques such as genetic programming.[192] In genetic programming, a population of small programs represented as formula trees (trees with operations in the nodes and values and variables as terminals) is kept at all times. In each step of the search, each tree is evaluated using a fitness function. Trees with low fitness are discarded and trees with high fitness are used to repopulate the discarded trees by changing single trees or by combining existing trees.

[†] http://docs.featuretools.com/

In earlier work, Heaton[146] showed that different learning algorithms need different AFE approaches and there are functions that NN cannot synthesize easily and others that are trivial. Rational differences and ratios were very difficult for NNs (cf., Figure 3.1 in Chapter 3). In his doctoral dissertation,[147] he performed a genetic programming stochastic search evaluating all the population at once using only one neural net. Moreover, as the genetic programming progresses, the weights in the evaluation NN are reused, reducing the amount of recomputation in the search. The thesis uses input perturbation as part of the fitness function of the GA.[46]

It runs the algorithm over the PROBEN1 dataset,[260] a collection of 13 datasets from the UCI repository, which has been widely used as a neural network benchmark on small data. It builds on his work on the Encog framework for genetic algorithms[145] but only deals with "low dimensional named features" (no more than two dozen features). From the 17 datasets, it only improved in a statistically significant manner in four. While the thesis is full of smart moves, it shows the complexity of the task. It will be interesting to see domain adaptations of this technique, for example, to human behaviour tabular data, such as Featuretools.

5.4.2 Unsupervised Feature Engineering

Unsupervised FE seeks to modify the feature space in ways that expose the structure present in the data. Similar to other unsupervised techniques, it contains a model of the object being worked upon and estimates the parameters of that model from the data. Usually, they require very large amounts of data. The model itself is a decision by the practitioner that captures domain knowledge about the feature space. Two approaches have been studied in detail in the literature: restricted Boltzmann machines[148] (RBMs) and autoencoders.[149] We will look into autoencoders.

Autoencoders train a neural network to predict its input, with a middle layer of smaller size than the input size, what is called a "bottleneck."[289] The structure present in the data is then concentrated in the smaller layer; see Figure 5.6 for an example.

The main question with autoencoders is how to achieve generalization. Simply packing the data into the middle layer will not help a ML task, as it will be akin to giving the ML algorithm a gzipped version of the training data (which is nothing that presents itself as a particularly good idea). What you really want is that similar representations in the centre layer produce plausible artificial (unseen) instances when run through the decoder side.

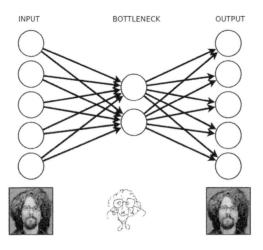

Figure 5.6 Example of autoencoders. The bottleneck generates an abstract representation of the image fed to the autoencoder.

Some techniques in active research to help this scenario involve injecting noise or variations during training, in the form of variational autoencoders[184] or denoising autoencoders.[317] Ultimately, they are also a dimensionality reduction technique similar to the ones described in Chapter 4.

5.5 Learning More

A great resource for staying up to date with new FE techniques is the write-ups for machine learning competitions in sites such as Kaggle, and conferences, such as the KDD Cup IJCAI or ECML. For variable-length feature vectors, I recommend the book, *Graph-Based Natural Language Processing and Information Retrieval* by Mihalcea and Radev.[232] For a recent review on graph kernels, see Ghosh and others.[121] Deep learning material is quite abundant these days. The main book on the topic is *Deep Learning* by Goodfellow, Bengio and Courville,[125] but many people might find *Hands-On Machine Learning with Scikit-Learn and TensorFlow* by Géron[120] easier to follow. For more practical matters, Ng's write-up on advice for applying ML is a great read.[242] There is also progress being made in better explaining DL models.[11]

For AFE, convolutional neural networks are studied in detail in DL for computational vision tutorials and books. For linear (non-bidimensional) approaches, I recommend the online lectures of Nils Reimers.[268] Another

AutoML framework of interest is TransmogrifAI,[307] which brings much needed type safety to FE.

Finally, for a more research-oriented perspective on FE, the book edited by Dong and Liu [132] is an excellent read. In particular, chapter 11 is devoted to DL, including a full review of different algorithms of the field. It also mentions that the first layers of the discriminator of a trained GAN [126] are a trained feature extractor, an insight that I believe deserves further attention in the FE field. On the AFE topic, chapter 9 in the same volume describes a system [181] using reinforcement learning to ponder the different FE transformations. I refer you to that chapter for the details; it encompasses both approaches discussed in the current chapter, plus a reinforcement layer on top, trained on thousands of ML datasets. Other topics covered in that volume that are not present in this book include FE for unsupervised learning and streaming data.

PART TWO

Case Studies

While domain-independent approaches can produce good-quality models very quickly, many times is a case "If you want to go fast, go alone; but if you want to go far, go together."[†] Tapping into domain expertise will allow you to get much farther than if you need to reinvent the wheel for every little quirk and problem in your target domain. Even more so in the amply studied domains we discuss in this part.

These domains are quite well studied and have many books written on each. Moreover, there might already be books on just feature engineering (FE) for each of these domains. The idea here is to learn from these well-studied domains and see whether aspects of the problem you are trying to solve will be enhanced by this knowledge. There is the obvious question of whether the information discussed here will be useful for people working with data on those domains. It is correct information and is useful *per se*. But when in doubt, I have focused in providing a narrative to take these techniques outside the domains than to keep them insularly useful.

All the code and data for these case studies is available under open source licenses at

`http://artoffeatureengineering.com`

The expectation is that the material should be understandable without looking at the Python notebooks, but references to the cells in the notebook are kept throughout. Not all the techniques presented here work well in the data at hand. FE involve much trial and error and that is reflected on these case studies. At about 50% success rate, these case studies still paint an optimistic view of FE. A rate between 10–20% is more likely.

These case studies reflect how I attempted to solve these problems through FE alone with the following constraints: Python code understandable for non-Python developers with as few Python dependencies as possible; running time under two days per notebook without a computer cluster or a GPU and using 8Gb of RAM or less; source dataset below 2Gb for all case studies combined. There are two obvious casualties from these decisions: not using a DL framework (like TF) nor performing hyperparameter search. This last item was a decision motivated by these constraints. **Do not copy that behaviour, hyperparameter search can account for almost 50% performance increase.** [175] When doing experiments for a publication or R&D for a production system, I would leave a hyperparameter search running for a week time or use a cluster with hundreds of cores to speed it up.

[†] And if you want to go really fast, ask somebody who knows the way.

6

Graph Data

This chapter focuses on feature engineering (FE) techniques for graph data as an example of FE techniques applied to structured data. The chapter also describes the creation of the base WikiCities dataset employed here and in the next three chapters. This dataset is used to predict the population of cities using semantic information from Wikipedia infoboxes. Semantic graphs were made popular in recent years thanks to the Semantic Web[33] initiative. Semantic graphs are an example of structured data. They exemplify the handling and the representation of variable-length raw data as fixed-length feature vectors, particularly using the techniques discussed in Section 5.1 in Chapter 5. Graph data itself is usually better dealt with by machine learning (ML) algorithms that operate directly over them, like graph kernels,[318] graph neural networks (NN)[256,271] using graph embeddings[283] or optimization techniques, such as the ones I employed in my own doctoral dissertation.[89]

The intention behind the creation of this dataset is to provide a task that can be attacked with structural features, with timestamped features, textual features and image features. A task that allows for all these approaches is that of calculating the population of a city or town based on their ontological properties (e.g., title of its leader or its time zone), based on its historical population and historical features (which involves a time series analysis), based on the textual description of the place (which involves text analysis, particularly as sometimes the text includes the population) and a satellite image of the city (which involves image processing). Each of these alternative takes of the problem will be addressed in the next chapters.

As each case study is quite detailed, a general overview section starts each case study with a high-level summary, together with a table of the different featurizations employed (Table 6.1). Other sources of information regarding ML over graphs in general conclude this chapter.

139

Table 6.1. *Feature vectors used in this chapter. (a) First featurization, 380 features (b) Second featurization, 325 features (c) Optimal feature set, 552 features (d) Conservative feature set, 98 features.*

1	rel#count
2	area#1
3	areaCode#count
4	areaLand#count
5	areaLand#1
6	areaLand#2
7	areaTotal#count
8	areaTotal#1
9	areaWater#count
10	areaWater#1
11	birthPlace?inv#count
12	city?inv#count
13	country#count
14	country#1=United_States
15	country#1=France
	...
34	country#1=OTHER
35	deathPlace?inv#count
36	department#1=Nord
37	department#=Yvelines
38	department#1=Pas-de-Calais
	...
377	seeAlso#3@OTHER
378	homepage#count
379	name#count
380	nick#count

(a)

1	rel#count
	... (identical to (a)) ...
34	country#1=OTHER
35	deathPlace?inv#count
36	department#1=Nord
37	department#1=Pas-de-Calais
	...
309	seeAlso#3@OTHER
310	homepage#count
311	name#count
312	nick#count
313	computed#defined
314	computed#value
315	country#1#TRE
316	department#1#TRE
317	leaderTitle#1#TRE
318	populationAsOf#1#TRE
319	region#1#TRE
320	timeZone#1#TRE
321	type#1#TRE
322	utcOffset#1#TRE
323	utcOffset#2#TRE
324	type#1#TRE
325	seeAlso#3#TRE

(b)

1	rel#count
	...similar to (b) without OTHER...
296	nick#count
297	computed#defined
298	computed#value
299	country#1=United_States+orig
	...similar to (b) with +orig...
552	seeAlso#3=OTHER+orig

(c)

1	rel#count
	...similar to (b) without country values ...
96	nick#count
97	computed#defined
98	computed#value

(d)

Chapter Overview

The WikiCities dataset is a resource put together (Section 6.1) for the purpose of exercising different FE techniques. It starts from DBpedia, a graph with entities and literals on its vertices and named relations on its edges. We use entities referring to human settlements (cities and towns, referred generally as cities in this discussion). Doing exploratory data analysis (EDA, Section 6.2), we drill down on specific relations useful for predicting the target population. We visualize 10 random city subgraphs and realize that the amount of information available is already a great indicator of population. Looking into the top relation counts, we settle for using relations that appear in at least 5% of all cities, resulting in 40+ relations. These relations have multiple values for them and are unordered. To deal with their set-based nature, we sort them by the frequency of its value then truncate them to their median length.

For the first feature set (Section 6.3), we introduce an OTHER category to handle categorical values that account for 20% of the occurrences. This nets 50 numeric and 11 categorical columns, which we then one-hot-encoded. A drill-down by feature ablation (Section 6.3.1) highlights the top contributors to the error are cities that have a rich history but are not necessarily that populated, like Dublin. This result makes sense for a system using ontological properties to predict population. An ablation study reveals that counts are misleading the algorithm. We can either drop these features or dampen their growth. We dampen their value with a log function, which helps performance. Moving into feature utility metrics (Section 6.3.1.3) that need a categorical target, we discretize the target variable into segments with an equal number of cities. For feature utility, we use mutual information (MI). The most informative features look very good, e.g., time zone features indicate that geographic location is important. Using random features to elicit uninformative features, we drop 68 features. To gain a broader picture, we use decision trees for feature analysis (Section 6.3.1.4) where we see that the country carries quite a bit of weight. It also uncovers a relation between areaTotal and populationDensity. Its product makes for a great computable feature. We then arrive to the second feature set (Section 6.4), where we make the categorical features more informative by doing target rate encoding (TRE). For categorical features representing whether a city is part of a country or not, TRE replaces a 1.0 with the mean size of the cities in that country. We also add the computed feature that is available roughly for one quarter of the instances.

Finally, we perform a feature stability study (Section 6.4.1) to create a conservative feature set that can withstand catastrophic variations in the training data. We then see how the trained model behaves under error perturbations over the features. It highlights country features as worrisome, but country is the most stable property of this domain. We leverage this realization to assemble the "conservative" feature set: non-categorical features plus categorical with country values. The high-performance feature set (Section 6.5) uses TRE and the rest of the features. This feature set achieves a performance equivalent to a four-way segmentation, that is, it can tell apart hamlets from small towns and small cities from large cities.

6.1 WikiCities Dataset

The WikiCities dataset (Figure 6.1) is a resource put together in this book for the purpose of exercising different FE techniques. It can be downloaded, together with all the source code for this and the following chapters from

$$\texttt{http://artoffeatureengineering.com}$$

It starts with the latest release of DBpedia[71] (October 2016), which is a curated ontological resource obtained from the infoboxes at Wikipedia. Infoboxes are the tabular information appearing next to the page content in each Wikipedia page.

The DBpedia project's mission is to transform the infoboxes into high-quality structured information in graph format, by cleaning and standardizing some of the information available in Wikipedia. DBpedia constitutes what is called a **semantic graph**, a graph with entities and literals on its vertices and named relations on its edges. Entities and relations are expressed using URIs,[32] a generalization of URLs, with their own namespaces and ontologies. It uses the resource description framework (RDF),[201] a graph-description language where graphs are represented as triples of source entity (also called the "subject"), named relation (also called the "verb") and target entity or literal (also called the "object"). DBpedia is thus distributed as files containing sets of triples. For example, a triple will be (New York City,

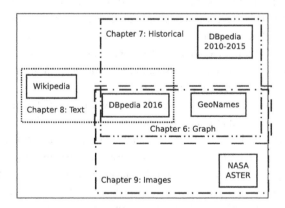

Figure 6.1 WikiCities dataset, with its dependencies in Part Two chapters.

leaderTitle, "mayor") with the entity "New York City" represented as the URI `http://dbpedia.org/resource/New_York_City`, the literal as `"mayor"@en` and the relation as `http://dbpedia.org/ontology/-leaderTitle`. I have tried to omit the full URIs whenever it is possible as they make the text more cumbersome. The subject is always an entity in the ontology, prefixed by the name space `dbpedia.org`. The verb is an ontological relation, of which there are several hundred (leader-name, type, population, etc). The object can be either another entity or a literal value (a string or a number).

The mapping between the infoboxes and the RDF output is also kept in a Wiki like resource. [205] While conceptually the graphs created in the DBpedia project are semantically rich and cleaner than the source Wikipedia pages, this is still a very noisy resource (a topic on which I have done some joint research [93]). You can expect many errors and inconsistencies, as the source material (Wikipedia) is the result of thousands of volunteers working semi-independently.

Besides the actual files, DBpedia also contains links to multiple other ontologies, like Freebase and [39] YAGO, [300] plus links to the original Wikipedia articles that resulted in the extracted information. For these case studies we will be using the files *instance_types_en.ttl.bz2*, *mappingbased_literals_en.ttl.bz2* and *mappingbased_objects_en.ttl.bz2*.

As the type information is derived from the infobox itself, it is noisy and the *city* or *settlement* types are not thoroughly annotated in the source Wikipedia. Therefore, one of the first challenges is to identify which entities in DBpedia are cities. Instead of relying on heuristics (such as "any entity with a location and a population," which are unreliable), Cell 1 in the accompanying Jupyter notebook uses an external, more reliable source through the GeoNames project. [323] GeoNames distributes a list of "cities or settlements with at least 1,000 people." It contains 128,000+ places (file *cities1000.txt*). Cell 1 links them back to DBpedia using the file *geonames_links.ttl.bz2* distributed also by DBpedia.

Using the available links to DBpedia, Cell 1 finds 80,251 of the GeoNames cities 1,000 in the DBpedia dataset. These 80,251 constitute the raw data for this problem. Following the methodology described in Chapter 1, Section 1.3.2, Cell 2 sets aside 20% of this data for final evaluation at the end of the FE process. That produces a development set of 64,200 cities with a held-out of 16,051 cities. The next step in the methodology is to do some EDA over these 64,200 settlements to decide basic featurization and the model to employ.

The key issue to resolve here is to drill-down on the specific relations that will be useful to predict the target variable (population). While DBpedia contains hundreds of relations, many are seldom expressed (meaning, there are few pages where a human editor feels the need to record information such as *distant-to-London*). Also, there might be value in relations that have a given city as its subject but there might also be value in relations that have the city as *its object* (that is, the inverse of certain relations). I then construct inverted relations by appending an ?inv at the end of the relation. This in itself is a design decision, as it will lose the connection between an actual relation and its inverse. This decision might be worth revisiting during the FE process.

Because processing the large files of DBpedia is a computationally onerous process, Cell 3 prefilters the triples related to all entities both forward and inverse, reducing the triples down to 2 million triples from 38 million. The next step is to produce a filtered version just for the development and held-out sets (Cell 4). These triples, close to 1.6 million in total, are the working set. Let us do some EDA over this working set.

6.2 Exploratory Data Analysis (EDA)

Cell 5 starts the EDA (cf., Section 1.4.1 in Chapter 1) by visualizing 10 random entities using the Graphviz package.[97] One of the entities appears in a Figure 6.2.

From here, I can see that many randomly sampled cities are all fairly small. This tell us that most instances will have very little data while others will contain the bulk of the triples. The amount of information available is already a great indicator of population, an insight that suggests *total number of triples* is a meaningful feature.

From looking at the graphs, we can see that certain places (like *Skudai*) do not contain population information. A reasonable next step is thus to filter out cities with no population information (as we cannot use them to build a regressor or a classifier).

The top relation counts are shown in Table 6.2 and the full list of 30 relations in file *ch6_cell5_rel_counts.tsv*. From the table we can see that some relations are defined for almost all cities (like *rdf type* or *is part of*). Looking at the full list of relations, I can see that some others are very rare (like *homepage* or *leader party*). The inverse relations are also quite rare but these places are all sparsely populated. Also note that taking a different sample produces quite different results, so it is easy to be misled. Still, the insights captured are useful and allow us to move forward.

Next, I need to know how population is expressed in DBpedia. From *Psevdas*, we can see it has a relation *populationTotal*. Would that be the

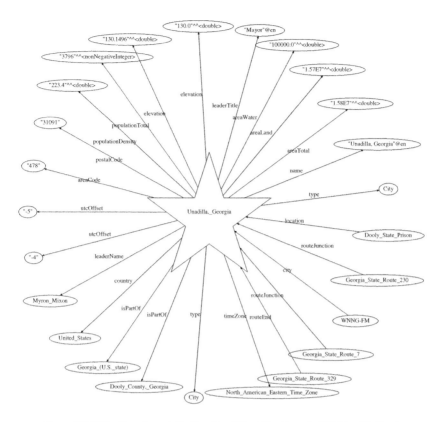

Figure 6.2   DBpedia subgraph for the city of Unadilla, Georgia (USA), with direct and inverse relations reachable from the city.

only way population is expressed? Let us see what relations contain the word population in their name (Cell 6), as shown in Table 6.3. From the table, it seems *populationTotal* is the right relation to use, but I want to remove *populationMetro*, *populationUrban* and *populationRural* as they will otherwise constitute a target leak (cf., Section 1.3.1). Also, if *populationTotal* is missing, either of those, if defined, could be used as surrogates of the target variable. At this stage we can filter out the cities without a defined population. We can collect also the population for the cities we keep (which will require cleaning type information in the literals[†]). This number will be the target value for regression, or a discretized version of it, the target class (Cell 7). That totals the cities with known population in the development set to 48,868.

[†] Such as ^^<http://www.w3.org/2001/XMLSchema#nonNegativeInteger>.

Table 6.2. *The most frequent 10 relations on
a sample of 10 cities from the first data round.*

Relation	Counts
utcOffset	10
isPartOf	10
timeZone	8
22-rdf-syntax-ns#type	7
name	7
country	7
populationTotal	5
areaTotal	4
leaderTitle	4
elevation	4

Table 6.3. *Relations with "population" in the
name.*

Relation	Counts
populationTotal	49,028
populationDensity	19,540
populationAsOf	5,410
populationPlace?inv	2,511
populationMetro	1,286
populationUrban	1,188
populationTotalRanking	1,057
populationMetroDensity	142
populationUrbanDensity	79
populationRural	42

Cell 8 repeats the plotting of 10 random cities now in the development set
with a known population. These cities with defined population have definitely
more things going on for them, including multiple *areaCode* relations (three
in the case of *Wermelskirchen*) and a variety of inverse relations.

At this stage in the EDA process I want to look into which of these relations
might be good features. From the discussion in Section 1.5.1 in Chapter 1,
**we want features that are simple, related to the target (population) and
readily available**. From the perspective of "readily available" I want to focus
on relations that are frequent enough that will be useful for a ML algorithm

Table 6.4. *Relation coverage for the cities in the development set. Last column is the percentage of cities with the given relationship defined. This table conveys a summary of the counts for the all 347 relations available.*

Position	Relation	Counts	%
First	buildingEndDate	1	0.00
At 10 percentile	sportCountry?inv	1	0.00
At 20 percentile	lowestState	3	0.00
At 30 percentile	inflow?inv	5	0.01
At 40 percentile	board?inv	9	0.01
At 50 percentile	riverMouth?inv	27	0.05
At 60 percentile	county?inv	78	0.15
At 70 percentile	knownFor?inv	209	0.42
At 80 percentile	populationTotalRanking	699	1.43
At 90 percentile	headquarter?inv	2,769	5.66
At 100 percentile	areaTotal	29,917	61.22
Last	22-rdf-syntax-ns#type	48,868	100.00

(Section 6.3 will look into the issue of "related to the target"). Therefore, their frequency over the whole set of entities is paramount. Cell 9 sorts the relations by the number of cities that have them defined. The relations with their counts at different percentiles is shown in Table 6.4.

To reiterate, which relations to use is key to success for the ML as each relation will span at least a feature, if not more. **At this early stage in the FE process, I want to overselect and then drill down to find a better subset.** But I still do not want to select unnecessarily too many, particularly we do not want relations that are not useful. Anything appearing less than 5% of the time is not really that useful, even if it looks very appealing (such as *populationTotalRanking*, only available for 1.4% of the cities in the devset).

Keeping only relations that appear in at least 5% of the cities (Cell 10), we are now down to 43 relations and 1.3 million triples for 48,000+ instances. But we still do not have features, as these **relations have multiple values for them and are unordered.** To deal with this situation, we can use the techniques from Section 5.1 in Chapter 5 for dealing sets, lists, graphs, etc. For the set-based (unordered) nature of the relations, we can sort them (Section 5.1.1). In this case we can sort them by the frequency of its value (object of the relation). If the object value is more frequent, it might be more informative to the ML. That leaves us then with a **list** of values for each relation. To represent lists, a common technique is to truncate it to a fixed length (Section 5.1.2). Cell 11

Table 6.5. *Arity of a sample of selected relations in the development set. The minimum column is not shown as it consists only of ones.*

Relation	Counts	Maximum count		Avg	Median
area	4803	Saint-Germain-Nuelles	1	1	1
areaCode	25417	Iserlohn	8	1.2	1
areaTotal	29917	Spotswood	2	1.3	1
birthPlace?inv	21089	London	6258	13.3	3
city?inv	13551	London	709	3.9	2
country	45977	Sada,_Galicia	8	1.1	1
district	5842	Waterloo,_Illinois	6	1	1
elevation	28669	Córdoba,_Argentina	4	1.3	1
ground?inv	3368	Vienna	134	1.9	1
isPartOf	32266	Baima	10	2	2
isPartOf?inv	3786	Shijiazhuang	296	7	1
leaderTitle	12322	Canora	8	1.5	1
nearestCity?inv	4136	Middletown	46	1.8	1
region	4711	Centralia,_Illinois	4	1	1
timeZone	28615	Jerusalem	4	1.4	1
utcOffset	27762	Lőrinci	3	1.7	2
rdf-schema#seeAlso	3426	Dubai	19	2.7	3
nick	2764	Davao_City	10	1.1	1

helps us see how many values a relation can take for a given city. I call this number the "fan-out" of a relation, borrowing from circuit design. It is shown in Table 6.5.

There are multiple things to note in Table 6.5. First, no relation has a minimum above one (this is ommitted from this printed table), which is good because it means no relation is inherently a relation commanding multiple values. We can also see that the inverted relations have substantive maximums, which make sense: cities such as London will be the birthplace of thousands of Wikipedia-worthy people in the English-language Wikipedia. Clearly, the most important signal here is the number of such inbound relations rather than the actual entities being referred, but I will leave that to be determined by some feature-selection techniques as the ones discussed in Section 4.1 in Chapter 4 or by feature-discretization techniques as discussed in Section 2.2 in Chapter 2. A broader analysis of the graphs might also pay off, for example, how many of the people born in the city received Oscars? I investigated such questions using optimization techniques when looking into semantic graph data for biography generation during my thesis work.[89] But such expansion is outside the scope of what is feasible with the techniques described here. Continuing with the table, **some of the averages are also high but they seem to be driven by a few megalopolis (big cities).** The medians are much more informative, with only a few beyond one. Cell 12 thus focuses on the medians and extracts them for featurization.

We are now almost ready for the first featurization. What is missing is to have global counts for all literals and entities that appear as objects of relations. These counts can then be used to sort the values and select the top ones according to the median fan-out computed in Cell 12. To such features I will also add the total count per relation (`relation name#COUNT`, e.g., `http://dbpedia.org/knownFor?inv#COUNT`) and a large total of all relevant relations (number of relations defined). Missing features are marked by the string "N/A." Adding the population produces the base featurization of the dataset (Cell 13). Some ML frameworks might be able to operate over this featurization directly (such as Weka[331]) but the ML framework being used in this use case (scikit-learn[253]) requires further encoding, which depends on the ML algorithm being used.

Therefore, now is a good time to think about which ML algorithm to employ over this data. The data contains almost 100 columns of different types and a numeric target. Cell 14 plots the target and its distribution, as shown in Figure 6.3(a). That curve is quite steep at the end. **To flatten it down, we can apply a logarithmic function as it helps put such growth processes in perspective, as discussed in Section 3.1** in Chapter 3. Instead of the default logarithm on base e I will use the more intuitive base 10 that tell us the number of digits in the population for a city. Figure 6.3(b) shows the result (Cell 15).

The first thing to notice in this figure is that there seems to be many cities in the dataset with less that 1,000 inhabitants (using base 10 makes

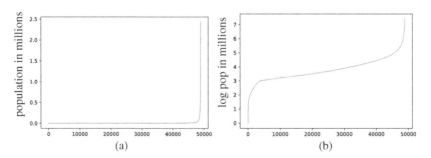

(a)   (b)

Figure 6.3 Population values in development set: (a) raw values (b) logarithmic values.

this realization straightforward). Some even with only one person! Looking a little bit into the triples, I can see that some are actual mistakes in Wikipedia (a city with 1,000,000 whose population has been erroneously written as 1.000.000, etc.). Others are small towns and hamlets that have less than a 1,000 people living on them (but might have more than a 1,000 at the time GeoNames built their list). **Following the discussion on outliers in Section 2.4 in Chapter 2, these are outliers that are worth removing from the data.** Cell 16 removes these outliers for a total of 44,959 cities. They are still in the held-out final test data as their impact in production needs to be seen and evaluated.

Now I can try some EDA for the ML algorithm to use, as I need to settle on the algorithm and decide how to featurize the string data present in the base featurization. **Let us try some regression models on it against the single feature of** *number of relations defined*. Let us start with support vector regression (SVR) using radial basis functions (RBFs) as kernels in Cell 17. SVR has two parameters C and epsilon, doing a grid search over them (which basically overfits them to the development set) we get to a RMSE 0.6179 with the curve fitting shown in Figure 6.4(a). Note that SVR needs its variables to be scaled to 1.0 and centred around zero, a technique discussed in Section 2.1 in Chapter 2.

While the RMSE is very promising for only one feature (less than one order of magnitude) and the flat bottom of the figure can be explained by the fact the SVR has only a single support vector (from its single feature), the figure still does not seem to track the curve that well. To see if this is still an issue with SVR or with the feature, Cell 18 plots one against the other. Figure 6.5 shows there is correlation but it is weak and **I conclude that the SVR algorithm is extracting just as good of information as is available in that one feature.** Settling for SVR, we are ready for the first feature set.

6.3 First Feature Set

The SVR algorithm (and SVMs in general) only takes numeric features as input. The first step is then to see which columns are numeric and whether the ones that are not numeric have a small number unique values, 100 or less, that can be represented using one-hot-encoding (Cell 19). Of the 99 columns, 54 are numeric but only 3 can be captured by 100 unique values. As I expect more of them to be quasi-categorical, Cell 20 employs the technique for category discretization, discussed in Section 2.2 in Chapter 2, introducing an *OTHER* category to handle the rest of the values **if they account for less than 20% of the total number of values.** That 20% is problem-dependent and choosing it

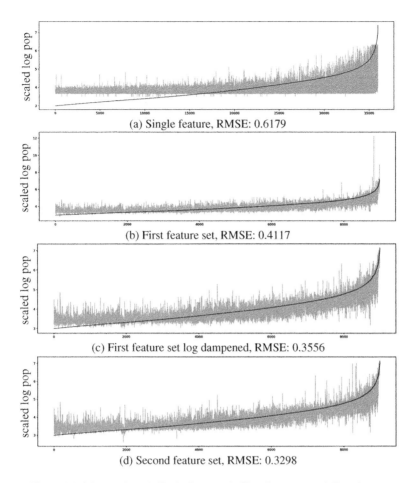

(a) Single feature, RMSE: 0.6179

(b) First feature set, RMSE: 0.4117

(c) First feature set log dampened, RMSE: 0.3556

(d) Second feature set, RMSE: 0.3298

Figure 6.4 SVR results. (a) Single feature. (b) First feature set. (c) First feature set after count dampening using a log function. (d) Second feature set.

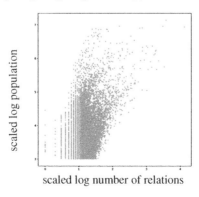

scaled log number of relations

Figure 6.5 Logarithm of relation counts vs. logarithm of population.

Table 6.6. *All the 11 categorical relations with their total number of categorical values and some example values.*

Relation	#	Example Categorical Values
country#1	21	United_States; France; Germany
department#1	59	Val-d'Oise; Yvelines; Pas-de-Calais
leaderTitle#1	4	Mayor; Alcalde; Municipal President
populationAsOf#1	15	2006-12-31; 2010-12-31; 2010-04-01
region#1	100	Île-de-France; Darmstadt; Jefferson_Parish
timeZone#1	14	Central_European_Time; China_Standard_Time
type#1	29	City; Town; Communes_of_Romania
utcOffset#1	7	−5; +2; +5:30
utcOffset#2	6	−4; +1; −6
22-rdf-syntax-ns#type#1	3	Settlement; City; OTHER
rdf-schema#seeAlso#3	73	List_of_twin_towns; Central_America; Argentina

involves considering how much of a difficult time we want to give the ML by dumping unrelated information under the same signal. A bigger percentage makes the *OTHER* a more confusing feature, as a smaller percentage will be able to represent less relations. **I also drop constant columns, as they are uninformative**, netting 50 numeric and 11 categorical columns. The remaining columns have a variety of values that cannot be discretized using these parameters. These columns will require text processing or are just uninformative for this ML approach. The selected categorical relations with their total number of categories is shown in Table 6.6.

Cell 21 performs one-hot-encoding of the categories (cf., Section 3.1 in Chapter 3) and imputes the missing values to the *OTHER* category for categorical features (cf., Section 3.2 in Chapter 3) or to 0 for numeric features. Imputing missing values to *the OTHER category,* rather than adding a new *MISSING* category, is a decision that might be worth also revisiting, based on error analysis later. This first featurization has a vector size of 380 features plus the target variable; see Table 6.1(a).

Cell 22 trains a SVR over this feature set, again with a grid search for its parameters, and saves intermediate data for error analysis. It results on a RMSE of 0.4117 and the curve shown in Figure 6.4(b). This figure and RMSE look better than the single feature that preceded it, but it has some strange spikes. Let us now perform error analysis on them, particularly, a drill-down by feature ablation on the error spike at the end of the figure.

6.3.1 Error Analysis

Using the intermediate data saved by Cell 22, Cell 23 plots the top contributors to the error as shown in Table 6.7 (a). From the table we can see that cities that have a rich history but are not necessarily that populated, like Dublin, get overshot by the system, in spite of regularization. This result makes sense for a system using ontological properties to predict population, but the hope is that we can do better.

Table 6.7. *Top contributors to the error: logarithmic error and actual error.*

(a) Logarithmic Error			
	Log	Population	
City	error	Actual	Predicted
Dublin	6.5	553,164	1,751,459,207,216
Saint-Prex	−2.09	312,010	2,485
Meads,_Kentucky	−2.08	288,648	2,351
Nicosia	2.03	55,013	5,931,549
Hofuf	−1.94	1,500,000	17,145
Mexico_City	1.93	8,918,652	761,989,297
Montana_City,_Montana	−1.88	271,529	3,513
Pikine	−1.82	1,170,790	17,470
Edinburgh	1.76	464,989	26,976,492
Isabela,_Basilan	1.74	1,081	60,349

(b) Actual Error			
	Log	Population	
City	error	Actual	Predicted
Dublin	6.5	553,164	1,751,459,207,216
Mexico_City	1.93	8,918,652	761,989,297
Edinburgh	1.76	464,989	26,976,492
Algiers	0.83	3,415,810	23,294,353
Prague	0.88	1,267,448	9,823,330
Milan	0.8	1,359,904	8,636,483
Amsterdam	0.98	842,342	8,094,965
Lisbon	1.15	545,245	7,776,212
Tabriz	0.74	1,549,452	8,586,162
Nicosia	2.03	55,013	5,931,549

Interestingly, Saint-Prex is actually about 5,000 people, the 300,000 number is an extraction error in the source DBpedia. Similarly, Meads, Kentucky, USA has a population listed in Wikipedia of 280,000 but it is being flagged as a mistake by an editor, as 280,000 is the total population in the full metropolitan area where Meads sits. The town itself is definitely less than 5,000 people in total.

Nicosia is a history-rich city populated for 4,500 years. Sadly, it is a divided city and one of its divisions has a population of 55,000 people listed on the table. A joint city would have a total of about 300,000 inhabitants. It has a historical record, however, of a 6,000,000-people city.

Therefore, we have history-rich, underpopulated cities and extraction errors. From here it makes sense to focus on real (not logarithmic) error and only cities where the system is overpredicting (Cell 24). This approach results in Table 6.7(b). The list looks informative: these cities are major contributors to the error and fall into the category of errors we have found the system is making. I will now do an ablation study (using wrapper methods) to see if we can find which features are contributing to this problem.

6.3.1.1 Feature Ablation

In this feature ablation study, we will eliminate one feature at a time and see whether it improves the cumulative error for these 10 cities. This approach falls into the class of wrapper methods for feature selection discussed in Section 4.1.1.4 in Chapter 4, as we are using the behaviour of the full ML system when performing variations over the feature set. **However, at this stage we are not doing the ablation with the purpose of selecting features.** As Dublin is so markedly overpredicted, it will dominate the aggregate error. Therefore, Cell 25 also keeps track of improvements per city. Feature ablation takes a long time to run even on a sample of the training data, but the results in Table 6.8 show that counts are misleading the algorithm. **Here I am presented with two options: either drop these features or dampen their growth by applying a squashing function to them.** As there seems to be value in them for the given task (a fact that will be confirmed in Section 6.3.1.3), Cell 26 dampens their value by applying a log function to them. The RMSE is better than before at 0.3556 and the spikes have reduced; see Figure 6.4(d). That is a nice improvement from the previous one, but **note that FE does not always succeed and you might encounter dead ends.** Taking the logarithm of these counts could have been done *a priori* based on the advice in Section 3.1 in Chapter 3 about target and feature transformations; it is interesting to arrive to the same conclusion by analyzing the errors.

Table 6.8. *Ablation study: this study was done on a 5% sample of training, as such the improvement numbers do not match Table 6.7(b).*

City	Improvement	Feature to remove
Dublin	0.85 to 0.6 (29.41%)	city?inv#count
Mexico_City	−0.53 to −0.92 (−73.81%)	seeAlso#3@List_of_tallest_buildings
Edinburgh	0.17 to −0.19 (212.89%)	leaderTitle#count
Algiers	−1.0 to −1.2 (−15.33%)	name#count
Prague	−1.3 to −1.7 (−30.56%)	seeAlso#count
Milan	−0.84 to −1.1 (−30.81%)	seeAlso#count
Amsterdam	−0.74 to −0.96 (−29.86%)	homepage#count
Lisbon	−0.6 to −0.88 (−46.54%)	seeAlso#3@Belarus
Tabriz	−0.75 to −1.2 (−57.17%)	seeAlso#count
Nicosia	0.3 to −0.028 (109.40%)	country#count
OVERALL	−4.5 to −6.3 (−40.69%)	seeAlso#count

Instead of continuing this route of feature ablation using a wrapper method, let us move to feature utility metrics, for which we will use a categorical target (like "big city" instead of a target variable of 5,000,000 inhabitants). I will thus discretize the target variable into segments with equal number of cities.

6.3.1.2 Discretizating the Target

When discretizing, an error will be incurred: you are replacing a given target variable value (for example, 2,513,170 people) by a value derived from its discretized class ("medium-sized city," for example, pegged to a population of 2,500,000 people). That incurs an error (13,170 people in this case). The more classes in the discretization, the smaller the error. For discretization, I use the algorithm described in Section 2.2 in Chapter 2, which involves sorting the values and splitting them into two segments using the mean value. The mean of each split is then the value chosen to represent the discretized class. Cell 27 tabulates the discretization error based on the number of splits. At two segments, the RMSE is 0.44, at four it is 0.29 and and eight it is 0.19, so discretization will not add a lot of error on its own. I thus proceed using four splits and also discretizing each feature into four bins.

Other techniques for discretization exist, such that, for example, the number of segments can be learned given a maximum discretization error. The simpler method presented here was chosen as it works well enough on this data and it is more straightforward to implement.

Table 6.9. *Top mutual information features: the feature* UTC offset *refers
to the time zone.*

#	Feature	M.I.		#	Feature	M.I.
1	utcOffset#count	.097		11	city?inv#count	.037
2	birthPlace?inv#count	.077		12	locationCity?inv#count	.034
3	country#1@OTHER	.071		13	location?inv#count	.034
4	areaTotal#1	.057		14	seeAlso#count	.032
5	type#1@City	.044		15	isPartOf#count	.031
6	hometown?inv#count	.044		16	rel#count	.030
7	leaderTitle#count	.041		17	leaderName#count	.030
8	ground?inv#count	.041		18	residence?inv#count	.029
9	isPartOf?inv#count	.038		19	utcOffset#1@"+8"	.029
10	headquarter?inv#count	.038		20	nick#count	.029

6.3.1.3 Feature Utility

With the discretized feature values and target, we are ready to compute feature
utility metrics (Cell 28). From the feature utility metrics discussed in Section
4.1.1.1 in Chapter 4, I chose MI. In earlier experiments, I tried chi-square but
this data is too biased, and chi-square found everything relevant (you can try
chi-square yourself by changing some parameters in the code). In a sense,
**chi-square values precision rather than recall and will select features
with a high association even though they are not necessarily that useful
(i.e., rare features). Therefore, MI is a better metric on this data.** The
top 20 features with their utility are shown in Table 6.9. The list of the
most informative features looks very good, particularly, the number of time
zones and actual time zones seems to indicate the geographic location is
important. Interestingly, while the Wikipedia page for most cities contains its
GPS coordinates, that information is not available in the DBpedia files we are
using (but it is available in the GeoNames file). Using GPS data is discussed in
the GIS case study in Chapter 10.

Cell 28 also introduces 10 random features and drops all features whose
MI falls below at least three random features using the intuitions discussed
in Section 4.1.2.2 in Chapter 4. This resulted in the dropping of 68 features,
particularly rare features for the *region* and *seeAlso* categories. The new feature
vector has 314 features, including name and target.

6.3.1.4 Decision Trees for Feature Analysis

Using individual feature utility is a fine way of doing feature selection
or getting some shallow insights about the feature set. To gain a broader
picture, I will move to use the Gini Impurity feature utility (Section 4.1.1.1
in Chapter 4) and recursively splitting the dataset based on the feature with

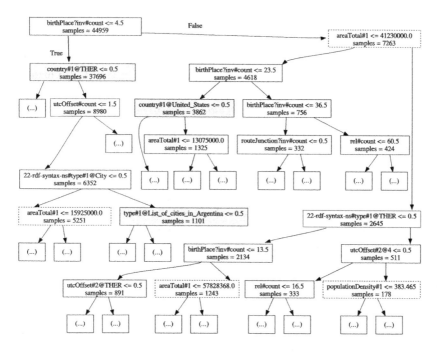

Figure 6.6 Decision tree over discretized first feature set.

highest utility. **While that sounds somewhat complex to program, luckily, that is the algorithm behind decision tree learning**[48] **and we can just plot the top-level branches of the tree to obtain great insights about the holistic behaviour of our features in the dataset.** Please note, I am not advocating using an unpruned single decision tree as a classifier, as they tend to consistently overfit. Here we are using them as a feature analysis tool. Other approaches using pruned sets of trees (forests) are perform quite well and they are used as regressors in other chapters.

Figure 6.6 shows the top-level branches of a decision tree trained on the discretized population at eight splits (Cell 29). In the tree we can see that the actual country where the city belongs carry quite a bit of weight. This information is represented in multiple ways within the data, for example, as the relation *country* but also as type *cities of Argentina*. It is highlighted as light grey in the figure. This is compatible with the ranking of features in Table 6.9 such as *is part of* and *country* but the signal is stronger and easier to discern in the decision tree. We will improve this behaviour using TRE in the next section.

A more intriguing relation appears between *areaTotal* and *populationDensity* (in dashed boxes in the figure). Clearly, the total population of a city is, by definition, the total area of the city times its population density. This product makes for a great computable feature, if both pieces of information are available. We will explore these two ideas (TRE and a computed feature from the product of *areaTotal* and *populationDensity*) in the next section.

6.4 Second Feature Set

Building upon the best variation of the first feature set (log counts and mutual information-filtered features), I proceed to make the categorical features more informative by replacing their value from 1.0 (present) and 0.0 (absent) to the mean value of the target variable for cities when the categorical value is defined or absent. This makes particular sense for categorical features representing whether a city is part of a country or not: it replaces a 1.0 with the mean size of the cities in that country. Of course, computing these mean values on training data will result in too much overfitting as we are blatantly offering the target variable to the learner. **The normal approach to handle this situation is to use cross-validation to compute these values using the out-of-fold technique discussed in Section 1.2.2.1** in Chapter 1: we split the training data into folds and for each fold, replace the 1.0 and 0.0 values by the mean target variable values in the **other** folds. It is important to use a relatively large number of folds, for instance, Cell 30 uses 10 folds. Using fewer folds risks picking very poor representative values that are not stable, for example, using two folds I ended up with a fold where the encoded value for 0.0 was **higher** than the encoded value for 1.0 *in the other fold* (basically reversing the meaning of the feature from fold to fold). That change renders the feature set uninformative to the ML algorithm. Note that I maintain the name TRE for consistency even though the name TRE only makes true sense for categorical target variables (i.e., for classification). For regressors, the more general "categorical encoding" name would be preferred.

Interestingly, because SVR needs scaled features, if we were to apply the TRE before the scaling, it will accomplish very little as the value computed for 0.0 will be scaled back to 0.0 and the same goes for the computed value for 1.0. Instead, **Cell 30 applies the TRE *after* the scaling, approximating the scaled target variable.** That way we can obtain meaningful TRE values that are also properly scaled.

Regarding the computed feature, while it is computationally as simple as multiplying *areaTotal* by *populationDensity*, it needs a little more finesse to deal with the rough nature of the dataset: first, **we want to add an indicator feature for the case when the feature is missing** (Section 3.2 in Chapter 3). Second, there are multiple ways the area information is rendered, that is, sometimes the area is distinguished as *areaTotal*, *areaRural*, etc. In the event the feature *areaTotal* is missing, Cell 30 uses any of the other areas as a surrogate (I did not go as far as computing the sum of the other areas, but that is a reasonable step, too). Finally, I want to take the logarithm of the computed feature so it is as similar as possible to the target variable. This feature is available for roughly one-quarter of instances.

Using the dataset with TRE nets a very modest improvement. Instead, **Cell 30 combines the TRE with the original non-TRE values, leaving it to the ML to decide what signal makes sense given the training data**; see Table 6.1(b). This approach performs much better, resulting in an RMSE of 0.3298, the best obtained on this dataset so far; see Figure 6.4(d).

6.4.1 Feature Stability to Create a Conservative Feature Set

To conclude this exercise, I want to look into feature stability when the training data has been erroneously sampled. Algorithmic stability is a subject closely studied in algorithmic learning theory,[42] from the perspective that small variations in the training data should produce models that make small variations in their predictions. **Here I am interested in building a conservative feature set that can withstand *catastrophic variations* in the training data.**

It is not unusual to have a training dataset that has been acquired with a sampling bias that invalidates a given feature (for example, asking whether a patient is thirsty when all the data was acquired during the winter). Therefore, it is good to see how the trained model behaves under error perturbations over the features. This is an understudied topic in ML, and I touch on it a little more in the next chapter. To simulate perturbations, I use a technique from privacy preserving data mining[3] where you swap the values of a given feature from one instance to another. That produces variations on the data that are compatible with the existing data. With this concept of perturbation, it is possible to control the amount of error introduced. To test whether a feature is pulling its own weight, we can see how much a feature helps (as measured using feature ablation) versus the feature's risk under catastrophic failure (measured using perturbations in the test set). I decided to arbitrarily set a perturbation percentage of 30% and drop features that drop performance more than they contribute to it. That is, a given feature, for example, *areaLand*, is responsible for a 0.05% increase in RMSE, when removed. Now, if that feature is perturbed at 30% using random swaps (for a total of $0.15 \times$ |training size| swaps, as each swap perturbs two instances), the RMSE increases by 0.07%, then I can conclude that, as 0.07 is bigger than 0.05, this feature is not worth the risk it entails.

To fully implement the concept, it would be necessary to retrain the full system after dropping each feature. Ablation and perturbation are computationally expensive to run. An ideal implementation will need a beam search (most probably informed by feature utility metrics) and the use of multiprocessing. I had no need to get to that level of finesse: an initial run of the proposed algorithm (Cell 31) produced hypotheses such as dropping USA or India as features. Indeed, these are very informative features. Clearly, if India became an aggregate of currently non-Indian cities, that will throw off the regressor dearly. But that is not compatible with this domain. Belonging to a particular country is one of the **most stable properties of this domain**. That is not to say that DBpedia properties themselves are stable; I discovered on my own research[94] that George W. Bush was a *politician* in some years, then an *elected official* in some others to become again a *politician* in later versions (that is, the *type* feature was very unstable for people).

Still, **the main takeaway from Cell 31 is the decision to not use its proposed results. Such perturbation makes sense if you suspect certain features might be wrongly sampled.** In this case, realizing that certain features are stronger than others is sufficient to assemble the "conservative" feature set: non-categorical features plus categorical with country values. This feature set is computed in Cell 32 for a RMSE of 0.3578 and only 98 feature; see Table 6.1(d). The resulting data files will be used in the next chapters as the starting point for more FE.

6.5 Final Feature Sets

We are thus left with two feature sets, the high-performance one (577 features, Table 6.1(c)), using TRE and all other features. This feature set achieves a performance roughly equivalent with the RMSE of a four-way segmentation, that is, it can tell apart hamlets from small towns, small cities and large cities.

The conservative feature set (98 features, Table 6.1(d)) achieves a worse RMSE and **the hope is that when mixing it with other data sources it will be able to surpass the high-performance set.**

For a final evaluation, the same steps are used to obtain the final sets ought to be performed, namely

- Typify the data using the type information computed in Cell 20.
- Filter the low MI features found in Cell 28.
- TRE using the full set of TRE values from Cell 30.
- Add the computed feature from Cell 30.
- Finally, to get the conservative feature set, keep only the features highlighted in Cell 32.

Of course this level of bookkeeping is error-prone and unattainable. This is why I advocate doing FE through a domain specific language (DSL), such as the DSL I wrote for the DeepQA project.[124]

This final evaluation is left to the reader. Do not forget to take these results with particular extra suspicion, as no exhaustive hyperparameter search was done at the different stages. As mentioned in the introduction of Part Two, hyperparameters search will take the running time beyond what I find reasonable for a case study in a textbook. But production models require it and will normally profit from a distributed ML architecture, such as SparkML.

Other ideas of interest to try on this dataset are discussed in the next section.

6.5.1 Possible Followups

Hopefully, this case study has provided inspiration for plenty of your own ideas. I do not presume the steps taken here were the best possible steps. Moreover, in light of a post hoc analysis of the results, we can even conclude the initial steps were suboptimal. **But we have approached a domain that was unknown to you and now you have a deeper understanding of the problem with plenty of things to try beyond blindly tweaking the ML parameters or the underlying model.** Here are some ideas of interesting things to try over this dataset.

By far my main gripe goes back to the decision of encoding the relations as lists of sets. An encoding as a set would have been more informative. In this encoding, instead of having a *seeAlso#1* and *seeAlso#2* meta-features, each with their own top categorical values, of which only one of them will take a value of 1 versus the rest with a value of 0, you will have a *seeAlso* meta-feature where each of the categorical values can take a 1 or a 0 depending on whether or not there is a relation to that categorical value. With this more compact representation, it should be possible to encode more values and relations. More importantly, the relation (?, *seeAlso*, Brazil) will not be aliased as *seeAlso#1@Brazil* and *seeAlso#2@Brazil* depending on the other relations.

Adding the GPS coordinates will also help, particularly a discretized version of them. Right now the system is relying on the UTC offsets to get some of that information. In the same vein, a good direction is to distill a high-quality *country* feature, from different sources present in the data.

Finally, for more complex ideas, it is possible to replace the discretization of values from one-hot-encoding to OOF clusters based on their behaviour with respect to the target value. Then (?, seeAlso, Brazil) gets encoded as (?, seeAlso, country-with-big-cities). By clustering the values, a wider variety of them can be made available to the ML. That is, through clustering it might be possible to realize that less-popular object values for a given relation verb, such as *seeAlso*, behave with respect to the target value similarly to more popular ones, and they might be worth representing explicitly. That will shed more light into the *seeAlso@OTHER* feature, reducing the amount of signal directed to that feature.

6.6 Learning More

For more specific material on ML over graphs, the book by Radev and Mihalcea[232] is a classic. In recent years, an embedding approach to RDF has been proposed.[271] For other takes on using ML over DBpedia, see the work of Esteban and others[100] as well as my recent joint work.[28]

For semantic graphs, relational learning[243] is a traditional methodology that exhibits quite a bit of success, including factorizing the YAGO ontology.[244] Also, as mentioned in Chapter 5, there is established work using graph kernels with kernel methods.[318]

Chapter 7 from the *Feature Engineering* book collection[132] discusses feature generation from graphs and networks in detail. In particular, the difference between global versus neighbourhood features. The approach followed in this chapter relies solely in local features. Other local features that can be extracted relate to the shape of the neighbourhood in the form of triangles and what is called the "egonet" of a node. It also analyzes the DL representations focused on random walks mentioned in Chapter 5, Section 5.1.4.

7

Timestamped Data

In his book, *Your Brain is a Time Machine,* Dean Buonomano says[54]

> Fields of science, like humans, undergo developmental stages: they mature and
> change as they grow. And in many fields one signature of this maturation process is
> the progressive embrace of time.

This is definitely our case in machine learning (ML), as we will see in this
chapter. The usual problems in ML explode when dealing with historical data.
The target class becomes mutable. Great features for a particular class have to
become acceptable features for a different class. To begin with, historical data
is not easy to find. It is the usual acquisition problem with a devilish twist:
you cannot go back in time (even if your brain is a time machine!); if you miss
acquiring data at the appropriate time, it is lost. You might have many gaps and
you will need special techniques to impute them (Section 7.2.1). Data cleaning
also becomes very complicated. Data errors in one version of the data may
not affect other versions that will make them harder to find. The set of entities
under study may change: your rows for classification might have a many-to-
many relation with past instances in the same problem.

In this chapter we will look into data with a time component, what falls
into the general term "timestamped data." We will look at two instances of
this phenomenon: when you have data from past observations of instance data
(historical data) and when you have past observations of the instance target
value or class (time series). I discuss other type of timestamped data (event
streams) in Section 7.7. Timestamped data is a domain that exemplifies: the
use of the past as a feature to predict the present, Markov assumptions and time
averaging. The main problems are past artifacts, variable-length raw data and
smart normalization, as the history provides a larger pool for normalization.
The takeaways in working with timestamped data are the value of representative statistics, the concept of windows or segments to compute such statistics.

Working with a past version of the DBpedia data used in the previous chapter, **the expectation is that places with a larger population will exhibit a bigger growth on their property coverage.** This information was captured by using historical versions of the existing features, which turned out to have a substantive amount of missing values. Most of the case study revolved around temporal imputation but the ML models did not find value on this data presented this way. Further, using the data for expansion did not help improve performance either. But there are plenty of follow-ups for you to try, as discussed in Section 7.5.2.

Time series concerns itself with modelling a variable (or variables) as a function of its past values. The observations are usually taken at specific intervals, and therefore, the time itself is left implicit (two observations before now can be two minutes or two years apart). I discuss them further in Section 7.6. While information about statistical time series analysis (TSA) is abundant, ML over timestamped data is not traditionally covered in ML books. A notable exception is Schutt and O'Neil's book, *Doing Data Science*,[278] and the Brink, Richards and Fetherolf book, *Real-World Machine Learning.*[49] This chapter implements some of the ideas found in the latter.

My intention was to study TSA using decades of census data for the cities on WikiCities. Alas, finding such data, even for particular countries, proved to be very challenging. To begin with, what a "city" is today tends to change quite often (for a recent example, the city of Montréal amalgamated 11 other municipalities in 2000 to de-amalgamate them again in 2010). And I had substantive problems finding this data under a license suitable for inclusion with the case studies. Instead, Section 7.6 uses 60 years of country population data from the World Bank against the DBpedia semantic graph.

Chapter Overview

This chapter contains two studies. The first one expands the WikiCities dataset with historical data from years 2010–2015. The second focuses on countries and time series and will be discussed later in this section.

For the historical WikiCities, we use six years of past data where as many as half of the cities are missing, possibly due to lower coverage in the earlier Wikipedia. Moreover, for cities present, they have up to 50% missing columns, possibly due to changes in the ontology. This enables the specific type of temporal imputation needed by timestamped data. An exploratory data analysis (EDA) (Section 7.1.1) starts by looking at the total number of relations year after year. They increased as DBpedia increased in size but there is a valley in

Table 7.1. *Feature vectors used in this chapter. BASE is the conservative graph feature vector from Chapter 6, Table 6.1 (d). (a) Imputed lag-2, 490 features (b) Simple moving average, 490 features (c) Exponential moving average, 490 features (d) Dataset expansion, 98 features (e) WikiCountries no TS, 2 features (f) Markov features, 3 features .*

1	2015_rel#count?is_defined
2	2015_rel#count
3	2015_area#1?is_defined
4	2015_area#1
5	2015_areaCode#count?is_defined
6	2015_areaCode#count
	...BASE double with ?is_defined for 2015...
195	2015_computed#value?is_defined
196	2015_computed#value
197	2014_rel#count?is_defined
	...BASE double with ?is_defined for 2014...
392	2014_computed#value
393	rel#count
	... BASE ...
490	computed#value

(a)

1	rel#count
	... (identical to (a)) ...
490	computed#value

(b)

1	rel#count
	... (identical to (a)) ...
490	computed#value

(c)

1	rel#count
	... BASE ...
99	computed#value

(d)

1	log #rels out
2	log #rels in

(e)

1	log #rels out
2	log pop 2015
3	log pop 2016

(f)

2013–2015. Imputing the timestamped data (Section 7.2.1) seems to complete the values quite well, but to test this in practice the first featurization (Section 7.2.2) adds the last two historical versions of each feature based on a Markov assumption. We also looked into differential features (Section 7.2.2.2), but they did not work with this setup. An error analysis (EA) (Section 7.2.3) on the lag-2 system using feature heatmaps asserts that instability on the number of relations might be a problem. We thus look into better smoothing using sliding windows that might help the 2013–2015 valley (Section 7.3). The second featurization (Section 7.3.1) with a simple moving average sees the performance to degrade, potentially due to an excess of smoothing.

In the third featurization (Section 7.4) we employ an exponential moving average from the present into the past, combining smoothing with imputation and curving the amount of smoothing. This produced a very small improvement. Finally, we looked into using the historical data as data expansion (Section 7.5) using the historical rows to obtain a more informed model. This approach is explored in the fourth featurization (Section 7.5.1), which further decreased performance, even if the training material increased seven-fold.

Looking into time series (TS) (Section 7.6), we created the WikiCountries dataset (Section 7.6.1), with two features per country: the number of out and in relations in DBpedia plus historical population over 59 years from the World Bank. An EDA (Section 7.6.2) plotting the relation counts finds a correlation. Looking into ten random countries and their time series data shows that fitting a TS for these curves seems hard to automate for feature engineering (FE). Detrending is key for this problem, but no technique easily helps for all countries. A baseline ignoring the time feature and using only the number of relations (Section 7.6.3) predicts the population within double of its actual number. The second featurization (Section 7.6.4) uses ML without TSA. We use the time series as lag features, including past versions of the target value for a given number of lags (Markov features). It achieves an almost perfect fit.

Finally, we attempt to use the time series model to predict the target variable and use that prediction as a feature (Section 7.6.6). But fitting a TS for each country using the ADF test works only for 4% of the countries. Without substantive and better TS modelling of the data, the SVR using Markov features performs better on this dataset.

7.1 WikiCities: Historical Features

Note that this chapter is not completely self-contained, thus if you have not read the previous chapter, you should read Section 6.1 for details on the task and motivation. For the running example used in these case studies, I looked into historical versions of the dataset, which allows us to explore FE concepts on historical features, including using time lagged features (Section 7.2) and sliding windows (Section 7.3). The historical data was extracted using the versions of DBpedia from years 2010–2015 (Table 7.2). The differences in terms of new relations being added will give an idea of the **velocity** of this data: bigger cities will probably have more people editing their pages.

Due to changes in the DBpedia extraction script (which changes the name of a city from "Phoenix%2C_Arizona" to "Phoenix,Arizona") and in the source Wikipedia (changing "Utrecht" to "Utrecht%28city%29"), the entity URIs change from year to year. I have tried to standardize them using the GeoNames

Table 7.2. *Historical data. The link size column is the size of Geonames link file. Current version has 80,199 settlements, with a Geonames link file 3.9M in size.*

Ver.	Year	Code	Link	Cities	found	Renamed	Rels	Ents
3.6	2010	dbpedia10	788K	32,807	40.9%	16,803	20m	1.7m
3.7	2011	dbpedia11	788K	32,807	40.9%	16,803	27m	1.8m
3.8	2012	dbpedia12	788K	32,807	40.9%	6,690	33m	2.4m
3.9	2013	dbpedia13	3.1M	73,061	91.1%	14,328	42m	3.2m
2014	2014	dbpedia14	3.3M	75,405	94.0%	14,587	61m	4.2m
2015/4	2015	dbpedia15	692K	32,807	40.9%	6,690	37m	4.0m
–	2016	–	3.9M	80,199	–	–	38m	5.0m

link file provided by DBpedia for each year, as done in Chapter 6. In the historical versions, however, the GeoNames data was limited and as many as half of the cities are missing. This might also be due to lower coverage in the source Wikipedia in the earlier years. Ultimately, these challenges are representative of dealing with historical data in production systems.

I have extracted the relevant triples from the data dumps for all years into separate files and from those files extracted the 98 conservative feature set from Chapter 6. Again, due to changes in the ontology many columns (sometimes up to 50% of the columns) are empty. Interestingly, this number changes from year to year, not necessarily linearly, as the provided linking files differ widely in size, as seen in the table. Therefore, it enables the specific type of temporal imputation needed by timestamped data. Note the extracted datasets also include the target variable (population) for each of these years, for the cities available for those years but it did not change enough to be useful as a TS. Let us start doing some EDA and see how this dataset behaves.

7.1.1 Exploratory Data Analysis

The first thing to take a look at is how the total number of relations behaves year after year in Figure 7.1(a), Cell 1 in Chapter 7 Jupyter notebooks. We see that the average number of relations (rels) has increased as DBpedia increased in size, for those years that had good linking data. There is a valley in 2013–2015 that might motivate a sliding window approach.

Let us see the behaviour of this number as compared to the last known year, 2016 (Cell 2). Figure 7.1(b) shows that convergence towards the current data, again with a valley in 2015. Let us now take a look at the number of identical

Table 7.3. *Whole missing columns and row sections that need to be imputed.*

Year	Missing Cols	Missing Cities
2010	37	9,990
2011	29	8,147
2012	29	6,808
2013	29	2,160
2014	62	1,538
2015	0	8,501

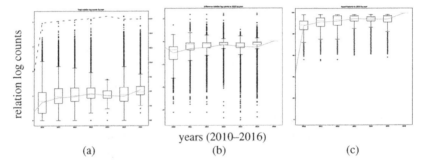

(a)   years (2010–2016)   (c)
                              (b)

Figure 7.1 (a) Logarithm of the total relation counts per years for cities between 2010–2016 (b) Difference on the logarithm over counts to 2016, per year from 2010–2016 (c) Percentage of features equal to the features for year 2016, per year, from 2010–2016.

features to the current year (Cell 3). Figure 7.1(c) shows that the trend is similar to the one observed in the relation counts alone. This data seems reasonable for trying lagged features (Section 7.2). Temporal smoothing, however, using a sliding window might provide better results given the bouncy behaviour of the data (Section 7.3).

There are two sources of imputation in this dataset: missing columns and missing sections of a row. The missing columns are due to relations not available in the source data; they total 186 columns, with the breakdown shown in Table 7.3. The other source are cities that are not present (or are present but linking through GeoNames or using the 2016 name failed to find them). For these cities and years, the data for the whole year is missing and needs to be imputed. The total number of such row sections is 37,144, with the breakdown shown in the same table. In this case, indicator features for imputed values

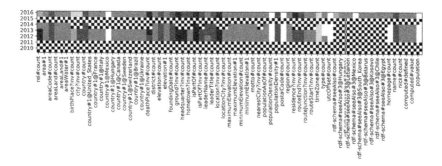

Figure 7.2 Historical features visualization using a feature heatmap (excerpt). This is for the Mexican city of Mérida, in Yucatán. The target variable, the logarithm of the population, is 5.986 (970,376 people). The chequerboard patterns are missing values.

(as discussed in Chapter 3) are very important and result in a feature vector double the size of previous vectors. Overall, 42% of the historical features need to be imputed. There is a significant amount of missing values. Let us see if we can visualize now individual entries.

We use a heatmap for visualization, discretizing features into up to six bins using k-Means clustering (described in Section 2.2.1.2, Chapter 2). The clustering is done per feature and the number of bins (six) was chosen for ease of visualization. Not all features produce six clusters. The top three clusters will be shown in green (in the notebook), the bottom in blue (in the notebook). The graph aligns features for each year to follow them, uncovering the story of the data (Cell 6). Missing values are shown in red. Figure 7.2 shows an excerpt converted to grey scale. Analyzing ten cities, I can see that the relation counts (first column in the heatmap) change from version to version but the target population (last column in the heatmap) seem to stay within the same range. There are plenty of missing features and the colours indicate a relative growth over time. The "seeAlso" features are missing for all years, that is a big loss as such features proved to be informative in Chapter 6.

7.2 Time Lagged Features

Let us start by using the value of a feature from a past version as a time lagged feature. Given the high percentage of missing values, we will need a way to impute them, discussed next.

7.2.1 Imputing Timestamped Data

Temporal imputation is quite different from general imputation as we can rely on values of the feature at different times to approximate its missing value. Care must be taken, though, to avoid the type of assumptions employed to complete the missing values to dominate the conclusions of the modelling process. The imputed data might result in a stronger and easy to pick signal that the signal in the normally occurring data. How to avoid imputation driving the results? In *Data Preparation for Data Mining*[263] Dorian Pyle offers the advice of checking whether the conclusions change significantly when adding imputed data, as such behaviour will be suspicious and unwanted. We will revisit this topic in the conclusions of this section. When discussing the general topic of imputation in Chapter 3 (Section 3.2), I discussed that the most principled way of solving imputation is to train a custom ML model to predict the value of the missing feature using the available features as input. This approach ends up being the most favoured one in the case of timestamped data, where an autorregressive model (Section 5.1.5) could be trained to predict the missing data based on the previous data. For simplicity, I will start repeating the last known value of the missing feature, giving preference to earlier values (Cell 7).

Of the 11 million feature values imputed, 16% were imputed with past values. Of the 84% imputed with future values, 23% are using present features. Therefore, most features are not present-imputed. That is important because otherwise there will be little value of the historical features. Cell 8 helps to visualize this. The figure is too big to include on a book format but it is available online at http://artfeateng.ca/u/71. The imputation looks to complete the values quite well, with a few places (e.g., *Watertown*) with some surprises in the centre. We are now ready for the first featurization.

7.2.2 First Featurization: Imputed Lag-2

For this, we will add the historical version of each feature based on a Markov assumption, discussed next.

7.2.2.1 Markov Assumption

A key assumption that can be made for dealing with timestamped data is that there is an underlying data generation process with limited "memory," that is, it depends only on a few number of previous states. Such processes are called **Markov processes** and the number of previous states needed to predict the current state is called the **order** of the Markov process. This lack of full memory helps alleviate the feature explosion problem and it is yet

Table 7.4. *RMSE for different feature lags using RFs. Trained on 35,971 cities. The last column is trained on differential features.*

Lag	Features	RMSE	Diff. RMSE
0	98	0.3594	–
1	294	0.3551	0.3599
2	490	0.3539	0.3588
3	686	0.3539	0.3588
4	882	0.3542	0.3584
5	1,078	0.3540	0.3583

another simplification of reality for modelling purposed. When doing FE for time series, the Markov assumption can be used two-fold: incorporating the target value (or class) from previous times, what I call **Markov features** and incorporating the value of the features from the past, known as **lag features**.

We will look into lag features now. For the first featurization, Cell 9 adds the historical version of each feature, for the last two versions plus a missing data indicator feature. As the number of features will explode, Cell 9 switches to random forests (RFs) as SVMs have a hard time a high number of features and the computational time explodes.[63] Training using 490 features (Table 7.1(a)), the resulting RMSE is 0.3539, which barely improves the SVR baseline of 0.3578. Let us see the RMSE for using other lags in Cell 10. **Keep in mind that too large of a lag might overfit as the number of parameters increases while the number of instances remains the same.** The results in the third column of Table 7.4 show that indeed the error start increasing after the third lag. Before doing EA, let us look at computing differences (Cell 11).

7.2.2.2 Differential Features

When working with lag features, the strongest signal might not lie in the feature itself but in its difference from, or the ratio to, the present value. In a differential feature, therefore, we replace the lag feature with its difference to the current value. These are a type of delta features, as described in Section 2.5 of Chapter 2. Instead of differences, ratios can also be very informative, if the features do not contain zero values. Our dataset contains plenty of zero values, so we will stick to differences and forego of ratios.

From the results in the last column in Table 7.4, we can see that differential features did not work in our case. Why did it not work? My hypothesis is that it is due to how RFs use a sample of the features when building each of the trees. In the case of differential features, it no longer has a way to put them

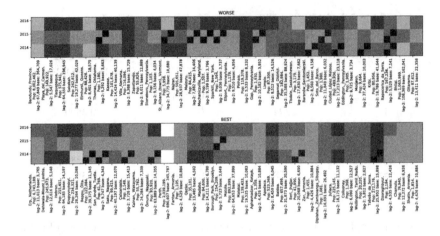

Figure 7.3 Historical features visualization using a feature heatmap for the total relation count for cities that got worse using lag-2 and cities that got better. We can see that the cities that got worse had very different number of relations in the three years plotted.

into perspective. If it picks Δf_{t-1} instead of f_t, the information in f_t is lost in the differential feature. Using the historical feature f_{t-1} seemed to work fine, as the feature values are close to each other. It seems f_{t-1} is just acting as a surrogate for f_t. If historical features are just a surrogate for the 2016 features (the last year present in this dataset) then all we are obtaining from this dataset is extra training data. But let us do some EA.

7.2.3 Error Analysis

For this EA, Cell 12 uses the feature heatmaps developed for the EDA to see which cities did worse with the lags than without them. See Figure 7.3 for just the first columns (number of relations). The full figure for this EA is too big to include in a book format but it is available online at http://artfeateng.ca/u/72. From this figure, I conclude that instability in the first column (number of relations) might be a problem, as I can see many cases where the value jumped to larger values then reduced again. Smoothing that behaviour could work.

7.3 Sliding Windows

Using lag features directly or their differences is problematic when variability in the feature values is high. A way to improve the data is to apply **temporal**

smoothing using a sliding window (see Section 2.1.2 in Chapter 2 for a general discussion about smoothing). For example, **replacing the feature value with the median or the average over the values in the window.** In our case, I will use a window of size 3. Note that we lose two years, for which the average is not defined. There are multiple ways to measure the average over the window. Some popular ways are arithmetic mean, weighted mean averages (where lags closer to the current value are given more weight) and exponential mean averages (where a "memory" average is updated as a weighted sum of the current value and the previous memory). You can also aggregate over different window sizes to obtain a temporal profile of the data,[76] that is, replace the smoothed feature by several features smoothed over different spans of time.

Using the mean for the values in the window is one of the different descriptive statistics described in Chapter 2. Other alternatives include standard deviation and metrics related to how similar to a normal distribution is the data in the window (kurtosis and skewness). In this context, these descriptive features are called **key features.** When computing means, you should be aware of the **Slutsky–Yule effect:** averaging will give you a sinusoidal curve when performed on perfectly random data.[61] This might mislead your ML into seeing a wave where there is none.

Let us see how the sliding windows approach fares on this data.

7.3.1 Second Featurization: Single Moving Average

A simple moving average (Cell 13) smoothed 17.8 million feature values. That is quite a bit of smoothing, with many features changed. Now let us try again with lag-2 over the SMA for the second featurization (Cell 14, Table 7.1(b)). The RMSE of 0.3580 is worse than before, which is not surprising given the level of smoothing. Let us try a different smoothing.

7.4 Third Featurization: EMA

Cell 15 uses an exponential moving average from the present into the past, combining smoothing with imputation. In **exponential moving average** (EMA), there is a memory m and the value smoothed at time t is a weighted average, controlled with a parameter α such that $0 < \alpha < 1$, between the value being smoothed and the memory. The memory is then set to the smoothed value:

$$\tilde{x}_t = \alpha x_t + (1 - \alpha)\tilde{x}_{t-1}$$

EMA is normally done from the past to the present. In our case, I am performing it from the present into the past, as the present values have fewer missing values and are of better quality. While computing the EMA, I am also imputing missing values to the current smoothed version, when found. As the past has not proved to be very useful in this data, I set $\alpha = 0.2$. This process smoothed 15.6 million feature values. Training a RF with a lag-2 RF (Cell 16, Table 7.1(c)) produced a RMSE of 0.3550, which is a very small improvement from before. It seems these techniques have failed to unveil value in the time dimension for this dataset.

7.5 Historical Data as Data Expansion

Finally, it is possible to disregard the time aspect in the data and simply use the history as a data expansion: **historical rows result in a more informed model**. When working with event data, this is equivalent to pivoting the data and switching from having events as columns to events as rows. [278] While the idea is straightforward, Schutt and O'Neil propose the following as a thought experiment: [278]

> What do you lose when you think of your training set as a big pile of data and ignore the timestamps?

An element you will definitely lose is any notion of causality implicit in the temporal ordering the data. If you believe this is not important in your case, then the dataset expansion makes perfect sense.

This conceptually simple approach poses challenges for evaluation, as it is now possible to have feature leaks by training on an instance and testing on a separate instance that is generated from the same row on the data. This problem becomes especially complicated in cross-validation, as discussed next.

Cross-Validating Temporal Data. To understand temporal feature leaks, assume that there is only one city in the dataset with an unusual property. For the sake of the argument, let us say it is close to some *pyramids*. In turn, the *pyramids* proximity means the city is much bigger than expected.[†] If the row with the historical data is split into five instances and four are used to train a model, when tested in the remaining instance, the fact that the *pyramids* are a good feature *for this particular city*, will be leaked from the test set into the training set. In production, that leak will not happen and special features of

[†] Due to *pyramids* reducing food shortage on growth by 25%, of course.

particular cities will drive the error rate higher. To avoid feature leaks, Cell 17 uses **stratified cross-validation**, splitting the cities into folds, then adding the instances derived from each city to the corresponding fold.

7.5.1 Fourth Featurization: Expanded Data

This last featurization involves using the extra rows as more training data (Cell 17, Table 7.1(d)). This increased the available training material seven-fold (from 35,000 to 250,000). However, things got worse, with an RMSE of 0.3722. At this stage, the experiments do not merit using the historical data for enhanced classification performance in this task.

7.5.2 Discussion

There are things left for the reader to try:

- A conservative feature set could be attempted just adding the EMA-smoothing for historical relation counts (and nothing else).
- Drop rows with too many imputed values or drop columns with too many imputed values.
- Use an imputed version of the features (e.g., the EMA version) instead of their current version. **This might improve the present data using its history.**
- Collect census data for the last 60 years for the 80,000+ cities in the dataset and add historical versions of the target as extra features (Markov features). These concepts are explored in the next section using a different dataset.
- **Computing the average over the window is just a particular type of convolution kernel. Other kernels are possible.** A potential kernel useful for this task is to use an indicator feature that outputs 1.0 if the change between the last two features increased by more than 10%.

Another use for historical data is to improve the robustness of the model over changes to the behaviour of the feature set together with the natural evolution of the data. Continuous growth of features is a common problem for many datasets. As the data changes, so do the coefficients that fit the data; the evolution of the coefficients speak of the stability of the data.[278] With the current dataset, it is possible to train on previous years and test on the following years. A more robust approach can take into account the expected growth of the features based in the overall behaviour in the dataset. **Differentiating which features will grow and which will not is a topic of research.**[28]

7.6 Time Series

The TS models from Section 5.1.5 in Chapter 5 can be used in a ML system:[49] first, you can use their predictions as extra features, and leave the ML to decide under which circumstances to trust them (Section 7.6.5). Second, you can use their internal parameters (their fitting polynomials or their order) as features. You can see how well the models seem to approximate the data as a feature (e.g., the confidence intervals for the model, but their AIC is preferred, cf., Section 4.1.3 in Chapter 4). Finally, you can train a model to predict their residuals, the error their prediction makes (Section 7.6.6). We will explore the first option.

7.6.1 WikiCountries Dataset

As mentioned in the introduction, the WikiCities dataset was not up to the task for TS and I switched to country-level data. There are not that many countries in the world, so I will only model two features over then: the number of out relations and the number of in relations for them in DBpedia (see Section 6.1 in the previous chapter for a definition of in and out relations). Having more features will not make sense with less than 300 datapoints without doing heavy feature selection and we want to focus on the time aspect.

Identifying all entities of type `dbpedia/Country` yields 3,424 entities (Cell 18). This includes historical countries (e.g., "Free State Bottleneck") and errors (e.g., "National symbols of Sri Lanka," which is an entity about symbols not a country). The historical population from the World Bank has information for 264 countries for 59 years (Cell 19). The number of countries also seems questionably high. Analyzing the intersection and missing countries (Cell 20), we can see the World Bank data includes many of regions (like North America), while many countries include republic designators that are handled differently in Wikipedia. The final mapping is done by hand in Cell 21, resulting in 217 countries. Finding those extra mappings sometimes required checking the source Wikipedia, as Georgia appears as *"Georgia (Country)"* and as *"Democratic Republic of Georgia"* (which ceased to exist in 1921). DBpedia also contains errors: Botswana and Uganda are not listed as having the type `dbpedia/Country`.

With these 217 countries, Cell 22 computes the in relations and out relations on DBpedia, resulting in a total of 1.3 million in relations, and 7,346 out relations. It makes sense that countries have lots of relations coming into them, with few standard relations departing from them. We can now merge the time series data with the relations data and split it into training data and final test data (Cell 23), for a development set of 173 countries.

With the data split properly, we can perform some EDA.

7.6.2 Exploratory Data Analysis

EDA is crucial when working with TS, particularly graphical visualizations. In the words of Dorian Pyle "[time] series data must be looked at."[263][†] In particular, by looking at different visualizations of the TS (graphs, correlograms, differences, spectra, etc.), we can conclude whether or not the data has a trend, the type of process involved (AR, MA, other, cf., Section 5.1.5 in Chapter 5) and their order. The main tool is the **correlogram**, a plot of the regression of the variable against a lagged version of itself. It has correlation values in the y axis (from -1 to 1) and lags in the x axis (from 1 to as many lags as you choose to plot). This is also called an ACF plot (for autocorrelation function). The second plot of importance is the PACF (the partial ACF plot), which plots the correlation coefficient *after* the effect of the previous lags has been removed. If the process is an AR process, then the ACF will drop slowly and the order could be then read from the PACF. For example, if the model is an AR(2) and we exclude the first two lags, the partial correlation for the third lag will be zero. If the process is a MA, then its ACF will be zero after its order. If both ACF and PACF decrease slowly, it might be an ARMA or an ARIMA with some differencing. Other things can be read from the correlogram, for example, whether there are seasonal fluctuations or the TS is alternating.

Let us start by plotting the relation counts and current population to see if there is a correlation (Cell 24). From Figure 7.4 we can see that the number of in relations is informative, but the number of out relations is not, as most of the countries are involved in the same number of standard relations. The level of correlation implied from the graph seems quite rich and looks very encouraging.

Let us now take 10 random countries and look at their time series data (Cell 25). In Figure 7.5 we can see trend reversal (Ireland in the 1980–1990, Slovak Republic in 2000–2010), missing data (Sint Maarten) and curves with a variety of behaviours. **Clearly, fitting a TS for one of these curves is a job in itself. This looks hard to automate for FE.** Let us take a look at the ACF and PACF (Cell 26). From these graphs, a sample of which is shown in Figure 7.6, we see no impact on the PACF, so MA will not be needed. But we can see also a strong trend effect.

[†] Chapter 9.

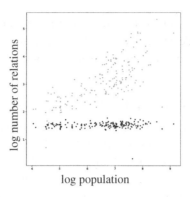

Figure 7.4 Logarithm of relation counts vs. logarithm of population on Wiki-Countries.

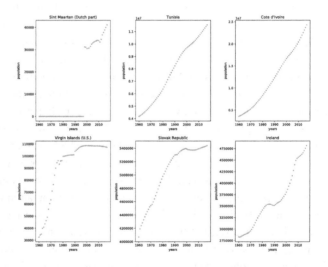

Figure 7.5 Sample WikiCountries population plots.

Detrending will be key for this problem, but the prevalent advice is to handle it with care as it can destroy the signal on the data. I looked graphically at detrending using a log function (Cell 27), a first-order differencing (Cell 28) and second-order differencing (Cell 29). Graphically, I cannot see a technique that easily helps for all the countries. Every curve looks quite different. I can see that concentrating on one single curve and trying different parameters and approaches will lead to a reasonable ACF/PACF and detrending. But **doing this by hand for 163 countries will only make sense if the models already**

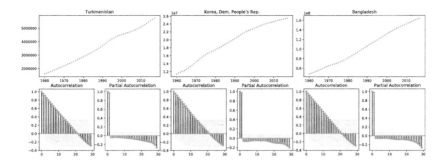

Figure 7.6 Sample WikiCountries population, ACF and PACF plots.

exist and were built for a different purpose. Clearly tapping on such models will give to any ML model a massive jolt of domain knowledge.

Let us move to test with ADF (Cell 30), an automatic stationarity test discussed in Section 5.1.5.3 in Chapter 5. Cell 30 tries a variety of approaches suggested in the literature for detrending and evaluates the resulting series using ADF. The results are summarized in Table 7.5. We can see that Ivory Coast did not achieve stationarity with differencing, log, linear nor quadratic regression. Other countries achieve stationarity only through specific methods. The most successful method was detrending using a quadratic regression after applying one order differencing. Using simpler methods like the base form and the log function and excluding the quadratic regression accounts for 50% of the countries in the sample.

A simple case is Turkmenistan, which is stationary on its log, so let us try to predict it using an AR model (Section 5.1.5 in Chapter 5). As Table 7.5 shows that the ADF autolag found stationarity at lag 11, Cell 32 uses an AR(11) process for a very good fitting. **The question is how to operationalize obtaining all these fitted models and predictions automatically.** A deeper question is whether this makes sense, a topic I will revisit at the end of this section. Let us start with a baseline, ignoring the time feature and another approach using ML without TSA. Given the EDA, it looks likely the TSA system will underperform compared to these other approaches.

7.6.3 First Featurization: NoTS Features

Let us start by using only the number of relations (Cell 33, Table 7.1(e)). The two hyperparameters of the support vector regression (SVR) are estimated on a held out using grid search, thus the SVR using them is tested on unseen

Table 7.5. *Achieving stationarity (ADF with $p < 0.1$) on a sample of 12 countries by various methods. The regression technique is in the columns and applying the regression to the population directly (base), its log or its differences is in the rows. Ivory Coast did not achieved stationarity. The number next to the country name is the number of lags needed to achieve stationarity.*

	no constant	constant	linear	quadratic
base		Virgin Islands 9 Trinidad and Tobago 11	Tunisia 8 Virgin Islands 9 Bangladesh 8 Seychelles 8	Ireland 9 Trinidad and Tobago 6 Tunisia 11 Virgin Islands 10 Seychelles 8
log	Bangladesh 8	Virgin Islands 9 Seychelles 0 Trinidad and Tobago 11 Turkmenistan 11 Bangladesh 11	Virgin Islands 9 Trinidad and Tobago 11	Ireland 9 North Korea 8 Virgin Islands 11
diff1	North Korea 8 Slovakia 2 Trinidad and Tobago 11 Sint Maarten 0	Sint Maarten 0 Ireland 9 Seychelles 0	Sint Maarten 0 British Virgin Islands 5 Trinidad and Tobago 10 Seychelles 0	North Korea 10 Seychelles 0 British Virgin Islands 11 Trinidad and Tobago 10 Sint Maarten 0 Tunisia 10

data. The RMSE of 0.6512 (equivalent with missing the target population at 230%) which is compatible with this poverty of features. It is still surprising that the number of links on DBpedia can predict the population of a country to about double its actual size. From Figure 7.7(a), though, we can see the approximation is still very choppy, particularly for smaller countries. Let us add the TS as extra features.

7.6.4 Second Featurization: TS as Features

This approach involves using the time series as lag features (discussed in Section 7.2), including past versions of the target value for a given number of lags, what I call **Markov features**. To find the number of lags that produces the best results, Cell 34 estimate on a held-out set the best hyperparameters for each lag. The best model is tested on unseen data. For an optimal lag of 2, we arrive to the second featurization: using the last two known values of the target value as features, and the numbers of out relations on DBpedia for a total of three features (Table 7.1(f)). For this, SVR obtains a RMSE of 0.0524 and the almost perfect fit shown in Figure 7.7(b). These results seem too good

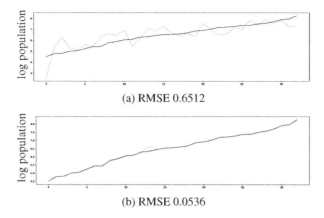

(a) RMSE 0.6512

(b) RMSE 0.0536

Figure 7.7 SVR results over 36 unseen countries, ordered by error: (a) no TS features (b) lag-2 features.

to be true until we realize the last known observation will produce a RMSE of 0.0536 when compared to the present year. It is going to be very difficult to improve upon these results using TS modelling. Let us give the TS a try.

7.6.5 Using the Model Prediction as a Feature

To combine the time series model and ML, we can use it to predict the target variable and use that prediction as a feature. This is in line with doing ensemble methods as feature expansion, as discussed in Section 3.1 in Chapter 3. The hope is that the ML will realize under which conditions the estimator is good and when to disregard it. Continuing the discussion from EDA, to get TS predictions, I will do the following: keep the target year (2017) unseen as it is the test data, and estimate the TS on 1960–2015, testing the TS on 2016.[†] In terms of detrending techniques, we will try three approaches: no detrending, log and linear regression. We iterate through the detrending approaches in order of complexity, preferring the simplest possible model. Note this implied running as many regressions as there are instances (countries). Luckily, excluding the quadratic regression resulted in fast execution. The code in Cell 35 is very involved as it tries to automatically fit a TS for each different country. This process is advised in the literature to be done manually, particularly relying on visual inspection. However, to be able to use the TS with ML, the process needs to be automated. The code applies

---

[†] The WikiCities dataset goes to 2016, but the population data comes from the World Bank that goes from 1960–2017.

the three detrending approaches, in increasing complexity until the ADF test of stationarity (Section 5.1.5.3) has a p-value under 0.1. For such stationary TS, it trains an ARIMA on the detrended TS and uses it to predict the population for 2016. If the error on this prediction is smaller than the error of the baseline (population(2015) + population(2015) − population(2014)), then the whole process is repeated to predict 2017 (which will be used as the ML feature).

The intention was then to train a model using the features from Section 7.6.4 and the prediction from the TS as an extra feature. However, over 163 countries, the code achieved stationarity for 96 (68%) of them, but the prediction improves over the baseline only for 6 countries (4%). At this stage, it is clear there will be no value using these particular TS features. Without substantive and better TS modelling of the data, the SVR using Markov features performs better on this dataset.

7.6.6 Discussion

Fitting TS models automatically without human supervision seems anathema to the TS material I have seen. If you have a quality TS model over your data and you want to expand it using features that will be better modelled using ML techniques, these approaches are worth pursuing:

TS Prediction as a Feature. Incorporate the prediction (as mined on Cell 35) as a feature and leave it to the ML to gauge its impact in comparison with other data.

Model Parameters as Features. The AR, regression and other model parameters can be incorporated as features. Even the conditions under which the TS achieved stationarity could be informative. Note that using the model parameters will result in a variable number of parameters per instance, as they depend on the type of regression and lags. A country that achieved stationarity after applying a log only requires one feature ("it used log for detrending") versus a country that needed a linear regression on two lags will need five features ("it used a linear regression," "it used two lags" and the three regression parameters).

Training Over the Errors. If the TS prediction were good enough, we can try to further improve them by training a ML over its residuals. This is an example of an ensemble learning technique. This is going back to error models where we believe the observed data is the sum of a well behaved, mathematically modellable process and some difficult to model error. We will be leaving the ML to model that error. This is called **training a model on the residuals**, a useful technique beyond time series.

Where do we go from here? Improving the TS fitting using a different regression approach or differencing are two good avenues for expanding this case study. Deviating from existing methods, I would train the SVRs for each year on a subset of the training (to be discarded afterwards), then compute residuals for all years and fit a TS on those residuals. Basically, we would be using the SVR as a detrending mechanism. I did not pursue that path as I felt fitting the TS automatically was enough transgression for one chapter. There are some marked methodological differences between the ML and statistical communities, some of which are discussed in Leo Breiman's article "Statistical Modeling: The Two Cultures."[47] Their reliance on model assumptions ought to be kept in mind when approaching methods from the statistical community.

Finally, I would also like to know how the population numbers are computed. It might be the case that the intermediate numbers are all interpolated and the SVR is just reverse engineering a mathematical function rather than real population numbers.

7.7 Learning More

A good introduction to TS from a computer scientist point of view is presented by Gupta and colleagues in their survey of outlier detection methods for TS.[133] Studying TSA is quite involved. Some textbooks I consulted for this chapter include Chris Chatfield's *The Analysis of Time Series*[61] and Alan Pankratz's *Forecasting with Dynamic Regression Models.*[252] However, online material that included code samples was equally informative. I recommend the blog posts by Brian Christopher[65] and Tavish Srivastava.[290] Research on incorporating TS data into classification systems currently focuses on turning the TS into features.[114]

DBpedia's changes can be used to model errors that are present in data and to study the impact of errors in knowledge-driven NLP algorithms, a topic on which I have done research with colleagues at the National University of Córdoba.[94]

Other topics not covered in the examples from this case study are:

Event Streams. Also known as *point processes*,[49] these are events that happen at different times and might be unrelated (e.g., one user clicking a link on a page vs. a different user clicking the same link). ML is now widely used to tackle these problems. Sometimes you can find a complementary view of your problem from an event stream into a time series (and to less an extent, vice versa). For example, each seismic reading is an event, therefore, it produces an event stream, while total number of micro-earthquakes per month as an aggregate of seismic readings over a certain threshold is a time series. Doing so can prove itself very valuable for FE.[49] I did not discuss event streams per se but Brink and others[49] mention they can be modelled as Poisson processes and non-homogeneous Poisson processes, which predict the rate of arrival of events, while afterwards the techniques in Section 7.6 can be used to inject them into the ML.

Time Dimension. Time has some very particular characteristics that should be taken into account when processing it. First, it is the issue of how to segment it (seconds? hours? days?). Second, time zone issues ought to be modelled and addressed (Do you think "lunch time" is a great feature? Make sure to accommodate customers in India, too), together with daylight savings times (and the disruptive change of time zones that many countries elect to perform over the years).[278] Finally, do not take arithmetic mean of time data, as it periodic. Use the periodic normal distribution (also known as von Mises distribution) instead.[76] While in this case study we seek to understand the data in time, it is possible to flip the question and study the effect of time on the data.[263†] For example, if you are trying to predict sales using the time of the day and other features, you can turn things around and use the sales data and the other features to predict the busiest times of the day. Such an approach is outside the scope of this case study.

Time Series Extensions to ML Algorithms. If you are working with TS data, many ML algorithms allow for extensions where the correlation between instances can be added. Examples include a TS extension to MARS (cf., Section 4.2.3 in Chapter 4) and TS extensions to LASSO. Outlier detection techniques have very specific TS adaptations, too,[133] as well as discretization algorithms.[83]

Seasonal Models. The trend plus the cycle tend to be combined, thus separating seasonal contributions is important, as removing the seasonal component allows the ML to not confuse seasonal with long-term change.[29] A seasonal term is different from a cycle: there is no "Christmasness," i.e., seasonal effects

---

† Chapter 9.

happen at very specific times.[263] The most common models for seasonal modelling assume the seasonal component has a stable pattern: it is strictly a periodic function with a periodicity of 12 months, 4 months or 7 days. The seasonal effect can be eliminated by differencing: $x_t - x_{t-12}$ or other techniques, including specially crafted moving averages.[61]

Transformations Into the Frequency Domain. The idea of changing dimensions from time to frequencies is productive and was not covered in these case studies, which lack any cyclic behaviour. A Fourier transform changes the data to be expressed as a combination of sines and cosines, which in turn has less parameters. It gives the minimum square error between the function and its approximation; their basis (sines and cosines) are orthogonal and can be estimated independently.[29] This is called the spectral representation, a decomposition into separate pairwise uncorrelated periodic oscillations where the total variance is distributed over frequencies.[29] The frequency domain equivalent of the correlogram is called a **periodogram**, which plots the Fourier power spectral density of a TS against its frequency of oscillation.[49]

8

Textual Data

In this case study I will use text problems as a domain that exemplifies a large number of correlated features, with feature frequencies strongly biased by a power law. Such behaviour is very common for many naturally occurring phenomena besides text. It is also a domain where ordering issues that are present in the raw data are important, as text is a sequence of words and meaning conveyed in the ordering: compare subject positions (Pacman eats Blinky) versus object positions (Blinky eats Pacman). **The very nature of dealing with sequences means this domain also involves variable-length feature vectors. Unique aspects of this domain are the types of correlations found in human languages, as their structure are specific to language itself.** Nevertheless, other macro-observations of the world at large might include such a level of correlation. What we observe are many rare events that account for 20% or more of the observed events. This distribution is known as a power law with a heavy tail or a Zipfian distribution.[236]

A central theme in this chapter is the concept of **context** and how to supply it within the enhanced feature vector in order to increase the signal-to-noise ratio available to machine learning (ML). Another theme is to benefit from my domain expertise, in my dual role of practitioner and domain expert in natural language processing (NLP).[89] **The advantage of domain expertise is that it allows for richer hypothesis building during error analysis (EA) and enables faster feature engineering (FE) cycles.** This can be seen in a total of six different featurizations accomplished in this case study (Table 8.1).

Among the methods exemplified in this domain we will cover feature selection (Section 4.1 in Chapter 4), particularly dimensionality reduction (Section 4.3 in Chapter 4); feature weighting (Section 2.1.3 in Chapter 2), in particular a text specific called TF-IDF; and computable features (Section 3.1 in Chapter 3) in the form of morphological features. NLP is one of the

Table 8.1. *Feature vectors used in this chapter. BASE is the conservative graph feature vector from Chapter 6, Table 6.1 (d). (a) Numbers-only, 131 features (b) Bag-of-words, 1,099 features (c) Stems, 1,099 features (d) Bigrams, 1,212 features (e) Skip n-grams, 4,099 features (f) Embeddings, 1,149 features*

1	rel#count
	... BASE ...
98	computed#value
99	logtextlen
100	Seg0: 1000-1126
	...
131	Seg31: 264716-24300000
	(a)

1	rel#count
	... (identical to (a)) ...
99	logtextlen
100	token=city
101	token=capital
	...
1,099	token=conditions
	(b)

1	rel#count
	... (identical to (a)) ...
99	logtextlen
100	stem=TOKNUMSEG30
101	stem=citi
	...
1,099	stem=protest
	(c)

1	rel#count
	... (identical to (c)) ...
1,099	stem=protest
1,100	bigram=NUMSEG31-urban
1,101	bigram=center-NUMSEG31
	...
1,212	bigram=grand-parti
	(d)

1	rel#count
	... (identical to (c)) ...
1,099	stem=protest
1,100	hashed_skip_bigram#1
1,101	hashed_skip_bigram#2
	....
4,099	hashed_skip_bigram#3,000
	(e)

1	rel#count
	... (identical to (c)) ...
1,099	stem=protest
1,100	embedding#1
1,102	embedding#2
	....
1,149	embedding#50
	(f)

older topics in artificial intelligence (AI) and commands many specialized technologies grounded in linguistics and separated from ML. Production quality NLP needs a quality text processing pipeline for feature extraction, particularly at the tokenization (word detection) level and segmentation of text into sentences, paragraphs, etc. In this case study, I have tried to avoid bringing heavy NLP dependencies to the code as they are unrelated to FE. NLP-specific issues are much better explained by the many excellent books in existence (see Section 8.10 for some of my favourites).

As always with FE, not everything I tried did improve performance. In particular, some of the more advanced techniques did not live up to expectations, but the hope is that with more tweaking of the underlying model used they might prove to be worthy (or maybe they do not apply to this domain and data). I do think there are better NLP-specific ways to deal with this raw data, and I lay out such a solution in Section 8.9.

Chapter Overview

In this chapter, we expand WikiCities with the text from full Wikipedia pages (Section 8.1). Benefitting from my domain expertise, we perform less error analysis (EA) for more coverage of NLP techniques. At the exploratory data analysis stage (Section 8.2), it is expected that bigger cities will have longer pages, so we add text length to see encouraging results. Looking at 10 cities at random, we see that most pages mention the population, albeit with punctuation. On to the whole dataset, this percentage reduces to about half. We thus start with using only the presence of numbers on a certain range as additional features in the first featurization (Section 8.3). We use the problem-dependent discretization data from Chapter 6, which results in only 32 extra binary features, producing a relative success (Section 8.3.3).

We then move into the bag-of-words (BoW) featurization (Section 8.4), which considers the words themselves as independent events. We do not want to drown the ML with tons of uninformative features, so we aggressively filter them down using mutual information (MI), keeping only the top 1,000 words (Section 8.4.2). The top 20 tokens look quite helpful (i.e., "capital," "major" or "international."). With this new feature vector, which is much longer than previous chapters, we obtain improved results. An EA (Section 8.4.2.1) looking at cities with top performance decreases or increases is then performed. The top winners are well-written, long documents for cities far from the western world, which might have less DBpedia property coverage (the features of the base system). The text thus might have helped to make up for the missing property coverage. The cities that lose performance inform us how to improve the features; some of the words that appear to be strong signals were not present in the top 1,000 terms. However, many stop words (words such as "the," "a," etc.) appear, so we decide to clean them up (Section 8.5.1), together with conflating morphological variations using a stemmer (Section 8.5.2). This results in the third featurization (Section 8.5.3). The top 20 stems by MI now assign greater importance to numbers, and we are getting closer to the best performance found on Chapter 6. We now see errors where the text contains the correct sentence "Population is 180,251." but the context is lost for the numeric token (Section 8.5.3.1). If the ML were made aware that these tokens are contiguous, it could pick them as a strong signal, which brings us to the concept of bigrams, pairs of words in order (Section 8.6.1) and the fourth featurization (Section 8.6.2). We aggressively filter bigrams that appear less than 50 times. This is as performant as using the stems themselves, so we do a more aggressive approach with skip bigrams of order six plus hash encoding (Section 8.7.2). That did not improve but it did not get worse either, which is quite informative in itself.

Finally, we explore dimensionality reduction using word embeddings (Section 8.8). To use these embeddings we take the weighted average embedding for the whole document, using TF-IDF as the feature weighting (Section 8.8.2). In the sixth featurization (Section 8.8.3), we add the embeddings to the stemmed top 1,000 MI terms as the embeddings visualization shows the embeddings alone will not be enough. We obtain a slightly worse error but it is unclear whether we can conclude this technique did not work. The type of dense features obtained from the embeddings are very different from the other featurizations in this case study.

8.1 WikiCities: Text

The text data we will be using in this case study are the Wikipedia pages for the different cities in the dataset from Chapter 6. Note that this chapter is not completely self-contained; if you have not read that chapter, you might read Section 6.1 for details on the task and motivation. Wikipedia text is not in plain format; it actually makes use of its own formatting, which makes the analysis difficult and may confuse the ML with formatting instructions instead of human language. Extracting plain text from Wikipedia is a computationally intensive task and better handled by specialized tools. In this case, I used the excellent software Wikiextractor[15] by Giuseppe Attardi to build the file *cities1000_wikitext.tsv.bz2* provided with the case study. It has one city per row and text lines separated by tab characters. That file totals 43,909,804 words and over 270,902,780 characters (that is an average of 558 words per document, or 3,445 characters). For some of the experiments using document structure, discussed in Section 8.9, I also kept the original markup in *file cities1000_wikiraw.tsv.bz2*. The total number of characters with markup climbs up to over 730 million characters.

First, many Wikipedia pages contain the population information mentioned within the text. Not necessarily all of them, but many do. At the exploratory data analysis (EDA) stage we might want to get an idea of how many do. Even for the ones that do, however, it might be indicated in many different ways, including punctuation (2,152,111 instead of 2152111) but most probably rounded up and expressed as intermixing digits with words (like "a little over 2 million"). In that sense, this task is representative of the NLP subfield of information extraction (IE), [78] where custom systems are built to extract specific types of information from texts with a specific style and type.

While NLP this decade has been overtaken by deep learning (DL) approaches, particularly using neurolanguage models, [31] this particular task can probably still benefit from non-DL techniques, as we are looking for a very small piece of evidence within a large amount of data. This is also a task representative of many potential enhancements to ML solutions using textual data. Tasks that are closer to text classification are better catered to by DL approaches, expanding on the embedding techniques in Section 8.8.

Following Chapter 6, it is expected that bigger cities will have longer pages, so a descriptive feature (cf., Chapter 2, Section 2.3) such as text length will most probably be a great feature. As base features, I will use the conservative feature set from Chapter 6, a feature set with 98 features based on the infobox properties of the cities. With the total text size close to 48 million words, aggressive feature selection will be needed. It is time to do some EDA.

8.2 Exploratory Data Analysis

Let us start by assembling a simple dataset with an extra feature (the text length) and see whether it helps to better predict the population. Cell 1 in the Chapter 8 Jupyter notebook reads the conservative features from Chapter 6 and joins it with the computed length of the associated Wikipedia article for a total of 99 features. The resulting RMSE of 0.3434 (Figure 8.1(a)) is an improvement of the one from Chapter 6 (0.3578), which is encouraging, but it is above using the full Chapter 6 graph information at 0.3298.

Let us look at 10 random cities to see whether their text descriptions include the population explicitly (Cell 2). Notice the code uses a regular Wikipedia dump, not a Cirrus dump. Wikipedia in recent years has moved to include tags expanded from the Wikidata project, and therefore, the exact population number might be absent, with a tag indicating to the page-rendering engine to fetch the number at rendering time. That does not seem to be a problem for the 2016 source data that corresponds to the DBpedia dataset employed.

From a random sample of 10-pages with highlights shown in Table 8.2, we can see that most pages mention the actual number, albeit with punctuation.

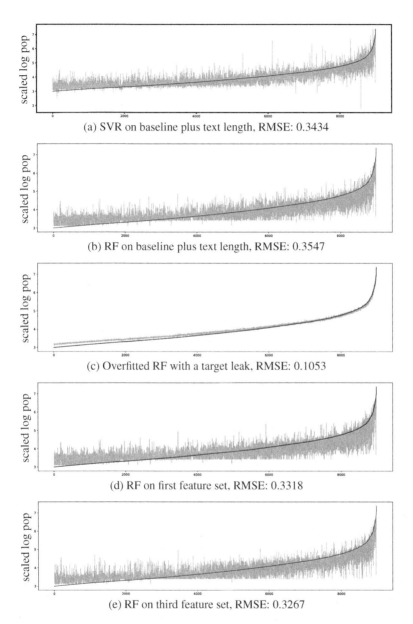

(a) SVR on baseline plus text length, RMSE: 0.3434

(b) RF on baseline plus text length, RMSE: 0.3547

(c) Overfitted RF with a target leak, RMSE: 0.1053

(d) RF on first feature set, RMSE: 0.3318

(e) RF on third feature set, RMSE: 0.3267

Figure 8.1 Results. The other featurizations are not included as they produce similar graphs. Note that, while the RMSEs are different, many of the graphs look quite similar.

Table 8.2. *Exploratory data analysis over the text of 10 random cities. The text column is example text where the population appears, if any. Two cities have no population information present in their description. The population column is empty if the correct population appears in the text.*

City	Pop.	Text Highlight
Arizona City		The population was **10,475** at the 2010 census.
Century, Florida		The population was **1,698** at the 2010 United States Census.
Cape Neddick		The population was **2,568** at the 2010 census.
Hangzhou		Hangzhou prefecture had a registered population of **9,018,000** in 2015.
Volda	8827	The new Volda municipality had **7,207** residents.
Gnosall		Gnosall Gnosall is a village and civil parish in the Borough of Stafford, Staffordshire, England, with a population of **4,736** across 2,048 households (2011 census).
Zhlobin		As of 2012, the population is **80,200**.
Cournonsec	2149	–
Scorbé-Clairvaux	2412	–
Isseksi		At the time of the 2004 census, the commune had a total population of **2000** people living in 310 households.

Eight out of 10 cities picked randomly mention the population, with one case having a different population (7,207 versus 8,827) and another with nonstandard punctuation (80.200 instead of 80,200). Clearly there is value on the textual data. Only one case (*Isseksi*) has the number verbatim (without any punctuation). Also, note that *Volda* is a very small town with plenty of text and a rich history. The page itself describes its population changes over the years, which might potentially confuse an algorithm (at least it made it difficult for me to find its current population).

Let us see if these percentages carry on to the whole dataset. Cell 3 goes through all the cities in the development set and checks whether its population appears on the page as different variations on the ways a number can be expressed as a string. From a total of 44,959 cities, the population is found verbatim in 1,379 of them (3%), with commas, in 22,647 pages (50%) and with periods instead of commas, only in 36 of them (less than 0.1%). Thus in 53% of the pages, the population appears either verbatim or with proper commas separating digit groups.

Therefore, half the cities contain their population in the page in numeric format. **Note how misleading the conclusions from the sample of 10**

documents were. The number of documents with the population was 53%, not 80% and the number of documents with periods instead of commas was not 10% but 0.1% (finding one of the documents in our sample was akin to winning a raffle). These types of misleading samples are very common in NLP and thus the risk of overfitting is very real, particularly for techniques using exact words and phrases, which are very rare in a statistical sense. **Each specific phrasing for a concept is an unlikely event, as there are many ways to say them.** This constitute a very large source of **nuisance variations** within the domain. Care must be taken not to distill such patterns from the test data, as they will invalidate the conclusions: **it is not unusual in NLP that even strong patterns observed in training will have absolutely no effect during test.** Distilling patterns is a hand-labour–intensive process and if the practitioner is not shielded from looking at the test documents (what is known as being "contaminated by the test data"), then the evaluation results will not be representative of the system in production.

From this analysis, I conclude that using rule-based information extraction techniques in the form of regular expressions and similar techniques, for example, using the rule-based text annotation (RuTA) system, [187] would work with at least half the cities. Instead, I will try more automated techniques, which might also apply for the cities where the number is not explicitly mentioned, or when it is mentioned erroneously.

A question is then what type of model to use. Many feature representations for NLP require algorithms that can handle a large number of sparse features. [49] This might be a good moment to move away from SVRs, as they could have trouble with a large number of features. I was also afraid that their strong tendency against overfitting might fail when any of those features contain the target value. However, their behaviour when confronted with a target leak (cf., Section 1.3.1 in Chapter 1) in Cell 4 renders a RMSE of 0.1053, indicating that this is not the case. **Target leaks are not an uncommon occurrence for FE. You might be well served to keep an eye on them and learn to recognize them early on.** The difference in the curve obtained in Cell 4 (Figure 8.1(c)) with any of the curves over this dataset should highlight how different a system behaves on their presence.

Sadly, when adding more features the training times get prohibitively long with SVRs. Cell 5 moves on to use a random forest regressor. The faster training time of random forests takes a performance hit, with the RMSE now at 0.3547 (Figure 8.1(b)). It produces worse performance than SVR but it trains much faster, so I settle for them. I can now proceed to the first featurization, where I will see the documents as sets of numerical categories.

8.3 Numeric Tokens Only

This first featurization builds on the intuition from the EDA that the presence of numbers in a certain range are indicative of the target value or, at least, that the target value is in a certain range. But before that, let us discuss tokenization, the splitting of text into what we can generically call "words," although the term "word" is ambiguous between occurrences of a given word type and the type itself, a topic also introduced in the next section.

8.3.1 Word Types versus Word Tokens

When operating with documents and vocabularies, it is important to distinguish the vocabulary size versus the total document size. Both are measured in "words" but the term "word" means different things in each case. Therefore, in NLP, we use the terms "word types" to refer to dictionary entries and "word tokens" to refer to document entries. You can think of the word types as a class in object-oriented programming and a word token as an instance of the class.

Because the vocabulary is fixed in the train set, there will be many words missing in the devset. That is when smoothing techniques (like Good–Turing's smoothing) comes handy (see Section 2.1.2, in Chapter 2).

8.3.2 Tokenization: Basics

By far the most crucial task for NLP and ML is that of tokenization: successfully splitting a sequence of characters or, in general, Unicode codepoints,[70] into subsequences representing the events (words) being observed is far from trivial. **Many ML books talk about refraining from doing complex tokenization and just splitting on white space and then rely on aggressive dimensionality reduction over large amounts of text. But tokenizing on white space involves already complex decisions**, as there are at least half a dozen different Unicode codepoints representing white space in wide use. Moreover, it will create as many aliases for words as the density of the available punctuation. Thus, "`city`" and "`city,`" (note the comma at the end) and "`city.`" (note the period) will be completely different events, as distinct as "`city`" is from "`town`" or any other token. Moreover, some of the punctuated versions will be extremely rare events, which even by using techniques such as SVD (cf., Section 4.3 in Chapter 4) might be impossible to conflate properly. In a sense, a dimensionality reduction technique that puts "`city,`" and "`town`" near to each other and far from "`dog`," "`the`," "`nevertheless`," etc., is already quite a successful algorithm. You might then be tempted to just split into any non-alphabetical character (notice that it will drop all numbers, so for the WikiCities domain I need to consider alphanumeric; **note how the tokenization becomes a central place to add domain-related insights**). However, in texts with proper nouns in multiple languages, that will result in splitting words with accented characters (e.g., "Martín") into multiple tokens (e.g., "Mart" and "n") and will render spurious tokens that are difficult to understand and will double the statistical impact of the original word. Instead, you can split the words into codepoints that are not alphabetical in any script. That is possible using regular expressions with Unicode classes, but the regular expressions are very laborious to write. Therefore, they are usually reused as part of the NLP frameworks; see FACTORIE for such an example.[227] You will be better off using existing tokenizers rather than writing your own. And I have not discussed multiword expressions (MWE) that also disrupt the statistical properties on the events being generated ("New York" should be seen as one event, not two, similar to "Mart" and "n").[49] The same goes with custom tokenizers for nonstandard domains; if you want to make sentiment analysis on Twitter data, be sure to represent "¬_(ツ)_/¯" as a token, otherwise your result will be represented by that kaomoji.

As discussed in the next section, tokenizing numbers is key in this domain. **In other domains it is important to find different variations**[†] **of words, which is known as "morphology,"**[6] and discussed in Section 8.5. The WikiCities problem presents a simpler case, where numbers might just do. For the purpose of our regression problem, **a difference between 12,001,112 and 12,001,442 constitutes a nuisance variation and needs to be addressed**, for example, by conflating it into the same representation. I can replace each number with a pseudo-word, indicating, for example, how many digits the number has (think "TOKNUM1DIGIT," "TOKNUM2DIGIT," etc., where "TOKNUM" indicates it is a numeric pseudo-token). That will produce about 10 tokens for all the population numbers we have (that range from 1,000 to 24 million). This might not be fine-grained enough, however. Instead, I can distinguish the first digit of the numbers (1TOKNUM3DIGIT represents 1,000 to 1,999; 2TOKNUM3DIGIT represent 2,000 to 2,999 and so on), which will create about 90 tokens, and in turn might be too many.

Instead, **I can make the decision problem-dependent and make use of the discretization data from Cell 27 in Chapter 6** (discussed in Section 6.3.1.2) and transform each number-like token into a TOKNUMSEG<*number*> for 32 distinct segments (Cell 5).

[†] *Derivations* rather than *variations* would be more technically correct from a linguistic perspective; thanks to Steven Butler for stressing this difference.

8.3.3 First Featurization

One of the most common approaches to using textual data with the ML is to supply the ML with a histogram of word types, what is called a bag-of-words approach (cf., Section 2.3.1 in Chapter 2) and discussed in the next section. In this case study, I am more interested in numbers rather than English words. Therefore, I will start by just looking at numeric tokens. From the EDA, we know the population numbers appear at most once; therefore, the total count for each number is not important, all we care is whether a number on a certain range appears in the document or not. This rationale can be translated to other, similar domains that you may encounter with lots of potential features: **just because your raw data presents itself naturally with thousands of features does not mean that you or domain experts you consult with will not be able to find a handful believed to have strong explanatory power.**

This will work even with other problems over text, as numbers are an example of typed entities that can be recovered via automatic methods using what NLP calls, for historical reasons, named entity recognition (NER). Other examples are colours, places, dates and many others.[240]

Using only the 32 numeric tokens expands the feature vector to include only 32 binary features indicating whether numbers in the given range appear, bringing the feature vector size to 131 (98 plus text length and 32 features, Table 8.1(a)). The resulting random forest has a RMSE of 0.3437 (Figure 8.1(c)). That improved over the baseline when adding only these 32 new features, but we are still not at the level of the best graph models (note that a SVR on this first feature set takes two hours to train, with only 131 features, and produces a RMSE of 0.3216).

Given the relative success of the numbers-only approach, I will now look at more traditional bag-of-words techniques, without doing an EA on this first featurization. It is obvious that more words need to be added, since from the EDA we know that the numbers appear in only half the cases.

8.4 Bag-of-Words

Text, as a sequence of Unicode codepoints, has a hierarchical structure; first there are words (or word-like structures, like in Chinese), then sentences, paragraphas, sections, etc. Exploiting this hierarchical structure is a formidable task. The simplest way to represent text and, by far, the most widely used, is to disregard the order between words and consider the words themselves as independent events. This, of course, makes very little domain sense; we know word ordering affects communication between humans. From there, we can further disregard the number of times a word appears in a document (i.e., a Boolean feature vector), or we can use the raw word counts or weight them appropriately. The weighting scheme can be related to properties of the language, the dataset or the general problem domain. This constitutes a form of feature normalization, as discussed in Section 2.1, in Chapter 2.

The bag-of-words approach represents each document as a fixed-size vector with size equal to the whole vocabulary (as computed on training). Again, the most important function in a bag-of-words approach is the tokenization function (discussed next).

I want then to extend the numbers from the first featurization with more words. However, **I do not want to drown the ML with tons of uninformative features, so I will aggressively filter them down using MI** (cf., Section 4.1.1.1 in Chapter 4), as implemented in Cell 7. I keep only the top 1,000 words, leaving it up to the feature selection to determine whether the numeric tokens are important or not. The feature filtering is done using train and test together, which introduces a source of potential overfitting that I find a reasonable risk in this case, however, a held-out dataset kept from Chapter 6 is available to double-check these assumptions.

Note that I first threshold the tokens to tokens that appear in a minimum of 200 cities. The total vocabulary without threshold is 408,793 word types, when adding thresholding it reduces 98% down to 6,254 word types. **This is a very strong thresholding and it is the reason I feel these results are not overfit.** I will further discuss this decision in Section 8.9.

8.4.1 Tokenization

To avoid adding a NLP dependency, I used a regular expression truncating in codepoints outside ASCII letters, numbers and **commas**. The commas are an added requirements for the WikiCities domain. Any trailing commas were removed from the tokens. Tokens are also lowercased, following standard practices.[49]

I have dropped capitalization to reduce the feature set plus some light punctuation removal. Further processing is possible by stemming (conflating "city" and "cities") and dropping stop words (uninformative words as understood by the NLP/IR community), but we will see if that is an issue through EA next.

I will be showing the behaviour of different tokenization approaches on the following description of Ganzhou:

> Its population was 8,361,447 at the 2010 census whom 1,977,253 in the built-up (or "metro") area made of Zhanggong and Nankang, and Ganxian largely being urbanized.

This example sentence would appear to the ML as the sequence of tokens:

['its', 'population', 'was', 'TOKNUMSEG31', 'at', 'the', 'TOKNUMSEG6', 'census', 'whom', 'TOKNUMSEG31', 'in', 'the', 'built', 'up', 'or', 'metro', 'area', 'made', 'of', 'zhanggong', 'and', 'nankang', 'and', 'ganxian', 'largely', 'being', 'urbanized']

Each word type will have its own associated feature (column in the feature vector). In this featurization, similar to the previous one with numbers, there will be an indicator feature (either 1.0 or 0.0) representing whether that particular word type appears in the full text. The practice of replacing the original sequence of characters for a token with a new sequence such that we knew it will not appear in the original text (pseudo-token) is very common in NLP and can be extended to other types of words with high variability besides numbers. For example, it is possible to represent unknown words (TOKUNK) or unknown word, capitalized (TOKUNKCAP). While a relatively poor engineering practice, it makes EA and understanding the tokenizer much easy for humans.

Filtering the top 1,000 MI word types, the final tokenization for the example sentence will be:

['its', 'population', 'was', 'at', 'the', 'TOKNUMSEG6', 'the', 'built', 'metro', 'area', 'of', 'and', 'and', 'largely', 'being']

Note how TOKNUMSEG31 is gone. That seems a mistake that I will let carry over for the time being. **Plenty of insights can be gained by looking at the tokenized output before proceeding to train a model. You might be able to iterate your feature set without even retraining.**

8.4.2 Second Featurization

The top 20 tokens listed in Table 8.3 look quite helpful, particularly words like "capital," "major" or "international." As discussed in the tokenization section, not all the discretized numbers were chosen, but most of them are in the top 1,000 (18 out of 32). That shows their value. The ones that are missing fall into a category that has them grouped with years or very large numbers. The use of NER [240] will help here, as years tend to appear in very different contexts than other numbers (and their range is also very specific), but I do not want to increase the running time and add a complex NLP dependency.

With this new feature vector, which at 1,099 features (Table 8.1(b)) is much longer than the ones employed in previous chapters, we obtain in Cell 8 a RMSE of 0.3318. That is an improvement, so let us drill down with EA to see what worked and what did not.

Table 8.3. *Top 20 tokens by MI on the second featurization.*

Position	Token	Utility	Position	Token	Utility
1	city	0.110	11	than	0.0499
2	capital	0.0679	12	most	0.0497
3	cities	0.0676	13	urban	0.0491
4	largest	0.0606	14	government	0.0487
5	also	0.0596	15	are	0.0476
6	major	0.0593	16	during	0.0464
7	airport	0.0581	17	into	0.0457
8	international	0.0546	18	headquarters	0.0448
9	its	0.0512	19	such	0.0447
10	one	0.0502	20	important	0.0447

Table 8.4. *Error analysis for the bag-of-words feature set over cities that lost performance.*

City	Comments
Bailadores	A big city (over 600,000 inhabitants) described as a "town."
Villa Alvarez	No text.
Koro	"Agriculture" most probably is linked to smaller places.
Curug	We got a TOKNUMSEG6 for the 2010 census and then the correct TOKNUMSEG30; I think the first TOKNUMSEG6 is confusing the ML.
Delgado	No usable terms.
Madina	Population of toknumseg30 should be gotten by a stop words plus bigram.
Banha	I think if "cities" were "city" it will work.
Dunmore	Small hamlet with lots of info in Wikipedia; the main signal "village" is not part of the feature vector.
Demsa	The "population TOKNUMSEG30" should do its magic.
Xuanwu	No idea. The token "capital" ought to have worked.

8.4.2.1 Error Analysis

I will now proceed to do an EA by looking at the documents that gained the most with the text features and the ones that were hurt more (Cell 9). From the full results in the notebook, the top winners are well written, long documents for cities far from the western world. These cities might have less property coverage in the English-speaking Wikipedia, and these properties are the ones in Chapter 6 that derives the non-text features used as the base system. The text might have helped make up for the missing property coverage. The cities that lose performance are more informative (see the overview in Table 8.4).

Interestingly, some of the words that appear to be strong signals were not present in the top 1,000 terms (and thus not available for the ML). For example, "census" appears in 21,414 cities but it is not picked as a top 1,000. The word in itself might not be population-related but it appears close to the actual population (so it might be useful later when we use surrounding tokens to provide context). However, many stop words (words such as "the," "a," etc.) appear, and it might be worth to clean them up and also remove variants to see if we can accommodate more meaningful terms in the top 1,000. In the same vein, "village" appears in 13,998 cities but it had an MI of 0.0025 (compare to an MI for city of 0.1108) and it was at the bottom 100 at position 2,881. I believe it should have been selected, as there are differences between "town," village" and "city" that might inform the model, but it might be that at a four-way splitting of the target population used for the MI it is not granular enough to pick a signal on the small population range.

The conclusion is then to conflate and filter the terms, maybe even to consider expanding the list until *census* and *village* are added, **and to increase the granularity for the MI discretization**. We can also look into bigrams (pairs of terms, see Section 8.6), and skip bigram (pairs of terms with intervening words removed, see Section 8.7). Let us start with filtering stop words and do some stemming to see if we can include *census* and *village*.

8.5 Stop Words and Morphological Features

The type of vocabulary conflation I am looking for can be rendered via two common NLP techniques,[43] which are discussed next: removing uninformative words and conflating morphological variations. We will also look into increasing the number of segments for the target feature, in order to see if it is possible to incorporate *village* into our feature set.

8.5.1 Stop Words

As discussed in Chapter 4, Section 4.1.3.2, **for certain domains there exist features known and understood to be unproductive. Lists of such features are compiled and used to improve the performance of classifiers.** These taboo features are especially important in NLP and IR where they receive the name of **stop words**. This common feature selection technique in NLP consists of dropping a small set of highly frequent function words with little semantic content for classification tasks. This is called **stop word removal**, an approach shared with IR. I use the stop words of the snowball IR system[224] for a total of 180 tokens to be dropped, available in the file *stop.txt*. Stop words can also be identified automatically based on word frequencies.[330] For the running example, this will result in the following tokenization:

['population', 'TOKNUMSEG31', 'TOKNUMSEG6', 'census', 'TOKNUMSEG31', 'built', 'metro', 'area', 'made', 'zhanggong', 'nankang', 'ganxian', 'largely', 'urbanized']

Note how semantically dense the output becomes.

8.5.2 Tokenization: Stemming

In some textual domains, it is useful to reduce the number of features by dropping the morphological variants for different words. For example, if you believe the word "city" is useful in this domain, its plural variant "cities" might be equally useful but rarer. **If you conflate both terms as the same feature, you could obtain better performance by boosting the main signal with the rarer variants. It is a very targeted type of dimensionality reduction.** Alternatively, this could be considered as computable features, where you are computing a stem of a word based on a base feature (the word itself). The computable feature view indicates that you can also combine stems and base words and present both to the ML, an approach that is sometimes viable.

To obtain morphological roots for words, we can use a dictionary of root forms (a **lemmatizer** approach), or we can instead use a simple approximation (a **stemmer** approach). A small lemma dictionary might be enough, as most frequent words have the most exceptions, while less frequent words tend to be regular. I will use a stemming approach using an implementation of the Porter stemmer[258] (Cell 10).

Morphological variants can also be identified using unsupervised ML techniques.[286] Certain languages with strong morphology like Spanish or Finnish truly require morphological processing, while agglutinative languages (like Turkish) require dedicated methods.

In the running example, the new tokenization will produce the following:

['popul-', 'TOKNUMSEG31', 'TOKNUMSEG6', 'census-', 'TOKNUMSEG31', 'built-', 'metro-', 'area-', 'made-', 'zhanggong-', 'nankang-', 'ganxian-', 'larg-', 'urban-']

This is quite an improvement, as now the correct population (TOKNUMSEG31) is also included. Notice that stems are traditionally shown with a dash at the end to highlight the fact that they are stems, not words.

Table 8.5. *Top 20 stems by MI on the third featurization.*

Pos.	Stem	Utility	Pos.	Stem	Utility
1	TOKNUMSEG30	0.0537	11	import-	0.0366
2	citi-	0.0513	12	largest-	0.0357
3	capit-	0.0482	13	TOKNUMSEG18	0.0356
4	airport-	0.0445	14	TOKNUMSEG19	0.0349
5	temperatur-	0.0420	15	TOKNUMSEG20	0.0346
6	climat-	0.0420	16	china-	0.0338
7	univers-	0.0404	17	institut-	0.0322
8	intern-	0.0398	18	major-	0.0318
9	TOKNUMSEG29	0.0371	19	TOKNUMSEG22	0.0318
10	urban-	0.0370	20	TOKNUMSEG14	0.0317

8.5.3 Third Featurization

The top 20 stems by MI are shown in Table 8.5, and there we can see that the numbers are now much more important. But "villag-" is not even in the top 2,000, so I keep 1,000 (expanding to 2,000 terms was tried, but did not help and increased the RAM requirements beyond 16Gb). Tokenization now takes much more time. It is the reason that NLP is usually done in batches using multiple machines, employing frameworks such as Apache UIMA[106] or Spark NLP.[343] Adding name entity recognition will make it much slower. Also, as I add more complexity, the results are more difficult to understand. What type of tokens does the stem "civil-" capture? "Civilization"? "Civilized"? Intriguing.

Evaluating the new feature set (Cell 11, Table 8.1(c)) produces a RMSE of 0.3267 (shown in Figure 8.1(e), but this is the last curve I will include here as, while different, they are not informative at this stage). With this result, we are getting closer to the best performance found in Chapter 6.

And now for the EA using similar techniques as before.

8.5.3.1 Error Analysis

From the EA in Cell 12, we see examples such as *Demsa*, 180,251 that is predicted at 2,865 when the text contains the sentence "Population is 180,251." that results in the two continuous tokens ⟨"popul-", TOKNUMSEG30"⟩. Similarly, the city of *Leiyang*, population: 1,300,000, is predicted as having 55,023 inhabitants when it contains the sentence "It has over 1.3 million inhabitants." which produces the contiguous tokens ⟨"million-", "inhabit-"⟩. In the current system "popul-" and "toknumseg30" might as well appear in completely different ends of the document. The fact they appear side by side ought to make them a strong signal, but that information is not available to the ML. If the ML were made aware that these tokens are contiguous, it should pick them as a strong signal, which bring us to the concept of bigrams and the fourth featurization.

8.6 Features in Context

To incorporate some ordering among the words, a common technique is to use bigrams, or pairs of words in order. This is one of the techniques I discussed for encoding lists in Section 5.1.2, in Chapter 5. **Bigrams capture local ordering relations.**

8.6.1 Bigrams

If we were to use bigrams directly, this will increase the vocabulary size significantly (close to 600,000 entries), therefore, Cell 13 thresholds their minimum occurrence to at least 50 times, which causes 99.98% of them to be dropped, to 113. A random sample of 30 bigrams appears in Table 8.6. Plenty of MWE and some TOKNUMSEG, but not that many of either. The 14 bigrams that contain numeric tokens are listed in Table 8.7.

From the table, we can see that many of the most popular bigrams are just multi-word expressions, like "modern-era" or "new European." From Table 8.7, only the first bigram ("TOKNUMSEG31-urban") strikes me as

Table 8.6. *Random sample bigrams.*

Bigram	Bigram	Bigram
,-former	town-TOKNUMSEG4	three-smaller
TOKNUMSEG31-urban	war-town	lie-former
center-TOKNUMSEG31	town-support	centr-music
TOKNUMSMALL-known	leader-movement	park-host
known-west	mall-high	activ-health
citi-TOKNUMSEG2	modern-era	new-europ
high-old	delta-group	far-downtown
attract-TOKNUMSEG13	rate-TOKNUMSEG0	park-left
type-passeng	fair-literatur	outsid-known
commerci-compani	wall-capit	grand-parti

Table 8.7. *All bigrams with numeric tokens in the total of 113 bigrams.*

Bigram	Bigram
TOKNUMSEG31-urban	center-TOKNUMSEG31
TOKNUMSEG31-product	found-TOKNUMSEG6
TOKNUMSMALL-known	citi-TOKNUMSEG2
TOKNUMSEG6-bomb	town-TOKNUMSEG4
TOKNUMSEG29-concentr	local-TOKNUMSEG6
attract-TOKNUMSEG13	rate-TOKNUMSEG0
around-TOKNUMSMALL	near-TOKNUMSMALL

population-related. Therefore, these bigrams, while frequent enough to be strongly mined on joint train and test, are too few to be *a priori* useful.

8.6.2 Fourth Featurization

Training on these 1,212 features (98 base, text length, 1,000 stems plus 113 bigrams, Table 8.1(d)) nets a RMSE of 0.3262, which is just as performant as using the stems themselves. But what I was trying to accomplish (*populatio-numeric_*token) is not among the picked bigrams for any of the population numbers. Let us try a more aggressive skip bigrams approach with hash encoding instead.

8.7 Skip Bigrams and Feature Hashing

We will now discuss an extension of bigrams, skip bigrams, that produce a feature explosion. To deal with the feature explosion we will look into feature hashing. Let us discuss these topics in order.

8.7.1 Skip Bigram

A skip bigram is a way of representing a list as a set of pairs, with two elements in the pair appearing in order in the list, the first element in the pair appearing before the second element at a distance of at most the order of the skip-bigram. For example, a skip bigram of order 3 will tolerate up to two tokens in between the elements of the pair. They were introduced in Section 5.1.2 in Chapter 5. **The idea behind skip bigrams is to remove nuisance variations introduced in natural language texts by the parentheticals, appositions and additional**

qualifiers. Compare, "the 500,000 inhabitants of . . ." versus "at 500,000, the inhabitants of . . .". Allowing these *wildcard* positions might elucidate a signal otherwise unavailable to the ML.

If we were to use skip bigrams directly, this will increase the size of the feature vector by quite a bit. To further reduce the size of the feature vectors, any dimensionality reduction technique, as described in Section 4.3 in Chapter 4, can be used. **A technique that is very useful with this type of feature is feature hashing** (cf., Section 4.3.1 in Chapter 4), **as there are very good hashing functions that distribute natural language words.**[12,109]

8.7.2 Fifth Featurization

Cell 14 combines skip bigrams of order 6 with feature hashing (cf., Section 4.3.1 in Chapter 4) with a target hash size of 3,000 to reduce the number of bigrams to a manageable size. With feature hashing, a large number of features (expected in the couple of millions for this case) gets mapped to a fixed-size vector. The expectation is that, in case of collitions, the ML will be able to discern away the ambiguous signal. For hashing function, Cell 14 uses Python's built-in hashing function. The final vector size is 4,099 (Table 8.1(e)). The RMSE of this approach is 0.3267.

That did not improve, but it is so radically different from previous approaches that the fact it did not get worse is quite informative. Parameter tuning here (in terms of hash size and order of the skip bigrams) can go a long way. Note that doing EA here will be harder; the very large number of skip bigrams will need to be recorded and each coordinate of the hash ought to be associated with a distribution of skip bigrams that map to that coordinate. With a system instrumented in this manner, you can then do a more traditional feature impact analysis.

8.8 Dimensionality Reduction and Embeddings

Finally, Cell 15 explores dimensionality reduction using word embeddings. Because the embeddings and TF-IDF scores might overfit, Cell 15 computes them on the train set only. To use these embeddings, Cell 15 takes the weighted average embedding for the whole document, building a document representation that is the same size as the embedding vector (Section 8.8.2).

Some authors equate FE in NLP as a synonym with dimensionality reduction,[147] **but I hope this case study showcased many other alternatives.**

8.8.1 Embeddings

Following Section 4.3.7 in Chapter 4, Cell 15 trains classic Word2Vec embeddings. Other embeddings would be possible and might have performed better but Word2Vec has been around longer and may have more widespread implementations (at the time of this writing, ELMO[257] and BERT[82] embeddings offer the greatest performance). I believe the difference between embeddings will be dwarfed by the difference of using a good ML (like NN) that can benefit from the embeddings. Given the relatively small amount of text, I picked a relatively small embedding size (50 dimensions), for a 80% train split on the data (about 30,000 cities), Word2Vec trained embeddings for 72,361 tokens, using a stemmed version of the Section 8.4.1 tokenizer. That is, tokens are stemmed with capitalization conflated and numbers conflated into 32 segments. For the running example this tokenizer produces the following:

['it', 'popul', 'was', 'TOKNUMSEG31', 'at', 'the', 'TOKNUMSEG6', 'census', 'whom', 'TOKNUMSEG31', 'in', 'the', 'built', 'up', 'or', 'metro', 'area', 'made', 'of', 'zhanggong', 'and', 'nankang', 'and', 'ganxian', 'larg', 'be', 'urban']

Other dimensionality reductions are possible, for example, SVD (Section 4.3.3 in Chapter 4) or LDA (Section 4.3.4).

A two-dimensional projection of the embeddings is shown in Figure 8.2. I have tried to make that projection as understandable as possible by heavy pruning and sampling, but it is still better understood using interactive

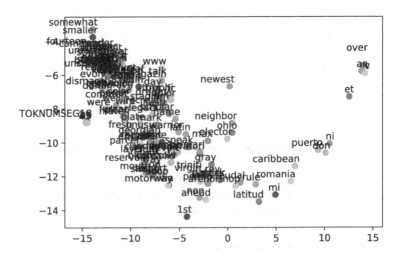

Figure 8.2 Two-dimensional rendering using the t-SNE algorithm on a sample of the 50-dimensional embeddings computed over the train set.

techniques. These projections are the main analysis techniques when using embeddings, together with listing the closer terms (using Euclidean distances) for a given term. From the figure, I concluded that the numeric tokens are clustered together and thus will not be particularly differentiated by the model if the embeddings are its sole information source.

8.8.2 Feature Weighting: TF-IDF

To obtain a representation for the whole document, the word embeddings need to be combined. Complex ways of combining them using RNN would be preferred (cf., Section 5.3.1 in Chapter 5). A simpler alternative, is just to consider them as a set (cf., Section 5.1.1), disregard their ordering and take their average. However, words that are more frequent will dominate the average, taking over the contribution from less-frequent, semantically rich words. This is a similar situation to the one encountered with stop words in Section 8.5.1. At this stage, it is not a matter of dropping less important words, but you can instead dampen their contribution using a feature-weighting scheme (cf., Section 2.1.3 in Chapter 2).

Therefore, instead of using raw counts, we can perform a traditional feature weighting employed in NLP/IR: adjust the counts by the inverse of the frequency of the word type over the corpus. **This is yet another way to do scaling based on statistics over the whole dataset** (cf., Section 2.1, Chapter 2).

We replace the term frequency (term is synonym with word type in IR) in the document with the TF times the inverse document frequency (IDF). To have more informed statistics, we can compute the IDF counts on a larger set (e.g., the full Wikipedia or a large web crawl). In this case study we will use the train set. (As we are using Boolean vectors, our TFs are either 0 or 1.)

The resulting weighted average might work due to the expectation that, if a particular set of dimensions are meaningful as a description of the document, the words with higher IDF might have those dimensions more strongly represented and the weighting will boost that signal.

For the word type "the" its IDF is 0.713, which is fairly low, compared to a content-bearing word such as "census," which is 1.13 or even "capital" at 8.0. As mentioned, IDF renders it somewhat unnecessary to filter stop words.

8.8.3 Sixth Featurization

From the embeddings visualization, it is clear that using the embeddings alone will be too poor a representation, so Cell 15 adds them to the stemmed top

1,000 MI terms from Section 8.5. Using this representation and training on 1,149 features (98 base, text-length, 1,000 top MI terms and 50 dimensions representing the document, Table 8.1(f)), we obtain a RMSE of 0.3280. The error is worse, but it is unclear whether we can conclude that this technique did not work. Maybe a different model might work or even a different parametrization of the random forest. The type of dense features obtained from the embeddings are very different from the other featurizations in this case study. **More worryingly, the results are unstable due to the randomness involved in the construction of the embeddings. This is a known and difficult problem.** The current advice[322] is to use a high-quality, external source for embeddings, such as GloVe.[255] Notice that this will not necessarily work in our case with custom numeric tokens, so we will need to abandon them on the embeddings side. The same goes with using any other pretrained **embeddings (BERT,[82] etc.), as they stop you from problem-specific customizations to the tokenizer.**

Note that EA here will be very difficult. Existing techniques for EA with embeddings focus more on understanding the contribution of the data to certain units in a neural network, for example, by leveraging attention maps. This, of course, is only available if the ML being used are neural networks. It can be argued that this difficulty is shared with other dimensionality reduction techniques. From my perspective, it depends on how easy it is to invert the reduction for interpretability purposes. The feature hashing can be reverse engineered, although it requires large amount of memory to do so.

8.9 Closing Remarks

In this case study, I have sought to work on a NLP problem beyond simple text classification (like topic detection or sentiment analysis). From the success of bigrams, we can see that context was indeed crucial in this domain. Some of the earlier decisions might not have been completely felicitous and I would like to highlight the tension between EA and "consuming" data in the sense of making yourself aware of particular wordings that work well on this data. My main gripe is the extraction of relevant words using MI over the joint train plus test sets. I do not think that the approach overfitted given the aggressive thresholding, but, on the other hand, the aggressive thresholding resulted in less words to inform the ML. Now, if I did not apply the thresholding, I could only use the test data once, as any iteration from there would be too targeted to it and would invalidate it for further testing. This brings an operational conundrum: to consume data while moving forward, you need to decide *ahead of time* how many cycles of FE you will undergo. Otherwise, you will consume all the data early on and the rest of your results will be too overfitted.

In terms of continuing the FE process on this dataset using more complex NLP technology, here are some things I would suggest to try the following:

- Go the NER route, for example, using spaCy[156] to distinguish 2016 as a year versus a regular number (potentially, the population).
- Segment the text and use only one segment to extract features. Topical segments (using classic algorithms such as TextTiling[144] as implemented in NLTK[37]), paragraphs or a sliding window of sentences would do. My favourite approach would be to use a small set of instances to find words in the vicinity of the actual population number (from the EDA, I would expect words such as "population," "inhabitants" and "census" to appear nearby), then pick a sliding window of three sentences that contain the higher density of such tokens (including numeric tokens). Alternatively, use the raw data with markup and extract sections of the data with specific headers and use those as target segments.
- Train a sequence tagger to identify populations as a specific typed entity. Building on the previous approach, as we have sentences where we can easily identify the right answer, we can use such sentences as annotated data and train a sequence tagger (building a custom NER, using for example, CRFs[198]) to identify populations on Wikipedia text. This approach of using an artifact of the text to extract labelled data and generalize from there to the rest of the instances is a trick I have used successfully in the past.[143]
- Delving deeper in to DL NLP, techniques like LSTM-CRFs[160] would most probably provide state-of-the-art performance for this problem, particularly when combined with universal language models.[157]

Smaller things to try, including the following:

- Add a feature indicating whether the numeric token had commas in it or not. From Table 8.2, it can be seen that year numbers are not split with commas, while population numbers are. As stressed in this chapter, domain-specific tokenization is a big source for adding domain knowledge. When working with biology texts,[143] I found that hyphenated structures such as "pB-actin-RL" were important to consider as both a single token and individual tokens (care had to be taken to adjust counts properly, though).
- Revisit using indicator features for numbers and words and move to using counts for them. Even for numbers, the actual population number seems to appear only once and that might be a signal in itself.

- Also regarding revisiting using the segments derived from the target values for numbers, I am not sure if that worked as well as I had hoped, as values from 600 thousands up to 24 million are conflated into the same token.
- Add MWE (for example, using the python gensim package functionality).
- When doing embeddings, you can also take the maximum and minimum for each coordinate over all entries in the document.

By far the biggest performance gain to be expected will be to do hyperparameter optimization for the ML used but I skipped that, as it is of less importance to FE topics. I will now discuss two topics that were not exemplified in this case study but are important when doing FE over textual data: content expansion and structure modelling.

8.9.1 Content Expansion

There are plenty of ways to make the available input data more informative and rich. For example, some of the statistics computed over the training data (like IDFs or the embeddings), could be computed over larger collections of related documents (**corpora**). In the case of hyperlinked documents such as Wikipedia,[49] it is possible to include pieces of text from linked documents. This expansion can also be done to entities identified through NER, for example, with DBpedia Spotlight.[230] The expanded data could be added back as regular text or kept as a separate set of features to avoid drowning the original signal. **This is a particularization to the textual domain of general expansion techniques, which were discussed in Chapter 3.**

8.9.2 Structure in Text

Finally, the hierarchical structure of text can be exploited in many ways. For example, a part-of-speech (POS) tagger can be run over the text (marking words to lexical–syntactic classes such as "noun" or "verb"). Then bigrams can be extended to have one or both entries in the bigram to be replaced by a POS tag, such as "NOUN-population" or "TOKNUMSEG3-VERB." **This domain-specific dimensionality reduction might help boost the signal, as it reduces the number of bigrams considerably.**

Another way to represent the structure of formatted documents is **to produce the Cartesian product of tokens in the section title with tokens in that section.** Therefore, a section with title "Demographics of India" and a sentence such as "Many ethnicities are present in..." will be represented as *demographics-many, india-many, demographics-ethnicities,* *demographics-india*, etc. The hope is that word titles that appear across documents will be picked up when such compound words are meaningful. **This is a particular version of the technique used to represent trees discussed in Section 5.1.3** in Chapter 5.

8.10 Learning More

As mentioned, using computers to process human text is almost as old as computers themselves, with applications appearing as early as the 1950s. It is also a field, until recently, well known for its reliance on heavy FE.[44] It is no surprise that starting in NLP spiked my interest in FE. There are a number of really good books in the field, starting with the classic *Foundations of Statistical Natural Language Processing* by Manning and Schütze;[220] which is both a great introduction to linguistics concepts as well as general statistics. For a more recent take on general concepts, the recently updated *Speech and Language Processing* by Jurafsky and Martin[172] is recommended. Finally, in the last few years, the field has been overtaken by DL approaches.[69] The book by Yoav Goldberg, *Neural Network Methods for Natural Language Processing*, is a great resource on the topic. For another worked-out NLP example, Brink, Richards and Fetherolf[49] show in Chapter 8 of *Real-World Machine Learning* a worked-out movie review case study. Chapter 2 from Dong and Liu's *Feature Engineering* book[132] discuss text representation as features in a general perspective. The last section discusses analyzing nontextual features as extra context for the NLP. This is an intriguing idea that deserves further investigation.

9

Image Data

The previous case studies have focused on discrete data. This chapter focuses on sensor data. As a NLP expert, this is far from my expertise. Luckily, there is plenty of material available on computer vision (CV) that we will be using in this case study. It can also be informative about how to tackle a domain when you have less expertise in it.

The visual perception on mammals is by now one of the better-understood components of the brain. [104] It started with Weibel and Hubel pioneering experiments in the 1950s. [335] We understand how the retina is wired with specific neurons transmitting signals from specific sections in the 2D space where the light lands on the retina. The parallelism with pixels and processing pipelines is no accident. The visual cortex contains a visual extraction pathway that builds a representation of increasing complexity. The information is processed by a precise architecture, with cells organized in layers that encode image characteristics. It is no surprise that deep learning (DL) started on image problems, as DL mimics very well our current understanding of the visual cortex.

When working with images, we have a representation of reality as quantized sensing intensity values provided by sensors. The same sensor will produce a different reading on the same exact scene. Allowing to transcend from these variations to capture high-level meaning (objects, people, etc.) is the monumental task set for CV. It starts as an exercise in smoothing. At this stage in the maturity of the field, new development in CV centres exclusively around DL. We are discussing feature engineering (FE) done over small datasets to provide you with information regarding techniques useful for dealing with sensor data. **As mentioned before, the point of this case study is not to teach you CV** (for that you will be much better served by the books discussed at the end of this chapter) **but to learn from the FE techniques used by CV practitioners to help you with the unique challenges presented by your domain.**

The main takeaway in FE on images is how to work with a large number of low-level features that are not understandable on their own. We need to deal with a high level of nuisance variations in order to normalize the features so that a small change in the way the information is acquired does not throw off your underlying ML mechanism. These takeaways are valuable for anybody working with sensor data where the acquisition process has a high variance. Particular to this case study and domain, another key lesson is to spend as much time as possible getting to know the data. Concentrating exclusively on the algorithm side is no silver bullet. Also in this domain, the issue of alignment between samples (images) is cornerstone, but it failed for this data, a topic we will revisit at the closing remarks in Section 9.8.

Chapter Overview

For this case study, we expand the WikiCities dataset with elevation satellite images. An exploratory data analysis (EDA) (Section 9.2) looking at histograms for 12 random cities highlights that places with more mountains seem to have less population and that city centres are unreliable. Each image adds hundreds of brittle new features (Section 9.3). The first featurization (Section 9.3.1) takes a square of 32×32 pixels centred on the city, with results below baseline. The error analysis (EA) (Section 9.3.1.1) maps the system behaviour back into images to ponder for further analysis and concludes that the model is not learning much. Moreover, nonimage features have an average importance of 40 times higher than image features. We then explore two variants: Gaussian blur, averaging a pixel with its neighbours to remove artifacts (Section 9.3.2), and whitening, which seeks to standardize and remove linear correlations from the data to allow only meaningful variations to remain (Section 9.3.3). Gaussian blur helps and we use it for the rest of the experiments. We then perform an EA on variations, trying to see if an image were to be modified slightly would that change the result of the ML prediction (Section 9.3.4)? We test the model by sampling different variations of the test images. The analysis shows how brittle this model is. Section 9.4 explores training on variations of the data to make the classifier more robust. We can generate feature vectors by automatically varying the data, expanding the training with variants (Section 9.4), which is an effective technique in CV to add domain knowledge on nuisance variations. In our case, these variations are affine transformations (Section 9.4.1), translations, scaling and rotations. The second featurization (Section 9.4.2) is expanded by using four instances per city, the base image plus three random variations. The transformations improve over the baseline and an

Table 9.1. *Feature vectors used in this chapter. BASE is the conservative graph feature vector from Chapter 6, Table 6.1 (d). (a) Pixels-as-features, 1,122 features (b) Variant-expanded, 1,122 features (c) Histogram, 354 features (d) Corners, 99 features (e) HOGs, 422 features.*

1	rel#count
	... BASE ...
98	computed#value
99	pixel at 0,0
131	pixel at 0,31
	...
1,122	pixel at 31,31

(a)

1	rel#count
	... (identical to (a)) ...
1,122	pixel at 31,31

(b)

1	rel#count
	... BASE ...
98	computed#value
99	counts for 0
100	counts for 1
	...
354	counts for 255

(c)

1	rel#count
	... BASE ...
98	computed#value
99	# of corners

(d)

1	rel#count
	... BASE ...
98	computed#value
99	HOG cell #1 histogram bin #1
100	HOG cell #1 histogram bin #2
	...
108	HOG cell #1 histogram bin #9
	HOG cell #2 histogram bin #1
	....
422	HOG cell #36 histogram bin #9

(e)

EA (Section 9.4.2.1) shows the model successfully focusing its attention to the centre of the city. For more robust processing, we move to descriptive features in the form of histograms (Section 9.5). The third featurization (Section 9.5.1) represents every city with its number of pixels with a particular value. This is robust to rotations, mildly robust to translations and still sensitive to scaling. In the evaluation, we see an improvement but it is still worse than not using images. Using coarser histograms achieves results very close to the baseline. An EA (Section 9.5.1.1) checks that the reduction of the impact of nuisance variations is in place.

We then move to local feature detectors in the form of corner detectors seeking to provide better context to similar features (Section 9.6). Corners are places in the image where the information changes in every direction, indicating a region with a geographical characteristic such as a lake or a mountain that will affect the inhabitable area. Using the Harris corner detector (Section 9.6.1) we arrive at the fourth featurization (Section 9.6.2) using the number of corners. This results in a slight improvement, the only one in this chapter. To conclude, as CV has its own gamut of domain-specific dimensionality reduction algorithms, Section 9.7 showcases the dimensionality reduction technique of histograms of oriented gradients, which computes a table of counts for different directions of growth per image segment. This fifth featurization (Section 9.7.1) produces a result that is better than using the raw pixels but worse than using histograms or corners, and it is also much worse than not using any image data at all.

9.1 WikiCities: Satellite Images

Note that this chapter is not completely self-contained; if you have not read Chapter 6, you should read Section 6.1 for details on the task and motivation. For this case study, I sought to expand the WikiCities dataset with satellite images, and then look into counting streets or buildings to estimate population. Counting cars from aerial photography even has its own standardized dataset provided by the Lawrence Livermore National Laboratory[238] and pretrained DL models have successfully been applied to it.

Satellite images are a valuable commodity and were hard to find with a good resolution and unrestricted distribution license. Moreover, satellite images for 80,000 cities with building-recognizable definition will push the expanded corpus into the terabyte range. Instead, I settled for sensor imaging as provided by NASA on the 31.25 meters per pixel range. These images were downloaded from the GIBS tile server. [†] Satellite images are usually distributed in HDF,[349] a custom image format that requires special tools; using the tile server further simplified not having to deal with HDF. The tile server has its tiles directly in the latitude and longitude format, which means the tiles are squeezed in the vertical direction depending on how close the city is to the poles. I have left this artifact in the data to represent the type of challenges in working with image data.

[†] We acknowledge the use of imagery provided by services from the Global Imagery Browse Services (GIBS), operated by NASA's Earth Science Data and Information System (ESDIS) Project.

These files contain sensor data captured in 14 bands of the electromagnetic spectrum using two cameras to record elevation features. These are images that are not in the visible spectrum. That also means that pretrained NN models would be of little expected value, for example, Venkatesan and colleagues found that fine-tuning models trained over regular images did not achieve good performance over medical images.[314] The raw data in this case study is a set of tiles, downloaded from NASA, based on the GPS coordinates distributed by GeoNames (Cells 1 and 2 in the Chapter 9 Jupyter notebooks). To transform these tiles into some initial data that can be appended to each row, Cell 3 extracts a 64×64 pixel range surrounding the latitude and longitude centre of each city as provided by GeoNames. The resulting 64×64 features are then available for further processing. Let us start with some EDA.

9.2 Exploratory Data Analysis

With these 80,199 tiles, we can do some EDA. Let us start by looking at some tiles and their histograms. Cell 4 plots 12 cities at random. As the tiles are not images, they contain a single channel with 256 levels of intensity (as compared with colour images, which contain three channel, red, green and blue). The human eye can only distinguish 60 shades of grey so this mono channel contains information lost to the human eye when shown in grey scale. To solve this problem, Cell 4 employs **false colour**, a visualization technique favoured for sensing data. By adding a colour to different parts of the scale, the information is made visible.

This satellite data has been criticized for having artifacts, which you can see as small black dots on the images.[150] The first row of Figure 9.1 shows a grey scale excerpt. I found no information about the meaning of the signal [†] but it is an elevation signal obtained from binocular-sensing elements on a satellite. The resolution does not seem fine-grain enough to capture manmade structures. We can see that places with more mountains have less population. Let us take a look at the histograms in Cell 5. From the second row in Figure 9.1, we can see that the different feature values are reflected well in the histogram. Plotting the city centre for a few known cities (not shown) informed us that the GeoNames city centre is sometimes a little off from what I would have considered the centre of the city.

We are ready to try ML using all pixels as features.

[†] While this might sound surprising, it reflects the many times I have been given a dump of a production database (and no further information) to address a data science question.

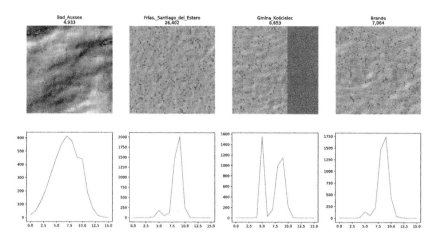

Figure 9.1 EDA: Four random settlements and histograms. The population is shown under their name. The elevation histograms are plots of frequencies versus 16 bins of elevation information. They show that Bad Aussee is in the Alps (elev. 600m), Gmina Kościelec (elev. 200m) downtown is next to a small pond and the other two places are relatively flat (not much variation in the histograms, elev. 300m and 100m).

9.3 Pixels as Features

We will now see a featurization using each pixel as different features plus some variants on the concept. This is the most popular approach these days, using DL to build more complex representations as layers. Let us see how non-DL approaches fare on it.

9.3.1 First Featurization

For a first featurization, Cell 6 takes a square of 32×32 pixels centred on the settlements, resulting in 1,024 extra features (Table 9.1(a)). I picked 32 pixels to cover about a kilometer around the city centre. As most of the settlements in the dataset are less than 10,000 inhabitants (the mean is 5,000), I would expect anything larger will encounter multiple settlements. We will revisit this decision in Section 9.8. For training, it uses a robust ML algorithm capable of handling thousands of features (random forests). Using SVMs on this data exceeded two days of training time. The final RMSE of 0.3296 is worse than the baseline of 0.3189, but we know from the EDA that there are projection issues as well as misplacement of the centre data. Another concern is the added complexity of using image data. Training took 60 times longer with the images.

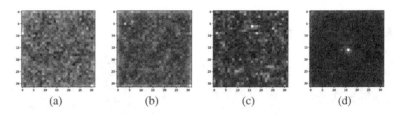

(a)   (b)   (c)   (d)

Figure 9.2 Graphical rendering of the Random Forest feature importance for each pixel. (a) Base RF. (b) Gaussian blur. (c) Whitening. (d) Expanded with affine transformations.

9.3.1.1 Error Analysis

Due to the large number of nondescriptive features, the most successful approach to understand CV systems is by mapping the system behaviour back into images that you can ponder for further analysis. Following this tradition, Cell 7 uses the feature importance computed by random forests to provide a visual guide to the relative importance of the different pixels as "seen" by the model (Figure 9.2(a)). The figure looks quite random, a signal that the model is not learning much. For a well-informed model, I would expect that central pixels have a higher importance, as a "focal centre" of the attention of the model. Graphically, that would have seen as a whiter element in the centre, but we will get to it. As this set has two components, regular features and image features, it is interesting to look at the maximum average feature importance of each block of features. For non-pixel features, the maximum importance value was 0.22702, with an average of 0.00775. For pixel features, however, the maximum is 0.00037 with an average of 0.00023. It is surprising the pixel-features still manage to worsen the RMSE. It all boils down to their sheer number. There are 10 times more pixel features than regular ones. Note that this visualization process could be extended to the EDA stage by leveraging other feature importance metrics, such as mRMR [254] or the techniques discussed in Chapter 4. Before moving to the next featurization, let's use the raw pixels as features that allow the two variants I want to explore now: Gaussian blur and whitening.

9.3.2 Computable Features: Gaussian Blur

As this satellite data is known to have artifacts, averaging a pixel with its neighbours could help remove some artifacts, even though it ultimately throws away information. In our case, as the images represent topographical information, it constitutes a case of geographical smoothing, as discussed in Chapter 2, in Section 2.1.2. Cell 9 implements these ideas and produces a tiny improvement on RMSE, which is still below baseline.

The pixel averaging technique employed, **Gaussian blur**, is a type of image filtering. In a CV context, filtering refers to running a function for each pixel using its neighbourhood. It is used to enhance the image, extract information from it (texture, edges, etc.) and to detect patterns.

Blurring a pixel involves replacing it with a combination of the values of the pixel and its neighbours. These operations are very useful and receive the name **convolutions**.[338] Given a matrix of weights, called a **convolution kernel,** and an anchor point within that matrix, convolution involves making a pass using each pixel of the image as the anchor point. For each pixel as anchor point, convolution takes the neighbours around it, for a context equal to the size of the kernel, and then multiplies the values by the kernel weights. Adding all these products is the value of the convolution for the source pixel. **A kernel is a great way to add local context information to the features.** In formula

$$C[i, j] = \sum_{u=0}^{w} \sum_{v=0}^{h} K[u, v] \, I[i - u + a_r, j - v + a_c]$$

where K is a $w \times h$ kernel with anchor at position (a_r, a_c), and I is the image pixels. This mathematical operation, usually denoted by a six-point asterisk ($*$), has many uses and properties.

Depending on the kernel, it can perform image sharpening, moving averages, weighted moving averages and compute correlations. It is shift-invariant, as its value depends on the pattern in the neighbourhood, not the position within the neighbourhood. It is also linear-invariant: $h * (f1 + f2) = h * f1 + h * f2$, and it operates well under scaling: $h * (kf) = k(h * f)$. It is commutative ($f * g = g * f$) and associative (($f * g) * h = f * (g * h)$). Finally, it works well with differentiation: $\frac{\partial}{\partial x}(f * g) = \frac{\partial f}{\partial x} * g$. That last property is used to approximate derivatives of any order in the Sobel operator.[288] Other important convolution filters for CV include Gabor filters, which allow for generic texture detection.[115]

Note that for the above definition to be applicable to all pixels in the image, it needs to deal with pixels outside the image. The missing pixels can be approximated by reduplicating the pixels at the border. Other alternatives include setting them to a constant value (all black or all white, for example) or using the values of the opposite side.

For Gaussian blur, the kernel is defined by a bidimensional Gaussian function:[245]

$$K(x, y) = \frac{1}{2\pi\sigma^2} e^{-\frac{x^2 + y^2}{2\sigma^2}}$$

In the 5×5 case and using the default $\sigma = 0.3 \times$ ((kernel_size $-$ 1) $\times$ 0.5 $-$ 1)$+$ 0.8 is equal to:

0.01400	0.02801	0.03430	0.02801	0.01400
0.02801	0.05602	0.06861	0.05602	0.02801
0.03430	0.06861	0.08404 *	0.06861	0.03430
0.01400	0.02801	0.03430	0.02801	0.01400
0.02801	0.05602	0.06861	0.05602	0.02801

Looking at the feature importance in Cell 10 (Figure 9.2(b)) we can see that now the borders of the image are lighter than before. That seems to indicate the blurring is not helping, as the borders are the elements that receive less blurring.

As this dataset is worse than the baseline, it is difficult to gauge improvements, as steering the ML away from the pixel data ought to produce better results. This might be what is at play here, as the feature importances for non-pixel features increased compared to the pixel features. The last technique popular on raw pixels is whitening. Let us take a look at it next.

9.3.3 Whitening

Whitening and ZCA were discussed in Chapter 2, Section 2.1.1, as normalization techniques. Whitening seeks to standardize and remove linear correlations from the data to allow only meaningful variations to remain. ZCA is a special type of whitening that produces results that are easier for humans to understand.

Cell 11 performs ZCA whitening with a formula different from the one in Chapter 2. It follows the approach present in the Keras package and performs the multiplication after the data.[†]

The results are disappointing as a result of shooting the RMSE to 0.3476 and almost doubling the training time. This was to be expected, given that whitening stabilizes the variance of the data, which is unnecessary for algorithms like random forests that operate on each feature independently.

Still, whitening remains a popular technique with DL and it might have helped here, too. To double-check the code correctly achieves whitening the data; Cell 12 computes the covariance and checks most correlations are zero.

[†] Computing a ZCA transformation on training and using it on test would need the matrix multiplication to happen **after** the data matrix, not before (it seems what Bradski and Kaehler[45] call a "scrambled" way of computing PCA).

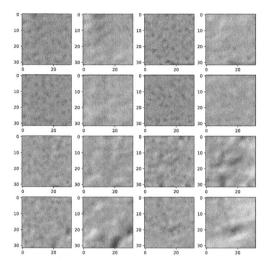

Figure 9.3 ZCA whitening results for eight settlements. The figure to the right is the whitened version of the figure to the left. The first two rows are from the train set, while the last two are unseen test examples.

It also checks that the columns have unit variance. These two properties indicate correct whitening. The main advantage of ZCA whitening with respect to other types of whitening is that the transformed images still resemble the original images, as seen in Figure 9.3 (computed also in Cell 12). The feature importance values look even more dark than before (Figure 9.2(c)). The average importance for the pixel features improved a tiny bit, though.

From these three approaches, I will now drill down on the Gaussian blur.

9.3.4 Error Analysis on Variations

From the EDA, we know this dataset has scaling issues and misplacement of city centres. How crucial are those issues? If an image was modified slightly, would that change the result of the ML prediction? To answer that question, Cell 14 splits the training data, trains a RF as per the Gaussian Blur model and then proceeds to test the RF on variations of unseen rows, sampling different variations of the source images:

• Scaling in the X and Y coordinates, from −10 to +10 pixels.
• Translation in the X and Y coordinates, from −10 to +10 pixels.
• Rotations from 20 to 340 degrees (in 20-degree increments).

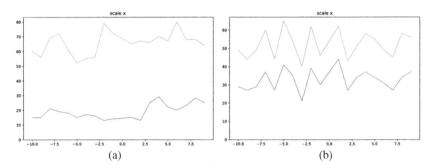

(a)   (b)

Figure 9.4 Impact of affine transformations on unseen data; the lower curve is an
error rate for improvement above 50% (excerpt). (a) All pixels. (b) Histograms on
32 bins. Note that (a) goes to 100 while (b) goes to 70.

These are called affine transformations and will be discussed in detail in the
next section. You may notice that almost all the transformations need pixels
outside the 32×32 square. This is why early on in Cell 3 we extracted 64×64
boxes, which Cell 14 uses fully, extracting the corresponding 32×32 square
afterwards. A sample of these variations is evaluated against the base image.
Cell 14 then records the number of times that the modified image produces
more accurate results when fed to the original regressor as compared to the
results using the base image. It also counts how many times it reduces the error
in half. The results are quite outstanding; of 13,649 attempts over almost 1,500
images, 6,072 resulted in an improvement of 1,777 in an improvement that
halved the error rate. **These results speak of a model where small variations
result in drastic changes in behaviour: a brittle model.** Cell 16 plots a
histogram of what parameters and techniques resulted in an improvement
(Figure 9.4(a)). It shows an improvement across the board, without any strong
parametric preferences that could be used for the automatic expansion next. Let
us make the model more robust it by expanding the training with these variants.

9.4 Automatic Dataset Expansion

An effective technique in CV is to add domain knowledge to the ML process
regarding which transformations do not carry information, or what are known
as **nuisance variations**.[280] In the case of satellite images, Cell 7 explores the
three transformations described in the previous section. These transformations
are part of what are known as **affine transformations**, which are discussed
next.

9.4.1 Affine Transformations

Affine transformations are linear transformations defined by mapping three points on the source plane to three points in the target plane. Mathematically speaking, they are defined by a 2×2 matrix multiplication followed by the addition of a 2×1 vector. They capture translations, scaling and rotations, which is the subset of affine transformations we will be using. In general, they can squeeze the image but they must maintain parallel lines, parallel.

In our case, the translations of up to 10 pixels reflect errors on the location of the city centre. The unrestricted rotations reflect different possible alignments of the city axes. Finally, scaling is particularly important in this dataset as we know the data presents uneven North–South compression.

9.4.2 Second Featurization

Cell 7 trains an RF on 143,884 instances, using four instances per city (Table 9.1(b)). The four instances are the base image plus three random variations with the same parameters shown in Section 9.3.4. Interestingly, using just the non-pixel features for a baseline model produced much worse results than the baseline model in the previous featurization: repeating rows verbatim leads the RF to trust certain feature configurations too much and to overfit. **This is a risk when doing dataset expansion without modifying the ML algorithm.** For that baseline, the transformations actually improve over it, albeit slightly, while being far from the baselines obtained without the duplicates.

9.4.2.1 Error Analysis

The feature importance in Figure 9.2(d) achieves the best possible result for this problem. It focuses the attention of the model to the behaviour at the centre of the city. Many settlements are very small and features far away from the centre may not be as informative. The figure shows how the feature importance reduces with the distance to the centre. I am quite pleased that it worked that well. At this stage, it is time to explore other alternatives.

9.5 Descriptive Features: Histograms

Another method to deal with nuisance variations is to represent the raw data in a way that it is robust to such variations. As discussed in Chapter 2, in Section 2.3.1, descriptive statistics that talk about the shape of the data distribution rather than the data itself are a popular way to concentrate the signal away from the noise. In the case of images and other sensor data, like sound, histograms are a great way to do that. If an image is rotated slightly, its histogram remains the same. If the image is translated slightly, the values at pixel positions change substantially but the histogram will change only as the result of the pixels lost and gained at the borders.

9.5.1 Third Featurization

Cell 18 thus represents every instance as 256 counts, indicating the number of pixels with a particular value present in the image (Table 9.1(c)). This will be robust to rotations, mildly robust to translations and still sensitive to scaling. Note that Cell 18 does not normalize the histograms, as all the images are of the same size. Neither does it scale over the actual range of a given image, but it scales using the maximum and minimum observed grey values, producing what is known as "equalizing" the histogram. The latter is a very common operation when working with histograms obtained under different illumination conditions, but it does not seem needed here.

At an RMSE of 0.3265, this is still worse than not using images. But the training time is now only nine times longer than the baseline. Cell 19 further reduces the granularity of the histogram by splitting it into 32 bins (instead of 256). Training on the total 130 features achieves a RMSE very close to the baseline at 0.3208 and just doubles the training time.

9.5.1.1 Error Analysis

The main objective in using histograms is to reduce the impact of nuisance variations and to make the model more robust. Cell 20 redoes the variations impact analysis from Section 9.3.4 over the histogram model (Figure 9.4(b)). The differences are substantive. The pixels-as-features model encountered variations that improved over the base image 45% of the time, while that percentage lowered to 28% when using histograms. Moreover, substantive improvements were only found 29% of the time for the model from Section 9.3.2, while in the case of histograms, that number goes up to 62%. That means that the model is more robust and if a variation helps, it does so in a more comprehensive manner. Regarding the parameters and conditions, it seems similar to Section 9.3.4. However rotations have a slight decline of relative effectiveness, which makes sense as histograms should be quite insensitive to rotations. **Ultimately, histograms are more robust, train faster and produce more accurate results. It is no surprise histograms are a favourite tool in CV.**

9.6 Local Feature Detectors: Corners

When you have plenty of seemingly similar features, the ML algorithm might get lost on a sea of information. Vision is about filtering and extracting the relevant from the general. Then, in this section, we will explore **local feature detectors** when the word feature in "local feature detector" is used in the CV sense; it is related to ML features but in a more abstract nature. A better term for our context would be image characteristic. Local feature detectors are functions run over the image that find regions of interest (ROIs). These ROIs are such that they exhibit some important property. Generally, these feature detectors can be also trained, for example, to recognize faces; descriptive studies, such as the histogram for backprojection, can be used to estimate their parameters, as we will see in the next chapter (Section 10.1 in Chapter 10). Representing images as local features is a standard technique in CV.[202]

For the WikiCities' case, we will look at an established algorithm to detect corners. **Corners are places in the image where the information changes in every direction.** They are different from flat areas, with no change, and edges, that exhibit change in only one direction.

Change is key to perception. In their experiments in 1950s, Hubel and Weibel realized, by accident,[161] that the neurons in the visual cortex of the mammal they were studying reacted to changes in the visual stimuli rather than the stable stimuli itself. **For our WikiCities problem, a corner indicates a region with a geographical characteristic such as a lake or a mountain that will affect the inhabitable area. Corners constitute a basic type of texture analysis.**[139]

9.6.1 Harris Corner Detector

The algorithm[141] is based on computing the gradient of the image, or in other words, the matrix of partial derivatives that captures the different directions of change. Areas of rapid change will have high derivatives. The detection algorithm then computes the eigenvalues of the gradient matrix to understand the directions of change independent of the axis of coordinates. Using the eigenvalues makes the filter rotation and translation invariant. It still remains affected by scaling and changes in illumination characteristics.

For a flat surface, the eigenvalues will be small. If one eigenvalue is much bigger than the other, then it is an edge. Otherwise, it is a corner. Because the change in direction in a corner is so marked, corners are among the most robust image characteristics to detect. Note the gradients can be calculated using convolution and the Sobel operator.

9.6.2 Fourth Featurization

The Harris Corner detection algorithm has some parameters that need to be chosen: context size and Harris k parameter. I also add blurring as a preprocessing step. **Noise kills derivatives, so it is important to smooth first before computing them.** Cell 21 plots some variants over the images used in the EDA. In total, 144 images are plotted in false colour, but the size and complexity of this plot is not suitable for a book format. However, the image can be seen online at http://artfeateng.ca/u/91. From there I can see that higher values of blurring and larger context produce less corners at 10% from the maximum value, but it becomes less discriminative. I thus choose a blurring of size 3, a context of size 2 and 0.05 for the Harris' k parameter. The Harris corner detector returns a score for each pixel representing the "cornerness" of the pixel. To obtain actual corners, it needs to be thresholded by picking a threshold that depends on the ilumination characteristics of each particular image. Also, a large corner results in many pixels with a large score. Therefore, besides thresholding it, it is recommended to perform non-maxima elimination, finding points near a maximum and dropping them. Instead of finding actual corners and to get away from needing to specify a threshold, I rank the values and add the top 100 values, obtaining an overall "cornerness" score for the image.

Cell 22 adds a cornerness feature to disappointing results. Other parameters of Harris produce worse results. Luckily, finding quality corners is hard enough that OpenCV has a function aptly named "goodFeaturesToTrack" (talk about truth in advertisement) that receives a single quality parameter and returns the main corners in the image. It uses a different corner algorithm built on similar ideas to Harris' and performs the non-maxima elimination. As a quality parameter, Cell 23 uses 0.01, a parameter proposed as a reasonable default. Using the length of the returned list of corners as an extra feature results in a slight improvement (Cell 23, Table 9.1(d)), from 0.3198 to 0.3188. This is the first improvement over the baseline in this chapter.

9.6.2.1 Error Analysis

For EA, Cell 24 plots population against number of corners detected (Figure 9.5). **Interestingly, the figure reveals that cities with many corners, reflecting a fractured terrain, are never of medium size.** This is as much geographical and demography commentary as I will venture, but it justifies the intuition behind the feature. Let us now take the gradients idea to the next level.

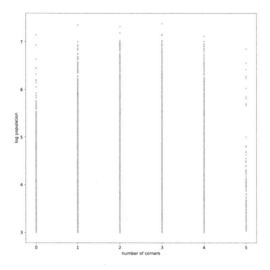

Figure 9.5 Number of corners detected versus population logarithm in base 10.

9.7 Dimensionality Reduction: HOGs

As corners produce a sudden gradient change, and are among the most robust local features to detect, it makes sense to compute histograms of gradients. The histogram of oriented gradients (HOG)[79] method involves computing a histogram of gradients, that is, a table that contains counts for different directions of growth for image segment. It constructs what in CV is called a "feature descriptor," a domain-specific dimensionality reduction intended to be invariant to nuisance variability and changes in illumination, yet discriminative enough to intrinsic properties of the scene like 3D objects, materials, shapes, even deformed.[85] HOGs are representative of a domain specific dimensionality reduction, an approach with a long history in CV, including SIFT, VLAD, GIST, BLP and many others.[171] From our perspective, they use the gradients to provide a context to the pixels and make them more information.[352][†]

Given a point and an angle, an unnormalized histogram of gradients is the amount of pixels whose gradient is in the direction of the angle.[85] Its main advantage is that it is invariant to a number of transformations, including rotations and scaling. The HOG method achieves illumination invariance by normalizing the histograms using neighbour cells, what the algorithm calls a "block."

[†] Chapter 9.

The algorithm starts by calculating the gradient of the whole image, dividing the image into cells and then calculating the orientation of the gradient per cells. The histogram of these orientations form the HOG. To compute orientation of the gradients, it uses the arc-tangent function. The resulting orientations are considered without direction, from zero to 180 degrees. Not using the directions has shown better results in practice. The range of 0–180 is then divided into nine bins. Each gradient is counted on each bin interpolated from its actual value (i.e., a gradient on 27 degrees contributes to bin 20 and, to a lesser extent, to bin 40). The counts on each bin also take into account the magnitude of the gradient by using "votes." These details seem to be key to the effectiveness of the algorithm. If you try to design something HOG-inspired for your domain, beware that finding the optimal parameters and mechanism over your data will not be an easy task.

Note that for our particular case, HOGs are not necessarily ideal, as they are still sensitive to changes in orientation. The same image rotated 90 degress will produce different features. We could further improve by expanding the training data or designing a custom HOG-like filter.

9.7.1 Fifth Featurization

At this stage, it is unclear whether there is a signal in this data that can help the task. Whether two settlements are geographically similar most likely does not affect their population as much as I would have thought *a priori*. Cell 25 puts the ideas behind HOG to test using 8×8 cells over the 32×32 tiles. It normalizes using 16×16 blocks resulting in 324 extra features (Table 9.1(e)). As each histogram uses nine bins (HOG's default), those are features for 36 histograms, obtained from the 16 cells in the tile as follows: four cells at the corners of the image that are normalized once, the eight cells at the edges of the image that are normalized twice (they account for two histograms on each normalization). Finally, the four cells in the centre are normalized four times each.

The final result of an RMSE of 0.3398. It is better than using the raw pixels but worse than using histograms or corners. It is also much worse than not using any image data at all. This is a good moment to wrap up this case study.

9.8 Closing Remarks

For a conservative feature set, I would pick the number of corners. A high-performance feature set is still to be found over this data, but I would go for a combination of the affine transformations and the number of corners.

The dataset and code leave plenty of space for you to experiment upon. Here are some straightforward ideas left to be explored:

- Deep convolutional networks. The amount of training data might just be barely enough, but it is definitely worth trying. It should be straightforward to adapt any of the many MNIST digit OCR tutorials to this data.
- Fix the scaling issue. It is a computable artifact on the data that can be easily addressed.
- Try traditional dimensionality reduction techniques, such as PCA. The PCA code is already there for the whitening.
- Perform supervised discretization over the histograms in Section 9.5. A greedy algorithm where two contiguous bins are joined, if using them together improves the error as measured on unseen test might work. Such an algorithm will be inspired by ChiMerge and adaptive quantizers discussed in Chapter 2, Section 2.2.
- Use "edgeness" rather than "cornerness." I discuss edge detection in the next section.

To make up for the lack of domain expertise as discussed in the introduction, at times, this case study became an informed exercise of trial and error. To highlight the value of domain expertise for FE, Dr. Rupert Brooks,[†] a CV expert and a friend, read this chapter and looked at the source data. He suggested exploiting texture features in the form of local binary patterns or LBPs.[247] He stressed that, for this dataset, neighborhood information is important, while absolute position, it is not. There are other problems of importance to CV, such as face recognition (the problem that originated HOGs), which do care about absolute positions, so picking the right techniques is key. Moreover, finding and ensuring a correct alignment of samples is cornerstone for CV. As this dataset lacks such alignment, nor can it be automatically built, an expert would have known beforehand that pixels-as-features and its variants had no chance of success (and avoided them). The Spanish proverb "el que no tiene cabeza, tiene pies" comes to mind.[‡]

I would like to conclude with a conversation that I had with a CV colleague back at IBM: I said how I envied CV because intermediate processes, such as finding corners, were useful on their own. NLP applications require end-to-end performance: finding good part-of-speech tags is not useful on itself. He countered that he envied NLP because feature detection and extraction were

---

[†] I am indebted to him for taking the time to do this. The approach in this chapter and any potential errors or oversights are all mine.
[‡] "He who lacks a head ought to have feet." If it cannot be smart, it will be laborious.

already done for us NLP practitioners. I can definitely relate to that comment after the work that was done for this chapter.

9.8.1 Other Topics in Computer Vision

I will very briefly mention other topics related to this chapter that might be of interest to other people working with sensor data.

Colour Manipulation. This chapter data was single channel. For multiple channels, it is possible to process different channels separately and obtain features per channel. It is also possible to transform the image to grey safle using the perception-derived formula: [45]

$$Y = (0.299)R + (0.587)G + (0.114)B$$

Besides red, green and blue channels, some images have an alpha (transparency) channel. While RGB format is common, it is not the only way to represent light sensor readings. Another representation is hue saturation and value (HSV), which can be computed from RGB as discussed in Chapter 3 (Section 3.1). Computing feature from H and S channels is the recommended approach for face recognition.

Edge Detection. In the same way that corners can be detected, changes in one direction can be extracted from the image gradients. The most widely used algorithm is the one proposed by John Canny. [56] Beside first-order derivatives, the algorithm makes use of the second-order derivatives (through the Laplacian operator), as a zero on the second order indicates a change of direction to the gradients, therefore finding an edge. The algorithm uses a high threshold to consider a detached pixel as part of an edge and a low one to continue an existing edge through a neighbour point. This idea is called **hysteresis** and can be used for other problems and domains.

Image Smoothing. If you control the acquisition mechanism, it is possible to acquire multiple images of the same scene and average them. [297] This is the same principle as the error models discussed in Chapter 7, Section 7.6. It reduces noise by a factor of $\sqrt{n}$ where n is the number of images. The satellite images employed in this chapter benefit from this technique, as they are the result of multiple passes made by the Terra satellite. A related technique is **chartless calibration**, which uses different exposure times for calibration. [297]

This approach might be transferable to other settings where there is a sensor that needs to be calibrated and you can vary its energy intake.

SIFT. Similar to HOG, SIFT[215] computes histograms of gradients but generates a local descriptor rather than a global descriptor. HOG gained popularity as an alternative to SIFT as the latter is patented.[216] Both belong to the histogram of gradient's family, which given a region centred on a point, produce histograms of the gradient with different normalizations.[85] SIFT approximates the optimal representation if the scene is flat, and what is important is to achieve invariance on translations parallel to the viewing plane. These assumptions are quite important for video processing.[85] SIFT also uses pyramids of images at different resolutions, which is what gives it a degree of scale independency.

Deep Networks as Feature Extractors. While you might not have enough training data to fit a deep network for your problem, reusing pretrained models can be very helpful. In a recent blog posting,[87] Arthur Douillard describes looking into aerial imagery for detecting cars and successfully deploying a COCO[210] pretrained model on them. Of the 82 objects that COCO tracks, cars is one of them and the model is robust enough to help identify them when all the car images are exclusively from it.

9.9 Learning More

Computer vision is a fascinating topic with decades of research and development behind it. As discussed, identifying higher-level structures ("features" in CV) over which to operate upon is a topic that has full books written about it. For example, Nixon and Aguado's *Feature Extraction & Image Processing for Computer Vision*.[245] For more basic concepts, I found Carsten Steger's *Machine Vision Algorithms*[297] very useful. For the OpenCV, the particular software library used in the notebooks, Bradski and Kaehler's *Learning OpenCV*[45] is a great resource that deeply informed this discussion, but this chapter would not have been made possible without the excellent tutorials put together by the OpenCV community, in particular, the ones by Ana Huamán Quispe.

Combining text and images have opened up exciting new directions of research. Take, for example, the Language and Vision series of workshops at the Conference on Computer Vision and Pattern Recognition.[26]

Chapter 8 of Zheng and Casari's *Feature engineering for machine learning*[352] also covers feature engineering for CV with an excellent detailed explanation of HOG. They also relate DL approaches like AlexNet[194] to HOGs, which can be very elucidating. Chapter 3 in Dong and Liu's *Feature Engineering* book of contributed chapters[132] discusses feature extraction from images. They present three approaches: handcrafted (the content of current chapter), latent (which we touched upon with HOGs) and DL. They also relate DL approaches to HOGs, particularly describing how feature extractors for pixels ought to be very local and thus have a small "receptive field." They conclude that fine-tuning a CNN architecture is akin to handcrafting feature extractors.

10

Other Domains: Video, GIS and Preferences

To conclude this book, let us take a look at some topics not covered in previous case studies due to the WikiCities' focus of the data employed. Having the same problem used throughout Chapters 6–9 has the advantage of putting different techniques in context, but it limits the problems that can be showcased. This chapter briefly presents three other domains, video data, geographical (GIS) data and preference data. As with the other case studies in Chapters 6–9, the point of this chapter is not to learn how to best apply feature engineering (FE) to video, GIS and preference data, but to get FE inspiration from these domains so you can apply these lessons to your unique domain, when you can find parallels from the three domains to your unique domain. I will discuss the data and provide an example featurization with discussion, without going into a full-fledged EDA nor error analysis (EA).

The first domain is video processing. **The main lesson is FE in a high data volume environment, focusing on computation reuse from related instances (previous frames) as much as possible.** We will look into tracking mouse cursor position on screencasts.

The second domain is GIS data, in this case, path data. **The main FE lesson is dealing with dynamic spatial data that changes over time.** We will look into predicting whether a migratory bird will be moving shortly or not, using animal tracking data from the movebank.org repository.

Finally, preference data demonstrate imputation techniques for large datasets with sparse features. We will discuss them over a mining software repository problem expressed as preferences.

The feature vectors used in these case studies are sketched in Table 10.1.

Table 10.1. *Feature vectors used in these case studies. (a) Video, 96 features (b) Geographical, 14 features (c) Preferences, 15,623 features.*

keyframe?		target moving?		MRR	
	features				
1	red bin$_1$ (prev)	1	year	1	file length
2	red bin$_2$ (prev)	2	month	2	# of includes
	...	3	day	3	# of structs
16	red bin$_{16}$ (prev)	4	day of year	4	# of char(0)
17	green bin$_1$ (prev)	5	hour (24)		...
	...	6	minutes	259	# of char(255)
33	blue bin$_1$ (prev)	7	seconds	260	pref. Torvalds
	...	8	latitude	261	pref. akpm
50	red bin$_1$	9	longitude		...
		10	distance city 1	15623	pref. Hemmelgarn
	...		...		
96	blue bin$_{16}$	14	distance city 5		
	(a)		(b)		(c)

10.1 Video

With the growth in the previous decade of easily available smartphones with large storage and advanced video capabilities, the amount of recorded and stored videos has skyrocketed. YouTube alone adds through user uploads more than 400 hours of content per second.[273] Doing machine learning (ML) over video is not necessarily much harder than the computer vision discussed in the previous chapter. For example, recognizing a person in one frame and in subsequent frames is a similar problem as deciding whether two persons are the same in two photographs. There is no difference in working with video frames than, for example, photos from Instagram.

However, the sheer number of images represented by the frames on a video means the computational power required is significant for a brute-force approach. To put things into perspective, the five-minute video used in this case study represents 9,276 images. That is roughly 10% of all the satellite images from the previous chapter and it occupies more space (as separate images), given the much higher resolution of the images. Moreover, most of the processing will be reduplicated: given the nature of video ("movies" was originally short for "moving images"), there is little change from most frames to the next. That speaks of reusing the feature computation from one instance to the next. **If you are facing a problem with large amounts of multidimensional sequential data, you may find lessons from video processing in this section helpful to you.**

Figure 10.1 Mouse cursor with the halo. The halo is in a very strong, easy to discern yellow tone.

The main problems in video processing are tracking changes over time, real-time processing and massive number of features. The main techniques include blobs, key frames and trajectories.

10.1.1 Data: Screencast

The video data used in this case study is a five-minute video on the use of a specific screencasting tool. This particular tool highlights the position of the mouse cursor with a bright yellow circle (a halo). The particular video was chosen for its high-definition quality and because its author, Xacobo de Toro Cacharrón, graciously chose to distribute it under a Creative Commons license.

Tracking the position of mouse cursors on screencasts is problematic for viewers. When operating a window environment, an user can always move the mouse and our movement-detecting cells in the eyes will quickly locate it. When watching a screencast, however, we do not control the mouse, so this approach is impossible. Moreover, the mouse cursor is the most likely place where important actions will happen next in the video. Due to this, the makers of this particular screencast highlighted the mouse position using a high-contrast yellow circle (Figure 10.1). That yellow circle is relatively easy to find on a frame. However, the screencast software allows for zooming of areas of the screen (the mouse cursor and its surrounding circle is also zoomed). This means that the artifact recognizer, mouse cursor in our case, will need to be able to handle scaling properly.

10.1.2 Key Frame Detection

Movies are composed of a set of scenes. At scene changes, there is an abrupt change on the whole screen. Any features precomputed on previous frames ought to be discarded. The same is true for non-scene changes, but camera changes, flashbacks or any other cinematic device that produces full-screen changes. The frames that correspond to scene changes are conceptually called **key frames**, at which point all features must be recomputed. Key frames are important for video compression and applications such as video summarization.

Identifying whether a frame is sufficiently different from the previous frame is a matter of computing a suitable distance over the images. Obviously, a simple pixel distance will not capture things like camera panning, but more robust features can be used, like the histograms used in the previous chapter; see Section 9.5 in chapter 9.

We will look into identifying key frames as a learning problem. As for training labels, compressed video contains key frames explicitly marked on what are called I-frames. Using the tool ffprobe, part of the ffmpeg set of tools, we can obtain labelled data that we can then express as frame indices. Most of the I-frames on the video, though, are marked at 160-frame intervals.[†] A volunteer annotated all the 41 key frames over the video for our use. Cell 11 in Chapter 10's Jupyter notebook computes the histograms of two nearby frames and their differences. It then uses the computed difference to decide whether the second frame is a key frame. Cell 12 contains a SVM using a polynomial kernel using these two histograms as features and trains it over the first three-quarters of the video. The model is tested on the last quarter of the video. Its feature vector is sketched in Table 10.1(a). This is a hard problem to tackle from only one video, as there are 9,000 frames, of which only 41 are key frames. Sampling the negative class, the final system in Cell 12 achieves a few successes with a recall of 65% on test. You are welcome to try it with more videos, of course.

The main takeaway for your unique domain is how the ML receives two nearby images (or instances in your domain) as input, which are featurized independently. Due to the nature of video data, we can get away with not featurizing one of the images, as we can reuse the histogram from the previous frame (see Section 9.5 in Chapter 9 for details on histograms). This looks obvious, but this cuts the featurization time in half. If the ML computation could be also reused partially, for example, the propagation of input values in neural networks, that would cut down the processing time even further. This optimization is only applicable if the features are computed independently for each frame. Note that computing a histogram is not an onerous task, but we might want to do more complex normalization that will require more computing time, for example, computing a histogram of oriented gradients, as discussed in Chapter 9 in Section 9.7.

[†] Thanks to Heri Rakotomalala for pointing this out.

Finally, note that key frame detection is similar to segmentation in event streams, which is a topic of importance nowadays.

The technique presented here is not necessarily the best way to do key frame extraction. A better approach is to maintain a probability distribution of the histograms of the frames seen so far, and then compute how likely is the new histogram to have been generated from that distribution.[14] This is closely related to the histogram back projection technique, which is described next.

10.1.3 Blobs Tracking: Mean-Shift

We are now ready to tackle tracking a mouse cursor surrounded by a yellow halo, also known as **blob tracking**. The first task is to find it on a frame, independent from other frames. A simple technique for this task is **histogram back projection**, discussed next. From the output of the back projection, we need to find the cursor as the most likely group of candidate points using k-means clustering. We will optimize the speed of that process by reusing the position of the cursor in the previous frame through the mean-shift algorithm. **The main takeway for your unique domain is to reuse computation from the previous frame by searching for a nearby solution, rather than starting from scratch.**

10.1.3.1 Histogram Back Projection

This algorithm[301] uses a sample image of the blob we want to track and then computes, for each pixel in the image, the probability that the pixel was generated by the histogram (i.e., the probability distribution) of the sample image. The algorithm is single channel. As the main signal in our case is the colour (yellow), Cell 15 applies the algorithm to the hue channel after transforming the image from RGB format to HSV format.

The output of the back projection is a probability value per pixel. To find the most likely centre of the data, Cell 15 uses k-means clustering to find the most likely centre to highlight. The resulting system makes some errors and takes a while to run, but it is surprisingly effective given its simplicity. It took 785.76 seconds and found 5,291 boxes on 9,276 frames. We can try to speed up the algorithm and improve its accuracy by reusing the output from the previous frame.

10.1.3.2 Mean-Shift

The mean-shift algorithm is a general algorithm to find local extrema on probability distributions.[113] For the particular case of blob tracking on videos, it takes the back projection probabilities for each pixel and moves the region of interest (ROI) from the previous frame towards the direction of greater density

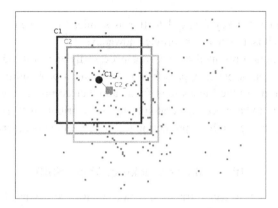

Figure 10.2 Mean-shift blob tracking algorithm. The algorithm computes the
current region of interest or ROI (C1) centre of mass C1_r and moves the ROI
in that direction. It iterates, changing the ROI until convergence.

of points (Figure 10.2). It stops when a maximum number of iterations has
been reached or when the centre of the ROI does not change.

To simplify visualization, Cell 16 slows down the video when the first ROI
is identified over the whole image to appreciate whether the mean-shift is
working properly. Cell 16 took 680.80s, almost 100s less than the original
algorithm and it found the same number of boxes, with 4,886 (92% of the
total) found by mean-shift. The execution shows places where mean-shift got
lost, though. It would be worth it to tune its parameters better.

10.1.4 Learning More

Video processing using ML is a relatively new discipline compared with
CV. Interestingly, video processing, when tackled with deep learning (DL)
techniques, exhibits a variety of neural architectures depending on how the
temporal aspect is merged with the video aspect. **The key takeaway is that
the architecture is task-dependent,[186] for example, the best architecture
for action recognition is not necessarily the best for object segmentation.
This can be applicable to your domain, e.g., if your data is a set of related
instances.**

Regarding the case study, two other tracking algorithms are worth mentioning, optical flow and camshift. These algorithms, including mean-shift are well
covered by Bradski and Kaehler in their *Learning OpenCV* book.[45]

Optical Flow. This algorithm determines the general movement of all points in the screen, distinguishing points that have moved from points in the background. This is further complicated by shadows of moving objects that affect points in the background, giving the impression they have moved.

CamShift. The mean-shift algorithm we have seen in this section has trouble when the region of interest zooms in or out, i.e., it is not scale-invariant. A natural progression from mean-shift is camshift, that explores changes in size and orientation besides changes in location of the data.

Datasets. In terms of datasets, a popular source for testing new video ML ideas and algorithms is the *Human Actions and Scenes Dataset,* as presented by Marszalek and colleagues in CVPR 2009.[223]

10.2 Geographical Features

Similar to how time presents special challenges and motivates special techniques such as the ones discussed in Chapter 7, so do locations on the surface of the planet. Particularly, while the earth looks quite flat from a human experiential perspective, it is a sphere (flat earth believers notwithstanding). That means the distance between two points on the planet is not a straight line but an arc. The other complication is that it is not a perfect sphere, as its rotation has resulted on a slight bulging towards the equator.

It is estimated that 80% of the daily 2.5 exabytes (2.5 billion gigabytes) generated by the planet are georeferenced.[319] Moreover, geospatial data is key to our understanding of the environment and the spread of diseases. These topics are at the forefront of the challenges facing humanity in the current century.

Working with locations falls into the domain of Geographical Information Systems (GIS). We distinguish between points on a map (static) and trajectories (dynamic). In GIS features, we will look at using representations based on distance to key points. **Even if your domain is not GIS, a key lesson to take away is to exploit geometrical properties on your data, for example, using distance-based features.**

10.2.1 Data: Animal Migration

We will be using the migration data through satellite telemetry for African cuckoos in Nigeria, kindly provided by Iwajomo and colleagues[166] as part of

Figure 10.3 Cuckoo paths, as shown on a map of Nigeria and Cameroon.

the movebank.org data repository.[165] It contains 12,563 tracking points for six individuals (birds) from May 29, 2013 until June 28, 2017. See Figure 10.3 for the datapoints on a map.

The problem we will look into is to predict whether a bird will move in the next two hours. Cell 21 splits the rows by individual, leaving two individuals for training, two for testing on development and one for final testing. That resulted in 3,199 rows for training and 4,329 rows for testing.

To obtain the target class, i.e., whether the bird has moved or not, Cell 22 parses the timestamps and assigns a class depending on the number of seconds between two entries. Cell 23 then separates the date and time as individual features and compute a "day in the year" feature. The intuition is that migration times would be better understood as a day in the year rather than as two features for day and month. The baseline featurization contains nine features: year, month, day, day of year, hours, minutes and seconds plus latitude and longitude. A RF trained on these features produce a precision of 70.2%, recall of 91.4% and F1 of 79.4%. Let us expand this with radial distances to landmarks.

10.2.1.1 Radial Distance to Landmarks

Points in latitude and longitude by themselves are not very informative. A better way to represent them is by taking as a feature the distance to a given point of importance in the domain. This can be further expanded with the distance and angle to a given number of landmark points. For example, in a case study on New York City tipping behaviour (further discussed in the next section), Brink and colleagues suggested using the distance to Time Square as a feature.[49] As landmarks, we will use the distance to nearby cities.

Cell 24 first computes the centre of the data as the average of their GPS coordinates. That is a flat-earth simplifying assumption that works well for points in close proximity that do not cross the antemeridian, on which longitudes go from −180 to 180 and on which averages will not work. With the centre computed, Cell 24 then filters a list of administrative units obtained from GeoNames for both Nigeria and Cameroon, keeping only cities less than 50 km away from the centre of the data and adding the features as the distance to each point in that list. As the exact distance to each of these points is key, it is computed using the precise orthodromic distance. It results in one feature per city.

This narrowing down to administrative units less than 50 km away from the centre of the points reduces their number from 850 to only 5. The distance from a datapoint to each of this administrative units becomes an extra feature, on top of the 9 features from the previous section. A RF trained on these 14 features produces a precision of 70.0%, a recall of 91.8% and a F1 of 79.5% (Cell 25). Its feature vector is sketched in Table 10.1(b). It improves recall and hurts precision, for a tiny improvement on F1. **The takeaway here is that if you are working on a problem where distances are crucial to the model, you can consider adding domain knowledge to the problem in the form of context to the distances by selecting special elements to compute distances against.** More generally, you may want to learn more about other techniques used in GIS, as is discussed next.

10.2.1.2 Learning More

Similar to time series analysis, the field of geospatial modelling has a long tradition of statistical methods. I would like to mention two in particular, **kriging**, a spatial interpolation technique, and **variograms**, an analysis tool similar to the auto-covariance function in time series analysis. In recent years, the need to handle multidimensional data has started mixing these statistical approaches with ML in what is known as GeoAI. That includes a recent workshop series organized by SIGSPATIAL.[158]

An early work from 2000 by Kobler and Adamic trained a decision tree to predict suitable bear habitats in Slovenia. They used a coarser model for locations (500m per pixel) and modelled inhabited areas rather than sightings to accommodate for noise. They expanded the data using various sources, including elevation information, forest coverage, settlements and human demographic information. The top node in the tree is whether the region has a percentage of 91% forest or not. For example, if the forest is dense but there are humans living nearby, then it is not a suitable habitat. Similar to this case study, Van Hinsbergh and colleagues predict whether a stationary car is waiting at a traffic light or has arrived to a destination using GPS traces.[312] Some interesting results in the field include empirical Bayesian kriging, an alternative to ordinary kriging that uses a composite of local models.[129] Also the work by Pozdnoukhov and Kanevski found that support vectors for spatial data represent the optimal places to put measuring stations in sensor networks.[259] More recently, Lin and colleagues[211] used OpenStreetMap features to enhance a PM2.5 model for California that predicts the presence of small particle pollutants in the air.

Finally, location data can be used to produce recommendations, a topic presented at length by Zhao, Lyu and King in *Point-of-Interest Recommendation in Location-Based Social Networks*.[348] We will look into recommendations in the next section.

10.3 Preferences

Recommendation systems are an instance of collaborative filtering,[249] where the system filters information using communities of users. The usual situation is to have lists of users with items and preferences for the said items.

The main challenge when incorporating preference data to a ML problem has to do with how humans express preferences: only very few items are appraised. Moreover, those few items reflect upon them latent preferences for a much larger set. From the ML perspective, preferences data manifests itself as extremely sparse features, with most of the feature values needing to be imputed. With such a large number of missing values, the imputation techniques from Chapter 3, Section 3.2 will not apply, either because they will produce poor results or they will take too long to run. Instead, I will present a simple item-based recommendation algorithm to do **opportunistic imputation.** More generally, if you are working on a domain with sparse features and plenty of missing values, learning from techniques on preference data might help you, including the technique discussed here or other techniques in the last section.

10.3.1 Data: Linux Kernel Commits

The preferred (pun intended) data source for showcasing recommendation systems is the University of Minnesota MovieLens dataset, as released by the GroupLens research group.[140] That dataset, however, is specifically earmarked for not-for-profit research and will require each reader to download their own copy of the dataset if they qualify for their license. Instead, I use some ideas from Ying et al.'s article, *Predicting Software Changes by Mining Revision History*[339] and analyze the commit history of the Linux kernel. We can think of the commit history as a committer versus source code file preference: a person that commits multiple changes to a file is expressing a preference or expertise over that file.

As the objective of this case study is to combine preference data with regular features, it is possible to enhance the data with information for each committer and try to predict a particular characteristic of them. I chose not to do so in order to respect their privacy. Instead, we will look at the files as having a preference for certain committers to work on them and we will use features on each file to predict whether the file will receive more attention than others (commits) during its lifetime. Predicting this information seems unnecessary as it is available when studying the history, but it could be an important piece of information to predict for new files. The features computed for each file on its source code at inception: character histogram, which captures features like number of open braces or open parentheses, number of #include, and number of structs, together with its full file length.

The preferences are computed using `gitrecommender`,[90] a Java tool I wrote for teaching purposes a few years ago. The preferences form a table of counts of committers versus files with the number of commits the committer has done. To capture the centrality of a file, we look at the date of the commits and group them by month. Cell 31 then ranks the files by number of commits and computes the reciprocal rank for them ($1/\text{rank}$). This metric assigns the score 1 for the file (or files in case of ties) that appears in most commits for a given month, $1/2$ to the second and so on. The mean reciprocal rank (MRR) is the target metric for regression. For the MRR for a particular file, the average is computed from the first known commit to the last observed commit. Files with less than 10 months of active range are discarded. Cell 32 plots the top MRR files (Table 10.2) and they seem to make domain sense, as plenty of commits add names to the maintainers list or tweak the build system.

To obtain preferences from the table of commit counts, Cell 33 normalizes it by committer and then proceeds to threshold the normalized values, obtaining a grand total of 8,000 preferences. With this data, Cell 36 does a first featurization and a baseline run on 51,975 instances with 15,662 features for a RMSE of 0.0010. The feature vector is sketched in Table 10.1(c). Training took 150 minutes using 32Gb of RAM and eight cores. This number of features is a departure from the other case studies and requires more memory than the other notebooks.

Table 10.2. *Top Linux kernel files according to monthly mean reciprocal ranks.*

File	MRR
MAINTAINERS	0.91181878
drivers/scsi/libata-core.c	0.31163823
Makefile	0.27082308
kernel/sched.c	0.13061257
net/core/dev.c	0.10050353
sound/pci/hda/patch_realtek.c	0.095225337
drivers/gpu/drm/i915/intel_display.c	0.090184201
drivers/scsi/libata-scsi.c	0.076660623
drivers/net/wireless/iwlwifi/iwl4965-base.c	0.066584964
drivers/net/tg3.c	0.064789696
Documentation/kernel-parameters.txt	0.060356971

10.3.2 Imputing Preferences

Many algorithms have been proposed to solve collaborative filtering. We will look into simple algorithms that work well over large datasets. Particularly, we will look into item-based recommendations. The idea behind item-based recommendation is as follows: if a user has expressed a preference for a given item i, then they might equally like an item j that is similar to i. To capture similarities among items, any distance metric from clustering algorithms can be used. Cell 37 computes the Tanimoto distance between two committers, also known as IoU (intersection over union). It does so by binarizing the preferences and then computing the size of the intersection over the union of files worked upon by the two committers. Intuitively, two committers will be more similar if they have worked over similar files. The imputation process itself is then the multiplication of the Tanimoto similarity matrix of committers by the preference table, which contains committers against files.

For files that have received a commit by a given committer (let us call this committer u), this multiplication gives us a score equal to this file preference for a different committer (let us call this other committer v) times the Tanimoto similarity between u and v. Thus, if a file has seen commits by many people all similar to an unknown one, we are led to believe the unknown committer would probably do commits to this given file. The underlying intuition here is to uncover teams of committers, a topic I will further discuss in the next section.

These weights obtained by multiplying the preferences with the similarities allow us to compare unknown committers among themselves, but are not valid

numbers for imputation: all preferences are between 0 and 1 while these values
can exceed 1. They are not comparable to the existing preferences. Instead,
Cell 38 uses them for opportunistic imputation: it picks the top n unknown
committers based on the multiplication by the Tanimoto matrix and imputes
them with the median preference for that file. This way popular files remain
popular and committers that have been shown to have a strong preference for a
file remain with a strong preference value. The resulting RMSE reduces from
0.0010 to 0.0008.

10.3.3 Learning More

The field of collaborative filtering has attracted plenty of attention in recent
years, driven by the Netflix challenge[306] and click-through models popularized
by search engines.[66] A practical resource on the topic is Owen, Anil, Dunning
and Friedman's *Mahout in Action*,[249] which informed the current discussion.
I would like to discuss two topics related to the case study: preferences for new
users and using nonnegative matrix factorization (NMF).

New Users. Recommendations for new users is very challenging, as there is
usually a lack of preference data to inform the model. In the case study, this is
akin to handling newly created files. A good way to handle these circumstances
is to define a vicinity of files and impute based on the centroid for the class.
A reasonable vicinity in the case study would be files in the same folder, for
example.

NMF. A great method for recommendation is the use of NMF. As discussed
in Chapter 4, Section 4.3.6, NMF seeks to replace the original preference
matrix by the multiplication of two matrices W and H such that no entry in
W and H is a negative number. The number of rows in W and columns in H
is a hyperparameter of the algorithm. For the case study, it encompasses the
concept of teams, matrix W indicates how likely it is for a given team to be
involved with a given file. Matrix H indicates how likely a given committer
is to belong to a given team. Computing W and H for imputation purposes
requires special modifications to the solver to disregard the missing entries.[345]
Also, note the solver in scikit-learn has trouble dealing with columns that are
not independent.[116]

Bibliography

[1] Martín Abadi, Ashish Agarwal, Paul Barham, Eugene Brevdo, Zhifeng Chen, Craig Citro, Greg S. Corrado, Andy Davis, Jeffrey Dean, Matthieu Devin, Sanjay Ghemawat, Ian Goodfellow, Andrew Harp, Geoffrey Irving, Michael Isard, Yangqing Jia, Rafal Jozefowicz, Lukasz Kaiser, Manjunath Kudlur, Josh Levenberg, Dandelion Mané, Rajat Monga, Sherry Moore, Derek Murray, Chris Olah, Mike Schuster, Jonathon Shlens, Benoit Steiner, Ilya Sutskever, Kunal Talwar, Paul Tucker, Vincent Vanhoucke, Vijay Vasudevan, Fernanda Viégas, Oriol Vinyals, Pete Warden, Martin Wattenberg, Martin Wicke, Yuan Yu and Xiaoqiang Zheng. TensorFlow: Large-scale machine learning on heterogeneous systems, 2015. Software available from tensorflow.org. Accessed: 2018-12-13.

[2] Charu C. Aggarwal. *Outlier Analysis*. Cambridge, MA: Springer, 2013.

[3] Charu C. Aggarwal and S. Yu Philip. A general survey of privacy-preserving data mining models and algorithms. In *Privacy-Preserving Data Mining*, pages 11–52. Cambridge, MA: Springer, 2008.

[4] Rakesh Agrawal, Ramakrishnan Srikant. Fast algorithms for mining association rules. In *Proc. 20th Int. Conf. Very Large Data Bases, VLDB*, volume 1215, pages 487–499, 1994.

[5] Alfred V. Aho, Ravi Sethi and Jeffrey D. Ullman. *Compilers: Principles, Techniques, and Tools*. Boston, MA: Addison-Wesley, 1986.

[6] Adrian Akmajian, Ann K. Farmer, Lee Bickmore, Richard A. Demers and Robert M. Harnish. *Linguistics: An Introduction to Language and Communication*. Cambridge, MA: MIT Press, 2017.

[7] E. Alpaydin. *Introduction to Machine Learning*. Cambridge, MA: MIT Press, 2010.

[8] Edoardo Amaldi and Viggo Kann. On the approximability of minimizing nonzero variables or unsatisfied relations in linear systems. *Theoretical Computer Science*, 209(1-2):237–260, 1998.

[9] Gene M. Amdahl. Validity of the single processor approach to achieving large scale computing capabilities. In *Proceedings of the April 18-20, 1967, Spring Joint Computer Conference*, pages 483–485. New York, NY: ACM, 1967.

[10] Michael R. Anderson and Michael J. Cafarella. Input selection for fast feature engineering. In *IEEE 32nd International Conference on Data Engineering (ICDE)*, pages 577–588, Helsinki, IEEE, 2016.

[11] Jacob Andreas, Anca D. Dragan and Dan Klein. Translating neuralese. In Regina Barzilay and Min-Yen Kan, (eds.), *Proceedings of the 55th Annual Meeting of the Association for Computational Linguistics* (volume 1: Long Papers) pages 232–242. Association for Computational Linguistics, 2017.

[12] Austin Appleby. MurmurHash 3.0. https://github.com/aappleby/smhasher, 2010. Accessed: 2018-12-13.

[13] David Arthur and Sergei Vassilvitskii. k-means++: The advantages of careful seeding. In *Proceedings of the Eighteenth Annual ACM-SIAM Symposium on Discrete Algorithms*, pages 1027–1035. Philadelphia, PA: Society for Industrial and Applied Mathematics, 2007.

[14] Yannick Assogba. Filmstrip, an opencv/python based set of scripts for extracting keyframes from video. https://github.com/tafsiri/filmstrip, 2014. Accessed: 2018-12-20.

[15] Giuseppe Attardi. wikiextractor. https://github.com/attardi/wikiextractor, 2018. Accessed: 2018-12-12.

[16] Giulia Bagallo and David Haussler. Boolean feature discovery in empirical learning. *Machine Learning*, 5(1):71–99, 1990.

[17] Ryan S. Baker. Week 6: Behavior detection and model assessment. www.youtube.com/watch?v=5DWZoXI5z-E, 2014. Accessed: 2018-06-11.

[18] Ryan S. Baker. Advanced Excel. www.columbia.edu/~rsb2162/FES2015/FES-AdvancedExcel-v1.pptx, 2015. Accessed: 2018-06-11.

[19] Ryan S. Baker. Data cleaning. www.columbia.edu/~rsb2162/FES2015/FES-DataCleaning-v1.pptx, 2015. Accessed: 2018-06-11.

[20] Ryan S. Baker. Data sets. www.columbia.edu/~rsb2162/FES2015/FES-SpecialSession1-DataSets-v2.pptx, 2015. Accessed: 2018-06-11.

[21] Ryan S. Baker. Feature adaptation. www.columbia.edu/~rsb2162/FES2015/FES-FeatureAdaptation-v2.pptx, 2015. Accessed: 2018-06-11.

[22] Ryan S. Baker. Feature distillation. www.columbia.edu/~rsb2162/FES2015/FES-FeatureDistillationpt2-v1.pptx, 2015. Accessed: 2018-06-10.

[23] Ryan S. Baker. Feature distillation I. www.columbia.edu/~rsb2162/FES2015/FES-FeatureDistillation-I-v1.pptx, 2015. Accessed: 2018-06-11.

[24] Ryan S. Baker. Iterative feature refinement. www.columbia.edu/~rsb2162/FES2015/FES-IterativeFeatureRefinement-v2.pptx, 2015. Accessed: 2018-06-11.

[25] Ryan S. Baker. Prediction modeling. www.columbia.edu/~rsb2162/FES2015/FES-SpecialSession-PredictionModeling-v1.pptx, 2015. Accessed: 2018-06-11.

[26] Andrei Barbu, Tao Mei, Siddharth Narayanaswamy, Puneet Kumar Dokania, Quanshi Zhang, Nishant Shukla, Jiebo Luo and Rahul Sukthankar. Language and vision workshop at CVPR 2018. https://languageandvision.com/. Accessed: 2018-2-1.

[27] V Barnett and T Lewis. *Outliers in Statistical Data*. Hoboken, NJ: Wiley, 3rd edition, 1994.

[28] Damián Barsotti, Martín A. Domínguez and Pablo A. Duboue. Predicting invariant nodes in large scale semantic knowledge graphs. In *Information Management and Big Data – 4th Annual International Symposium, SIMBig 2017*, Lima, Peru, September 4–6, 2017, Revised Selected Papers, pages 48–60, 2017.

[29] Estela Maria Bee de Dagum. *Models for Time Series*. Ottawa: Information Canada, 1974.

[30] Anthony J. Bell and Terrence J. Sejnowski. Edges are the 'independent components' of natural scenes. In *Advances in Neural Information Processing Systems*, pages 831–837, 1997.

[31] Yoshua Bengio, Réjean Ducharme, Pascal Vincent and Christian Jauvin. A neural probabilistic language model. *Journal of Machine Learning Research*, 3(Feb):1137–1155, 2003.

[32] T. Berners-Lee, R. Fielding and L. Masinter. Uniform resource identifiers (URI): Generic syntax. RFC Editor, United States, 1998.

[33] Tim Berners-Lee, James Hendler and Ora Lassila. The semantic web. *Scientific American*, 284(5):34–43, May 2001.

[34] Alberto Bietti. What is feature discretization? From Quora. www.quora.com/ What-is-feature-discretization, 2013. Accessed: 2019-01-27.

[35] Daniel M Bikel. Intricacies of collins' parsing model. *Computational Linguistics*, 30(4):479–511, 2004.

[36] Misha Bilenko. Big learning made easy – with counts! Microsoft Machine Learning Blog. https://blogs.technet.microsoft .com/machinelearning/2015/02/17/big-learning-made-easy-with-counts/, 2015. Accessed: 2019-07-11.

[37] Steven Bird, Ewan Klein and Edward Loper. *Natural language processing with Python: Analyzing text with the natural language toolkit*. New York: O'Reilly Media, Inc., 2009.

[38] David M. Blei, Andrew Y. Ng, and Michael I. Jordan. Latent dirichlet allocation. *Journal of Machine Learning Research*, 3(Jan):993–1022, 2003.

[39] Kurt Bollacker, Colin Evans, Praveen Paritosh, Tim Sturge and Jamie Taylor. Freebase: A collaboratively created graph database for structuring human knowledge. In *Proceedings of the 2008 ACM SIGMOD International Conference on Management of Data*, SIGMOD '08, pages 1247–1250, New York: ACM, 2008.

[40] Leon Bottou. COS 424: Interacting with Data. Princeton CS Class 18, Feature Engineering. www.cs.princeton.edu/courses/archive/ spring10/cos424/slides/18-feat.pdf, 2010. Accessed: 2018-05-01.

[41] Alexandre Bouchard-Côté. CS 294: Practical Machine Learning. Princeton EECS class Feature Engineering and Selection. https://people.eecs .berkeley.edu/~jordan/courses/294-fall09/lectures/ feature/slides.pdf, October 2016. Accessed: 2018-05-02.

[42] Olivier Bousquet and André Elisseeff. Stability and generalization. *Journal of Machine Learning Research*, 2(Mar):499–526, 2002.

[43] Jordan Boyd-Graber. Digging into data - feature engineering (spoilers). www
    .youtube.com/watch?v=oYe03Y1WQaI, 2016. Accessed: 2018-06-11.

[44] Jordan Boyd-Graber. Machine learning: feature engineering. www.youtube
    .com/watch?v=0BGAD23_mhE, 2016. Accessed: 2018-06-06.

[45] Gary Bradski and Adrian Kaehler. *Learning OpenCV: Computer Vision with the
    OpenCV Library.* New York: O'Reilly Media, Inc., 2008.

[46] Leo Breiman. Random forests. *Machine Learning*, 45(1):5–32, 2001.

[47] Leo Breiman. Statistical modeling: The two cultures. *Statistical Science*,
    16(3):199–215, 2001.

[48] Leo Breiman, Jerome H. Friedman, Richard A. Olshen and Charles J. Stone.
    Classification and Regression Trees. The Wadsworth Statistics/Probability
    series. Monterey, CA: Wadsworth & Brooks/Cole Advanced Books & Software,
    1984.

[49] Henrik Brink, Joseph W. Richards and Mark Fetherolf. *Real-World Machine
    Learning.* Shelter Island, NY: Manning, 2017.

[50] Gavin Brown, Adam Pocock, Ming-Jie Zhao and Mikel Luján. Conditional
    likelihood maximisation: A unifying framework for information theoretic feature
    selection. *Journal of Machine Learning Research*, 13(Jan):27–66, 2012.

[51] Jason Brownlee. Discover feature engineering, how to engineer features
    and how to get good at it. https://machinelearningmastery
    .com/discover-feature-engineering-how-to-engineer-
    features-and-how-to-get-good-at-it/, oct 2014. Accessed:
    2018-05-02.

[52] Bruce Buchanan and David Wilkins. *Readings in Knowledge Acquisition and
    Learning.* New York, NY: Morgan Kaufmann, 1993.

[53] Chris Buckley. trec eval ir evaluation package. https://github.com/
    usnistgov/trec_eval, 2004. Accessed: 2019-11-11

[54] Dean Buonomano. *Your Brain Is a Time Machine: The Neuroscience and Physics
    of Time*, chapter 1. New York, NY: WW Norton, paperback edition, April 2018.

[55] Arno Candel. Anomaly detection and feature engineering. www.youtube
    .com/watch?v=fUSbljByXak, 2014. Accessed: 2018-06-10.

[56] J. Canny. A computational approach to edge detection. *IEEE Transactions on
    Pattern Analysis and Machine Intelligence*, 8(6):679–698, 1986.

[57] Jean Carletta. Assessing agreement on classification tasks: The kappa statistic.
    Computational Linguistics, 22(2):249–254, 1996.

[58] Joseph E. Cavanaugh. Unifying the derivations for the akaike and corrected
    akaike information criteria. *Statistics & Probability Letters*, 33(2):201–208,
    1997.

[59] Joseph E. Cavanaugh and Andrew A. Neath. Generalizing the derivation of
    the schwarz information criterion. *Communications in Statistics-Theory and
    Methods*, 28(1):49–66, 1999.

[60] C.-C. Chan, Celai Batur and Arvind Srinivasan. Determination of quantization
    intervals in rule based model for dynamic systems. In *Decision Aiding for Com-
    plex Systems, Conference Proceedings. 1991 IEEE International Conference on
    Systems, Man, and Cybernetics*, volume 3, pages 1719–1723. Charlottesville,
    VA: IEEE, 1991.

[61] Chris Chatfield. *The Analysis of Time Series: An Introduction*. Boca Raton, FL: CRC Press, 2016.

[62] Jim X. Chen. The evolution of computing: Alphago. *Computing in Science and Engineering*, 18(4):4–7, 2016.

[63] Jingnian Chen, Houkuan Huang, Shengfeng Tian and Youli Qu. Feature selection for text classification with naïve bayes. *Expert Systems with Applications*, 36(3):5432–5435, 2009.

[64] David Chiang, Aravind K. Joshi and David B. Searls. Grammatical representations of macromolecular structure. *Journal of Computational Biology*, 13(5):1077–1100, 2006.

[65] Brian Christopher. Time Series Analysis (TSA) in Python: Linear models to GARCH. www.blackarbs.com/blog/time-series-analysis-in-python-linear-models-to-garch/11/1/2016, 2016. Accessed: 2019-01-15.

[66] Aleksandr Chuklin, Ilya Markov and Maarten de Rijke. An introduction to click models for web search: Sigir 2015 tutorial. In *Proceedings of the 38th International ACM SIGIR Conference on Research and Development in Information Retrieval*, pages 1113–1115. ACM, 2015.

[67] Edgar F. Codd. A relational model of data for large shared data banks. *Communications of the ACM*, 13(6):377–387, 1970.

[68] William Cohen. Learning trees and rules with set-valued features. In *Proceedings of the 14th Joint American Association for Artificial Intelligence and IAAI Conference (AAAI/IAAI-96)*, pages 709–716. American Association for Artificial Intelligence, 1996.

[69] Ronan Collobert, Jason Weston, Léon Bottou, Michael Karlen, Koray Kavukcuoglu and Pavel Kuksa. Natural language processing (almost) from scratch. *Journal of Machine Learning Research*, 12(Aug):2493–2537, 2011.

[70] Unicode Consortium, et al. *The Unicode Standard, Version 2.0*. Boston, MA: Addison-Wesley Longman Publishing Co., Inc., 1997.

[71] DBpedia Contributors. DBpedia. http://dbpedia.org, 2018. Accessed: 2018-11-05.

[72] Quora Contributors. What are some best practices in feature engineering? www.quora.com/What-are-some-best-practices-in-Feature-Engineering, 2016. Accessed: 2018-05-02.

[73] Weka Mailing List Contributors. Mutual information feature selection. Retrieved from http://weka.8497.n7.nabble.com/Mutual-Information-Feature-Selection-tp8975.html, 2007. Accessed: 2019-01-10.

[74] Drew Conway and John Myles White. *Machine Learning for Hackers*. Sebastopol, CA: O'Reilly Media, 2012.

[75] Thomas H Cormen, Charles E Leiserson, Ronald L Rivest and Clifford Stein. *Introduction to Algorithms*. Cambridge, MA: MIT Press, 2009.

[76] Alejandro Correa Bahnsen, Djamila Aouada, Aleksandar Stojanovic and Björn Ottersten. Feature engineering strategies for credit card fraud detection. 51, 01 2016. *Expert Systems with Applications*, 51(01), 2016.

[77] Andrew Cotter, Joseph Keshet and Nathan Srebro. Explicit approximations of the gaussian kernel. Technical report, arXiv:1109.4603, 2011.

[78] Jim Cowie and Wendy Lehnert. Information extraction. *Commun. ACM*, 39(1):80–91, January 1996.

[79] Navneet Dalal and Bill Triggs. Histograms of oriented gradients for human detection. In *Computer Vision and Pattern Recognition, 2005. CVPR 2005. IEEE Computer Society Conference on*, volume 1, pages 886–893. San Diego, CA: IEEE, 2005.

[80] A. P. Dempster, N. M. Laird and D. B. Rubin. Maximum likelihood from incomplete data via the EM algorithm. *Journal of Royal Statistical Society, Series B (Methodological)*, 39(1), 1977.

[81] Joanne Desmond and Lanny R. Copeland. *Communicating with Today's Patient: Essentials to Save Time, Decrease Risk, and Increase Patient Compliance*. San Francisco, CA: Jossey-Bass, September 2000.

[82] Jacob Devlin, Ming-Wei Chang, Kenton Lee and Kristina Toutanova. Bert: Pre-training of deep bidirectional transformers for language understanding. *arXiv preprint arXiv:1810.04805*, 2018.

[83] Elena S. Dimitrova, M. Paola Vera Licona, John McGee and Reinhard Laubenbacher. Discretization of time series data. *Journal of Computational Biology*, 17(6):853–868, 2010.

[84] Pedro Domingos. A few useful things to know about machine learning. *Communications of the ACM*, 55(10):78–87, 2012.

[85] Jingming Dong, Nikolaos Karianakis, Damek Davis, Joshua Hernandez, Jonathan Balzer and Stefano Soatto. Multi-view feature engineering and learning. In *Proceedings of the IEEE Conference on Computer Vision and Pattern Recognition*, pages 3251–3260, Burlington, MA: Morgan Kaufmann, 2015.

[86] James Dougherty, Ron Kohavi and Mehran Sahami. Supervised and unsupervised discretization of continuous features. In *Proceedings of the Twelfth International Conference on Machine Learning*, pages 194–202, Tahoe City, California, Burlington, MA: Morgan Kaufmann, 1995.

[87] Arthur Douillard. Object detection with deep learning on aerial imagery. `https://medium.com/data-from-the-trenches/object-detection-with-deep-learning-on-aerial-imagery-2465078db8a9`. Retrieved Jan 20, 2019, 2018.

[88] Petros Drineas and Michael W. Mahoney. On the Nyström method for approximating a gram matrix for improved kernel-based learning. *Journal of Machine Learning Research*, 6(Dec):2153–2175, 2005.

[89] Pablo A. Duboue. *Indirect Supervised Learning of Strategic Generation Logic*. PhD thesis, Computer Science Department, New York, NY: Columbia University Press, June 2005.

[90] Pablo A. Duboue. gitrecommender. `https://github.com/DrDub/gitrecommender`, 2014. Accessed: 2018-12-12.

[91] Pablo A. Duboue. Automatic reports from spreadsheets: Data analysis for the rest of us. In *Proceedings of the 9th International Natural Language Generation conference*, pages 244–245. Association for Computational Linguistics, 2016.

[92] Pablo A. Duboue. Deobfuscating name scrambling as a natural language generation task. In *Argentinian Symposium on Artificial Intelligence (ASAI)*, Buenos Aires, Argentina, 2018.

[93] Pablo A. Duboue and Martin A. Domínguez. *Using Robustness to Learn to Order Semantic Properties in Referring Expression Generation*, pages 163–174. Cham: Springer, 2016.

[94] Pablo A. Duboue, Martin A. Domınguez and Paula Estrella. On the robustness of standalone referring expression generation algorithms using rdf data. In *WebNLG 2016*, page 17, Edinburgh, UK, 2016.

[95] Olive Jean Dunn. Multiple comparisons among means. *Journal of the American Statistical Association*, 56(293):52–64, 1961.

[96] D. Eastlake and P. Jones. US Secure Hash Algorithm 1 (SHA1). RFC 3174, IETF, 9 2001.

[97] John Ellson, Emden Gansner, Lefteris Koutsofios, Stephen North and Gordon Woodhull. Graphviz – Open source graph drawing tools. In *Lecture Notes in Computer Science*, pages 483–484. New York, NY: Springer-Verlag, 2001.

[98] Thomas Elsken, Jan Hendrik Metzen and Frank Hutter. *Neural Architecture Search*, In Frank Hutter, Lars Kotthoff, and Joaquin Vanschoren (eds.), *Automatic Machine Learning: Methods, Systems, Challenges*, pages 63–77. Cambridge, MA: Springer International Publishing, 2019. Available at http://automl.org/book.

[99] David Epstein. Feature engineering. www.slideshare.net/odsc/feature-engineering, 2015. Accessed: 2018-06-10.

[100] C. Esteban, V. Tresp, Y. Yang, S. Baier and D. Krompass. Predicting the co-evolution of event and knowledge graphs. In *2016 19th International Conference on Information Fusion (FUSION)*, pages 98–105, July 2016.

[101] Martin Ester, Hans-Peter Kriegel, Jörg Sander, Xiaowei Xu, et al. A density-based algorithm for discovering clusters in large spatial databases with noise. In *Kdd*, volume 96, pages 226–231, 1996.

[102] Virginia Eubanks. *Automating Inequality: How High-Tech Tools Profile, Police, and Punish the Poor*. New York, NY: St. Martin's Press, 2018.

[103] Usama Fayyad and Keki Irani. Multi-interval discretization of continuous-valued attributes for classification learning. In *Proceedings of the 13th International Joint Conference on Artificial Intelligence*, pages 1022–1029, Tahoe City, CA: Morgan Kaufmann, 1993.

[104] Kate Fehlhaber. Hubel and wiesel and the neural basis of visual perception. https://knowingneurons.com/2014/10/29/hubel-and-wiesel-the-neural-basis-of-visual-perception/, 2014.

[105] C. Fellbaum. *WordNet – An Electronic Lexical Database*. Cambridge, MA: MIT Press, 1998.

[106] David Ferrucci and Adam Lally. Uima: An architectural approach to unstructured information processing in the corporate research environment. *Natural Language Engineering*, 10(3-4):327–348, 2004.

[107] John Rupert Firth. A synopsis of linguistic theory 1930–1955. In *Studies in Linguistic Analysis*, pages 1–32. Oxford: Blackwell, 1957.

[108] J. L. Fleiss. Measuring nominal scale agreement among many raters. *Psychological Bulletin*, 76(5):378–382, 1971.

[109] Glenn Fowler, Landon Curt Noll, Kiem-Phong Vo, Donald Eastlake and Tony Hansen. The fnv non-cryptographic hash algorithm. *Ietf-draft*, 2011.

[110] Eibe Frank. Mutual information. Retrieved from `http://weka.8497 .n7.nabble.com/Mutual-information-tt41569.html#a41580`, 2017. Accessed: 2019-01-10.

[111] Jeffrey E. F. Friedl. *Mastering Regular Expressions*. Sebastopol, CA: O'Reilly & Associates, Inc. 2nd edition, 2002.

[112] Jerome H. Friedman. Multivariate adaptive regression splines. *The Annals of Statistics*, pages 1–67, 1991.

[113] Keinosuke Fukunaga. *Introduction to Statistical Pattern Recognition*. Computer Science and Scientific Computing. Cambridge, MA: Academic Press, 2nd edition, 1990.

[114] Ben D. Fulcher, Max A. Little, and Nick S. Jones. Highly comparative time-series analysis: The empirical structure of time series and their methods. *Journal of the Royal Society Interface*, 10(83):20130048, 2013.

[115] Dennis Gabor. Theory of communication. part 1: The analysis of information. *Journal of the Institution of Electrical Engineers-Part III: Radio and Communication Engineering*, 93(26):429–441, 1946.

[116] Piotr Gabrys. Non-negative matrix factorization for recommendation systems. `https://medium.com/logicai/non-negative-matrix-factorization-for-recommendation-systems-985ca8d5c16c`, 2018. Accessed 2019-22-1.

[117] William A. Gale and Geoffrey Sampson. Good-turing frequency estimation without tears. *Journal of Quantitative Linguistics*, 2(3):217–237, 1995.

[118] Salvador Garcia, Julian Luengo, José Antonio Sáez, Victoria Lopez and Francisco Herrera. A survey of discretization techniques: Taxonomy and empirical analysis in supervised learning. *IEEE Transactions on Knowledge and Data Engineering*, 25(4):734–750, 2013.

[119] Andrew Gelman. Analysis of variance–Why it is more important than ever. *Ann. Statist.*, 33(1):1–53, 2005.

[120] Aurélien Géron. *Hands-on machine learning with Scikit-Learn and TensorFlow: Concepts, tools, and techniques to build intelligent systems*. Sebastopol, CA: O'Reilly Media, 2017.

[121] Swarnendu Ghosh, Nibaran Das, Teresa Gonçalves, Paulo Quaresma and Mahantapas Kundu. The journey of graph kernels through two decades. *Computer Science Review*, 27:88–111, 2018.

[122] Xavier Glorot and Yoshua Bengio. Understanding the difficulty of training deep feedforward neural networks. In Yee Whye Teh and D. Mike Titterington, (eds.), *AISTATS*, volume 9 of *JMLR Proceedings*, pages 249–256, 2010.

[123] David Goldberg. What every computer scientist should know about floating-point arithmetic. *ACM Computing Surveys (CSUR)*, 23(1):5–48, 1991.

[124] D. C. Gondek, A. Lally, A. Kalyanpur, J. W. Murdock, P. A. Duboue, L. Zhang, Y. Pan, Z. M. Qiu and C. Welty. A framework for merging and ranking of answers in DeepQA. *IBM Journal of Research and Development*, 56(3.4):14:1 – 14:12, 2012. Digital Object Identifier: 10.1147/JRD.2012.2188760.

[125] Ian Goodfellow, Yoshua Bengio and Aaron Courville. *Deep Learning*. Cambridge, MA: MIT Press, 2016. `www.deeplearningbook.org`.

[126] Ian Goodfellow, Jean Pouget-Abadie, Mehdi Mirza, Bing Xu, David Warde-Farley, Sherjil Ozair, Aaron Courville and Yoshua Bengio. Generative adversarial nets. In Z. Ghahramani, M. Welling, C. Cortes, N. D. Lawrence, K. Q. Weinberger (eds.), *Advances in neural Information Processing Systems*, pages 2672–2680, Cambridge, MA: MIT Press, 2014.

[127] Josh Gordon. What makes a good feature. www.youtube.com/watch? v=N9fDIAf1CMY, 2016. Accessed: 2018-06-06.

[128] Pablo M. Granitto, Cesare Furlanello, Franco Biasioli and Flavia Gasperi. Recursive feature elimination with random forest for ptr-ms analysis of agroindustrial products. *Chemometrics and Intelligent Laboratory Systems*, 83(2):83–90, 2006.

[129] Alexander Gribov and Konstantin Krivoruchko. *New Flexible Non-parametric Data Transformation for Trans-Gaussian Kriging*, pages 51–65. Dordrecht, The Netherlands: Springer Netherlands, 2012.

[130] Aditya Grover and Jure Leskovec. node2vec: Scalable feature learning for networks. In *Proceedings of the 22nd ACM SIGKDD international conference on Knowledge Discovery and Data Mining*, pages 855–864. San Francisco, CA: ACM, 2016.

[131] Quanquan Gu, Zhenhui Li and Jiawei Han. Generalized fisher score for feature selection. In Fábio Gagliardi Cozman and Avi Pfeffer, (eds.), *UAI*, pages 266–273. Barcelona, Spain: AUAI Press, 2011.

[132] Huan Liu Guozhu Dong, (ed.). *Feature Engineering for Machine Learning and Data Analytics*. Series: Chapman/Hall/CRC Data Mining and Knowledge Discovery Series. Boca Raton, FL: CRC Press, 1st edition, April 2018.

[133] Manish Gupta, Jing Gao, Charu C. Aggarwal and Jiawei Han. Outlier detection for temporal data: A survey. *IEEE Transactions on Knowledge and Data Engineering*, 26(9):2250–2267, 2014.

[134] Isabelle Guyon and André Elisseeff. An introduction to variable and feature selection. *Journal of Machine Learning Research*, 3(Mar):1157–1182, 2003.

[135] Isabelle Guyon, Steve Gunn, Masoud Nikravesh and Lofti Zadeh, (eds.). *Feature Extraction, Foundations and Applications*. Series Studies in Fuzziness and Soft Computing, Heidelberg, Germany: Physica-Verlag, Springer, 2006.

[136] Isabelle Guyon, Jason Weston, Stephen Barnhill and Vladimir Vapnik. Gene selection for cancer classification using support vector machines. *Machine Learning*, 46(1-3):389–422, 2002.

[137] Maria Halkidi, Yannis Batistakis and Michalis Vazirgiannis. On clustering validation techniques. *Journal of Intelligent Information Systems*, 17:107–145, 2001.

[138] Nathan Halko, Per-Gunnar Martinsson and Joel A Tropp. Finding structure with randomness: Probabilistic algorithms for constructing approximate matrix decompositions. *SIAM Review*, 53(2):217–288, 2011.

[139] Robert M. Haralick et al. Statistical and structural approaches to texture. *Proceedings of the IEEE*, 67(5):786–804, 1979.

[140] F. Maxwell Harper and Joseph A. Konstan. The movielens datasets: History and context. *ACM Transactions on Interactive Intelligent Systems (tiis)*, 5(4):19, 2016.

[141] C. Harris and M. Stephens. A combined corner and edge detection. In *Proceedings of The Fourth Alvey Vision Conf.*, pages 147–151, 1988.

[142] John A. Hartigan and Manchek A. Wong. Algorithm as 136: A k-means clustering algorithm. *Journal of the Royal Statistical Society. Series C (Applied Statistics)*, 28(1):100–108, 1979.

[143] Vasileios Hatzivassiloglou, Pablo A. Duboue and Andrey Rzhetsky. Disambiguating proteins, genes and RNA in text: A machine learning approach. *Bioinformatics*, 17(Suppl 1):97–106, 2001. PubMedID: 11472998.

[144] Marti A. Hearst. Texttiling: Segmenting text into multi-paragraph subtopic passages. *Computational Linguistics*, 23(1):33–64, 1997.

[145] Jeff Heaton. Encog: Library of interchangeable machine learning models for Java and C sharp. *Journal of Machine Learning Research*, 16:1243–1247, 2015.

[146] Jeff Heaton. An empirical analysis of feature engineering for predictive modeling. In *SoutheastCon, 2016*, pages 1–6. Norfolk, VA: IEEE, 2016.

[147] Jeff Heaton. *Automated Feature Engineering for Deep Neural Networks with Genetic Programming*. PhD thesis, Nova Southeastern University, 2017.

[148] G. E. Hinton and R. R. Salakhutdinov. Reducing the dimensionality of data with neural networks. *Science*, 313(5786):504–507, 2006.

[149] Geoffrey E. Hinton and Richard S. Zemel. Autoencoders, minimum description length and helmholtz free energy. In *Advances in Neural Information Processing Systems*, pages 3–10, 1994.

[150] C. Hirt, M. S. Filmer and W. E. Featherstone. Comparison and validation of the recent freely available aster-gdem ver1, srtm ver4.1 and geodata dem-9s ver3 digital elevation models over australia. *Australian Journal of Earth Sciences*, 57(3):337–347, 2010.

[151] Victoria Hodge and Jim Austin. A survey of outlier detection methodologies. *Artificial Intelligence Review*, 22(2):85–126, 2004.

[152] A. E. Hoerl and R. W. Kennard. Ridge regression: Biased estimation for nonorthogonal problems. *Technometrics*, 12:55–67, 1970.

[153] Martin Hoffman. Kernels and the kernel trick. www.cogsys.wiai.uni-bamberg.de/teaching/ss06/hs_svm/slides/SVM_and_Kernels.pdf, 2006. Accessed: 2018-08-19.

[154] Thomas Hofmann. Unsupervised learning by probabilistic latent semantic analysis. *Machine Learning*, 42(1-2):177–196, 2001.

[155] Daniel Holden. My neural network isn't working! what should i do? http://theorangeduck.com/page/neural-network-not-working, August 2017. Accessed: 2019-01-10.

[156] Matthew Honnibal and Ines Montani. spacy 2: Natural language understanding with bloom embeddings, convolutional neural networks and incremental parsing. *To appear*, 2017.

[157] Jeremy Howard and Sebastian Ruder. Universal language model fine-tuning for text classification. In *Proceedings of the 56th Annual Meeting of the Association for Computational Linguistics (Volume 1: Long Papers)*, volume 1, pages 328–339, 2018.

[158] Yingjie Hu, Song Gao, Shawn Newsam and Dalton Lunga, (eds.). *GeoAI'18: Proceedings of the 2Nd ACM SIGSPATIAL International Workshop on AI for Geographic Knowledge Discovery*, New York: ACM, 2018.

[159] Chao Huang. Meaning of the spectral norm of a matrix. From Mathematics Stack Exchange. https://math.stackexchange.com/questions/188202/meaning-of-the-spectral-norm-of-a-matrix, 2012. Accessed: 2018-12-17.

[160] Zhiheng Huang, Wei Xu and Kai Yu. Bidirectional LSTM-CRF models for sequence tagging. *CoRR*, abs/1508.01991, 2015.

[161] DH Hubel and TN Wiesel. Receptive fields of single neurones in the cat's striate cortex. *The Journal of Physiology*, 148(3):574–591, 1959.

[162] Darrell Huff. *How to Lie with Statistics*. New York: Penguin Books, 1954.

[163] Aapo Hyvärinen, Juha Karhunen and Erkki Oja. *Independent Component Analysis*. Hoboken: NJ: Wiley, 2001.

[164] Grant S. Ingersoll, Thomas S. Morton and Andrew L. Farris. *Taming text: How to find, organise, and manipulate it*. Shelter Island, NY: Pearson Education, 2013.

[165] Soladoye B. Iwajomo, Mikkel Willemoes, Ulf Ottosson, Roine Strandberg and Kasper Thorup. Data from: Intra-african movements of the african cuckoo cuculus gularis as revealed by satellite telemetry. www.datarepository.movebank.org/handle/10255/move.714, 2017. Accessed: 2018-1-20.

[166] Soladoye B. Iwajomo, Mikkel Willemoes, Ulf Ottosson, Roine Strandberg and Kasper Thorup. Intra-african movements of the african cuckoo cuculus gularis as revealed by satellite telemetry. *Journal of Avian Biology*, 49(1), 2018.

[167] Giri Iyengar. CS 5304: Data science in the wild. Cornell EECS, class Feature Engineering. https://courses.cit.cornell.edu/cs5304/Lectures/lec5_FeatureEngineering.pdf, March 2016. Accessed: 2016-10-01.

[168] Nathalie Japkowicz, Catherine Myers, Mark Gluck, et al. A novelty detection approach to classification. In *IJCAI*, volume 1, pages 518–523, 1995.

[169] Nathalie Japkowicz and Mohak Shah. *Evaluating Learning Algorithms: A Classification Perspective*. New York, NY: Cambridge University Press, 2011.

[170] George H. John. Robust decision trees: Removing outliers from databases. In *KDD*, pages 174–179, 1995.

[171] Jacob Joseph. How to improve machine learning: Tricks and tips for feature engineering. http://data-informed.com/how-to-improve-machine-learning-tricks-and-tips-for-feature-engineering/, 2016. Accessed: 2016-30-01.

[172] Dan Jurafsky and James H. Martin. *Speech and Language Processing*. to appear, 3rd edition, 2020.

[173] Inc. Kaggle. Titanic: Machine learning from disaster. www.kaggle.com/c/titanic, 2012. Accessed: 2018-08-28.

[174] James Max Kanter. As someone who works with a lot of people new to machine learning, i appreciate... Hacker News: https://news.ycombinator.com/item?id=15919806, 2017. Accessed: 2019-01-12.

[175] James Max Kanter and Kalyan Veeramachaneni. Deep Feature Synthesis: Towards automating data science endeavors. In *2015 IEEE International Conference on Data Science and Advanced Analytics*, DSAA 2015, Paris, France, October 19-21, 2015, pages 1–10. New York, NY: IEEE, 2015.

[176] Saurav Kaushik. Introduction to feature selection methods with an example (or how to select the right variables?). www.analyticsvidhya.com/blog/2016/12/introduction-to-feature-selection-methods-with-an-example-or-how-to-select-the-right-variables/, 2016. Accessed: 2018-10-15.

[177] John D. Kelleher, Brian Mac Namee and Aoife D'arcy. *Fundamentals of Machine Learning for Predictive Data Analytics: Algorithms, Worked Examples, and Case Studies*. Cambridge, MA: MIT Press, 2015.

[178] Tom Kelley. *The Art of Innovation: Lessons in Creativity from IDEO, America's Leading Design Firm*, volume 10. New York, NY: Broadway Business, 2001.

[179] Randy Kerber. Chimerge: Discretization of numeric attributes. In *Proceedings of the Tenth National Conference on Artificial intelligence*, pages 123–128. AAAI Press, 1992.

[180] Roman Kern. Knowlede discovery and datamining i. kti graz university of technology. class feature engineering. http://kti.tugraz.at/staff/denis/courses/kddm1/featureengineering.pdf, November 2015. Accessed: 2018-05-03.

[181] Udayan Khurana, Horst Samulowitz and Deepak Turaga. Feature engineering for predictive modeling using reinforcement learning. In *Thirty-Second AAAI Conference on Artificial Intelligence*, 2018.

[182] Sangkyum Kim, Hyungsul Kim, Tim Weninger, Jiawei Han and Hyun Duk Kim. Authorship classification: A discriminative syntactic tree mining approach. In *Proceedings of the 34th International ACM SIGIR Conference on Research and Development in Information Retrieval*, pages 455–464. New York, NY: ACM, 2011.

[183] Stephen King. *On Writing: A Memoir of the Craft*. New York: Scribner, 2010.

[184] Diederik P. Kingma and Max Welling. Auto-encoding variational bayes. In *Proceedings of the 2nd International Conference on Learning Representations (ICLR)*, 2013.

[185] Kenji Kira and Larry A. Rendell. The feature selection problem: Traditional methods and a new algorithm. In *AAAI*, volume 2, pages 129–134, 1992.

[186] B. Ravi Kiran. How can deep learning be used with video data? From Quora. www.quora.com/How-can-deep-learning-be-used-with-video-data, 2017. Accessed: 2019-01-11.

[187] Peter Kluegl, Martin Toepfer, Philip-Daniel Beck, Georg Fette and Frank Puppe. Uima ruta: Rapid development of rule-based information extraction applications. *Natural Language Engineering*, 22(1):1–40, 2016.

[188] Thomas Kluyver, Benjamin Ragan-Kelley, Fernando Pérez, Brian E Granger, Matthias Bussonnier, Jonathan Frederic, Kyle Kelley, Jessica B Hamrick, Jason Grout, Sylvain Corlay, Paul Ivanov, Damian Avila, Safia Abdalla, Carol Willing, and Jupyter development team. Jupyter notebooks: A publishing format for reproducible computational workflows. In Fernando, Loizides and Birgit

Schmidt (eds.), *Proceedings of the 20th International Conference on Electronic Publishing*, pp. 87–90, Amsterdam, The Netherlands: IOS Press, 2016.

[189] Ron Kohavi and George H. John. Wrappers for feature subset selection. *Artificial Intelligence*, 97(1-2):273–324, 1997.

[190] Risi Imre Kondor and John Lafferty. Diffusion kernels on graphs and other discrete structures. In *Proceedings of the 19th international conference on machine learning*, volume 2002, pages 315–322, 2002.

[191] Sotiris Kotsiantis and Dimitris Kanellopoulos. Discretization techniques: A recent survey. *GESTS International Transactions on Computer Science and Engineering*, 32(1):47–58, 2006.

[192] J. Koza. *Genetic Programming II*. Cambridge, MA: MIT Press, 1994.

[193] Nicholas Kridler. Data agnosticism - Feature Engineering without domain expertise. www.youtube.com/watch?v=bL4b1sGnILU, June 2013. Accessed: 2018-06-04.

[194] Alex Krizhevsky, Ilya Sutskever and Geoffrey E. Hinton. Imagenet classification with deep convolutional neural networks. *Commun. ACM*, 60(6):84–90, May 2017.

[195] Max Kuhn. Feature engineering versus feature extraction: Game on! www.r-bloggers.com/feature-engineering-versus-feature-extraction-game-on/, 2015. Accessed: 2018-05-03.

[196] Ashish Kumar. Feature engineering: Data scientist's secret sauce ! www.datasciencecentral.com/profiles/blogs/feature-engineering-data-scientist-s-secret-sauce-1, 2016. Accessed: 2018-06-11.

[197] Lukasz A. Kurgan and Krzysztof J. Cios. Caim discretization algorithm. *IEEE Transactions on Knowledge and Data Engineering*, 16(2):145–153, 2004.

[198] John D. Lafferty, Andrew McCallum and Fernando C. N. Pereira. Conditional random fields: Probabilistic models for segmenting and labeling sequence data. In *Proceedings of the Eighteenth International Conference on Machine Learning*, ICML '01, pages 282–289, San Francisco, CA: Morgan Kaufmann, 2001.

[199] Jean Laherrere and Didier Sornette. Stretched exponential distributions in nature and economy: "fat tails" with characteristic scales. *The European Physical Journal B-Condensed Matter and Complex Systems*, 2(4):525–539, 1998.

[200] Mirella Lapata. Invited keynote: Translating from multiple modalities to text and back. www.slideshare.net/aclanthology/mirella-lapata-2017-translating-from-multiple-modalities-to-text-and-back, 2017. Accessed: 2019-01-12.

[201] Ora Lassila and Ralph R. Swick. Resource description framework (RDF) model and syntax specification. www.w3.org/TR/REC-rdf-syntax, February 1999. Accessed: 2018-20-1.

[202] Victor Lavrenko. Machine learning = Feature engineering. www.youtube.com/watch?v=CAnEJ42eEYA, 2016. Accessed: 2018-06-06.

[203] Daniel D. Lee and H. Sebastian Seung. Algorithms for non-negative matrix factorization. In T. G. Dietterich, S. Becker, and Z. Ghahramani (eds.) *Advances*

in neural information processing systems, pages 556–562, Cambridge, MA: MIT Press, 2001.

[204] Jeff Leek. *The Elements of Data Analytic Style*. Victoria, British Columbia: Leanpub, 2015.

[205] Jens Lehmann, Robert Isele, Max Jakob, Anja Jentzsch, Dimitris Kontokostas, Pablo N. Mendes, Sebastian Hellmann, Mohamed Morsey, Patrick van Kleef, Sören Auer and Christian Bizer. DBpedia - A large-scale, multilingual knowledge base extracted from wikipedia. *Semantic Web Journal*, 6(2):167–195, 2015.

[206] Chun-Liang Li. Feature engineering in machine learning. `www.slideshare.net/tw_dsconf/feature-engineering-in-machine-learning`, 2015. Accessed: 2018-06-11.

[207] Chun-Liang Li, Hsuan-Tien Lin and Chi-Jen Lu. Rivalry of two families of algorithms for memory-restricted streaming pca. In *Artificial Intelligence and Statistics*, pages 473–481, 2016.

[208] Ping Li, Trevor J Hastie and Kenneth W Church. Very sparse random projections. In *Proceedings of the 12th ACM SIGKDD International Conference on Knowledge Discovery and Data Mining*, pages 287–296. ACM, 2006.

[209] Chih-Jen Lin. Support vector machines and kernel methods: Status and challenges. `www.csie.ntu.edu.tw/~cjlin/talks/kuleuven_svm.pdf`, 2013. Accessed: 2018-08-27.

[210] Tsung-Yi Lin, Michael Maire, Serge Belongie, James Hays, Pietro Perona, Deva Ramanan, Piotr Dollar and Larry Zitnick. Microsoft coco: Common objects in context. In *ECCV. European Conference on Computer Vision*, September 2014.

[211] Yijun Lin, Yao-Yi Chiang, Fan Pan, Dimitrios Stripelis, José Luis Ambite, Sandrah P Eckel and Rima Habre. Mining public datasets for modeling intra-city pm2. Five concentrations at a fine spatial resolution. In *Proceedings of the 25th ACM SIGSPATIAL international conference on advances in geographic information systems*, page 25. New York, NY: ACM, 2017.

[212] Nick Littlestone. Learning quickly when irrelevant attributes abound: A new linear-threshold algorithm. *Machine Learning*, 2(4):285–318, 1988.

[213] Huan Liu, Farhad Hussain, Chew Lim Tan and Manoranjan Dash. Discretization: An enabling technique. *Data Mining and Knowledge Discovery*, 6(4):393–423, 2002.

[214] Huan Liu and Hiroshi Motoda. *Computational Methods of Feature Selection*. Boca Raton, FL: CRC Press, 2007.

[215] David G. Lowe. Object recognition from local scale-invariant features. In *Proc. of the International Conference on Computer Vision*, Corfu, 1999.

[216] David G. Lowe. Method and apparatus for identifying scale invariant features in an image and use of same for locating an object in an image. US Patent US6711293B1, 2004.

[217] Prasanta Chandra Mahalanobis. On the generalized distance in statistics. *Proceedings of the National Institute of Sciences (Calcutta)*, 2:49–55, 1936.

[218] Dandelion Mané. Hands-on tensorBoard (TensorFlow Dev Summit 2017). `www.youtube.com/watch?v=eBbEDRsCmv4`, 2017. Accessed: 2018-11-30.

[219] Christopher D. Manning, Prabhakar Raghavan and Hinrich Schutze. *Introduction to Information Retrieval*. New York: Cambridge University Press, 2008.

[220] Christopher D. Manning and Hinrich Schütze. *Foundations of Statistical Natural Language Processing*. MIT Press, 1999.

[221] Ivan Markovsky. *Low Rank Approximation - Algorithms, Implementation, Applications. Communications and Control Engineering*. New York, NY: Springer, 2012.

[222] Bernard Marr. Twenty-Seven incredible examples of AI and Machine Learning in practice. Forbes sites: www.forbes.com/sites/bernardmarr/2018/04/30/27-incredible-examples-of-ai-and-machine-learning-in-practice/, 2018. Accessed: 2019-01-12.

[223] Marcin Marszalek, Ivan Laptev and Cordelia Schmid. Actions in context. In *Computer Vision and Pattern Recognition, 2009. CVPR 2009. IEEE Conference on*, pages 2929–2936. San Diego, CA: IEEE, 2009.

[224] Andrew Macfarlane Martin Porter and Richard Boulton. Snowball stop words list. http://snowball.tartarus.org/algorithms/english/stop.txt, 2001. Accessed: 2018-12-12.

[225] Viktor Mayer-Schonberger and Kenneth Cukier. *Big Data: A Revolution That Will Transform How We Live, Work and Think*. Boston, MA: Houghton Mifflin Harcourt, 2013.

[226] Andrew McCallum, Kamal Nigam and Lyle H. Ungar. Efficient clustering of high-dimensional data sets with application to reference matching. In *Proceedings of the Sixth ACM SIGKDD International Conference on Knowledge Discovery and Data Mining*, KDD '00, pages 169–178, New York, NY, ACM, 2000

[227] Andrew McCallum, Karl Schultz and Sameer Singh. Factorie: Probabilistic programming via imperatively defined factor graphs. In *Advances in Neural Information Processing Systems*, pages 1249–1257, 2009.

[228] C. McCormick. Word2vec tutorial part 2 - Negative sampling. Retrieved from www.mccormickml.com, 2017. Accessed: 2018-12-22.

[229] Prem Noel Melville. *Creating diverse ensemble classifiers to reduce supervision*. PhD thesis, Department of Computer Sciences at the University of Texas at Austin, 2005.

[230] Pablo N. Mendes, Max Jakob, Andrés García-Silva and Christian Bizer. Dbpedia spotlight: Shedding light on the web of documents. In *Proceedings of the 7th International Conference on Semantic Systems*, pages 1–8. San Diego, CA: ACM, 2011.

[231] James Mercer. Xvi. functions of positive and negative type, and their connection the theory of integral equations. *Philosophical Transactions of the Royal Society of London A: Mathematical, Physical and Engineering Sciences*, 209(441-458):415–446, 1909.

[232] Rada F. Mihalcea and Dragomir R. Radev. *Graph-Based Natural Language Processing and Information Retrieval*. New York: Cambridge University Press, 1st edition, 2011.

[233] Tomas Mikolov, Ilya Sutskever, Kai Chen, Greg S Corrado and Jeff Dean. Distributed representations of words and phrases and their compositionality. In

C. J. C. Burges, L. Bottou, M. Welling, Z. Ghahramani, and K. Q. Weinberger, (eds.), *Advances in Neural Information Processing Systems 26*, pages 3111–3119. Vancouver, British Columbia: Curran Associates, Inc., 2013.

[234] Tom M. Mitchell. *Machine Learning*. New York: McGraw-Hill, 1997.

[235] Olivier Moindrot and Guillaume Genthial. Cs230 – Theory: How to choose the train, train-dev, dev and test sets. https://cs230-stanford.github.io/train-dev-test-split.html, 2018. Accessed: 2019-07-07.

[236] Marcelo A. Montemurro. Beyond the zipf–mandelbrot law in quantitative linguistics. *Physica A: Statistical Mechanics and its Applications*, 300(3-4):567–578, 2001.

[237] Alexander MacFarlane Mood and Franklin Arno Graybill. *Introduction to the Theory of Statistics*. International student edition. New York: McGraw-Hill, 2nd edition, 1963.

[238] T. Nathan Mundhenk, Goran Konjevod, Wesam A. Sakla and Kofi Boakye. A large contextual dataset for classification, detection and counting of cars with deep learning. In Bastian Leibe, Jiri Matas, Nicu Sebe, and Max Welling, (eds.), *ECCV (3)*, volume 9907 of *Lecture Notes in Computer Science*, pages 785–800. New York, NY: Springer, 2016.

[239] Glenn J. Myatt and Wayne P. Johnson. Making sense of data i: A practical guide to exploratory data analysis and data mining, 2nd edition, Hoboken, NJ: John Wiley & Sons, 2014.

[240] David Nadeau and Satoshi Sekine. A survey of named entity recognition and classification. *Lingvisticae Investigationes*, 30(1):3–26, 2007.

[241] Alexey Natekin and Alois Knoll. Gradient boosting machines, a tutorial. *Front. Neurorobot.*, 7(21), 2013.

[242] Andrew Ng. Advice for applying machine learning. https://see.stanford.edu/materials/aimlcs229/ML-advice.pdf, 2015. Accessed: 2018-20-1.

[243] Maximilian Nickel, Kevin Murphy, Volker Tresp and Evgeniy Gabrilovich. A review of relational machine learning for knowledge graphs. *Proceedings of the IEEE*, 104(1):11–33, 2016.

[244] Maximilian Nickel, Volker Tresp and Hans-Peter Kriegel. Factorizing yago: scalable machine learning for linked data. In *Proceedings of the 21st international conference on World Wide Web*, pages 271–280. New York, NY: ACM, 2012.

[245] Mark Nixon and Alberto S. Aguado. *Feature Extraction and Image Processing for Computer Vision*. Cambridge, MA: Academic Press, 2012.

[246] Sarah Nogueira, Konstantinos Sechidis and Gavin Brown. On the stability of feature selection algorithms. *The Journal of Machine Learning Research*, 18(1):6345–6398, 2017.

[247] Timo Ojala, Matti Pietikäinen and David Harwood. A comparative study of texture measures with classification based on featured distributions. *Pattern Recognition*, 29(1):51–59, 1996.

[248] Michael L. Overton. *Numerical computing with IEEE floating point arithmetic*, Philadelphia, PA: Siam, 2001.

[249] Sean Owen, Robin Anil, Ted Dunning and Ellen Friedman. *Mahout in Action*. Shelter Island, NY: Manning Publications, 1st edition, 2011.

[250] Afelio Padilla. Practical machine learning - 2.3 - Feature engineering. www .youtube.com/watch?v=78RUW9kuDe4, 2016. Accessed: 2018-06-10.

[251] Ashwini Kumar Pal. Diving deeper into dimension reduction with independent components analysis (ICA). https://blog.paperspace .com/dimension-reduction-with-independent-components-analysis/, 2017. Accessed: 2018-12-15.

[252] Alan Pankratz. *Forecasting with Dynamic Regression Models*. Hoboken, NJ: Wiley, 1991.

[253] F. Pedregosa, G. Varoquaux, A. Gramfort, V. Michel, B. Thirion, O. Grisel, M. Blondel, P. Prettenhofer, R. Weiss, V. Dubourg, J. Vanderplas, A. Passos, D. Cournapeau, M. Brucher, M. Perrot and E. Duchesnay. Scikit-learn: Machine learning in Python. *Journal of Machine Learning Research*, 12:2825–2830, 2011.

[254] Hanchuan Peng, Fuhui Long and Chris Ding. Feature selection based on mutual information: criteria of max-dependency, max-relevance, and min-redundancy. *IEEE Transactions on Pattern Analysis & Machine Intelligence*, (8):1226–1238, 2005.

[255] Jeffrey Pennington, Richard Socher and Christopher D. Manning. GloVe: Global vectors for word representation. In *Empirical Methods in Natural Language Processing (EMNLP)*, pages 1532–1543, 2014.

[256] Bryan Perozzi, Rami Al-Rfou and Steven Skiena. Deepwalk: Online learning of social representations. In *Proceedings of the 20th ACM SIGKDD international conference on Knowledge discovery and data mining*, pages 701–710. New York, NY: ACM, 2014.

[257] Matthew E. Peters, Mark Neumann, Mohit Iyyer, Matt Gardner, Christopher Clark, Kenton Lee and Luke Zettlemoyer. Deep contextualized word representations. In *NAACL-HLT*, pages 2227–2237. Stroudsburg, PA: Association for Computational Linguistics, 2018.

[258] M. F. Porter. An algorithm for suffix stripping. In Karen Sparck Jones and Peter Willett, (eds.), *Readings in Information Retrieval*, pages 313–316. San Francisco, CA: Morgan Kaufmann Publishers, 1997.

[259] Alexei Pozdnoukhov and Mikhail Kanevski. Monitoring network optimisation for spatial data classification using support vector machines. *International Journal of Environmental and Pollution*, 28(3-4):465–484, 2006.

[260] L. Prechelt. Proben1: A set of neural network benchmark problems and benchmarking rules. Technical Report 21/94, Univ., Fak. für Informatik, September 1994.

[261] Frank Puk. How is ANOVA used for feature selection. www.quora.com/ How-is-ANOVA-used-for-feature-selection, 2016. Accessed: 2018-08-27.

[262] James Pustejovsky and Amber Stubbs. *Natural Language Annotation for Machine Learning - A Guide to Corpus-Building for Applications*. Sebastopol, CA: O'Reilly, 2012.

[263] Dorian Pyle. *Data Preparation for Data Mining*. San Francisco, CA: Morgan Kaufmann Publishers, 1999.

[264] Ali Rahimi and Benjamin Recht. Random features for large-scale kernel machines. In *Advances in Neural Information Processing Systems*, pages 1177–1184, 2008.

[265] Ali Rahimi and Benjamin Recht. Weighted sums of random kitchen sinks: Replacing minimization with randomization in learning. In *Advances in Neural Information Processing Systems*, pages 1313–1320, 2009.

[266] Carl Edward Rasmussen and Christopher K. I. Williams. *Gaussian Processes for Machine Learning (Adaptive Computation and Machine Learning)*. Cambridge, MA: MIT Press, 2005.

[267] Christopher Ré, Amir Abbas Sadeghian, Zifei Shan, Jaeho Shin, Feiran Wang, Sen Wu and Ce Zhang. Feature engineering for knowledge base construction. *arXiv preprint arXiv:1407.6439*, 2014.

[268] Nils Reimers. Deep learning for nlp - Lecture 5 - convolutional neural networks. www.youtube.com/watch?v=nzSPZyjGlWI, 2015. Accessed 2018-20-1.

[269] Ehud Reiter, R. Robertson and Liesl Osman. Knowledge acquisition for natural language generation. In *Proceedings of the Fist International Conference on Natural Language Generation (INLG-2000)*, pages 217–224, 2000.

[270] Isidore Rigoutsos and Aris Floratos. Combinatorial pattern discovery in biological sequences: The teiresias algorithm. *Bioinformatics (Oxford, England)*, 14(1):55–67, 1998.

[271] Petar Ristoski and Heiko Paulheim. Rdf2vec: Rdf graph embeddings for data mining. In Paul Groth, Elena Simperl, Alasdair Gray, Marta Sabou, Markus Krötzsch, Freddy Lecue, Fabian Flöck, and Yolanda Gil, (eds.), *The Semantic Web – ISWC 2016*, pages 498–514, Cham: Springer, 2016.

[272] Stephen J. Roberts. Novelty detection using extreme value statistics. *IEE Proceedings-Vision, Image and Signal Processing*, 146(3):124–129, 1999.

[273] Mark R. Robertson. 300+ hours of video uploaded to youtube every minute. https://tubularinsights.com/youtube-300-hours/, 2015. Accessed: 2019-01-10.

[274] Yvan Saeys, Thomas Abeel and Yves Van de Peer. Robust feature selection using ensemble feature selection techniques. In Walter Daelemans, Bart Goethals, and Katharina Morik, (eds.), *ECML/PKDD (2)*, volume 5212 of *Lecture Notes in Computer Science*, pages 313–325. Cham: Springer, 2008.

[275] Magnus Sahlgren. A brief history of word embeddings (and some clarifications). www.linkedin.com/pulse/brief-history-word-embeddings-some-clarifications-magnus-sahlgren/, 2015. Accessed: 2018-12-20.

[276] Steven Schmatz. When should i use pca versus non-negative matrix factorization? www.quora.com/When-should-I-use-PCA-versus-non-negative-matrix-factorization, 2018. Accessed: 2018-12-18.

[277] Bernhard Scholkopf and Alexander J. Smola. *Learning with Kernels: Support Vector Machines, Regularization, Optimization, and Beyond*. Cambridge, MA: MIT Press, 2001.

[278] Rachel Schutt and Cathy O'Neil. *Doing Data Science: Straight Talk from the Frontline*. Stroudsburg, PA: O'Reilly Media, Inc., 2013.

[279] Konstantinos Sechidis. *Hypothesis Testing and Feature Selection in Semi-Supervised Data*. PhD thesis, School of Computer Science, University Of Manchester, UK, November 2015.

[280] Alireza Shafaei, James J. Little and Mark Schmidt. Play and learn: Using video games to train computer vision models. In *Proceedings of the British Machine Vision Conference BMVC*, York, UK, September 2016.

[281] Matthew Shardlow. An analysis of feature selection techniques. Technical report, The University of Manchester, 2016.

[282] Noel E. Sharkey, (ed.). *Connectionist Natural Language Processing*. Intellect, Oxford, England: Intellect, 1992.

[283] Blake Shaw and Tony Jebara. Structure preserving embedding. In *Proceedings of the 26th Annual International Conference on Machine Learning*, pages 937–944. New York, NY: ACM, 2009.

[284] Raphael Silberzahn, Eric L Uhlmann, Daniel P Martin, Pasquale Anselmi, Frederik Aust, Eli Awtrey, Štěpán Bahník, Feng Bai, Colin Bannard, Evelina Bonnier, R. Carlsson, F. Cheung, G. Christensen, R. Clay, M. A. Craig, A. Dalla Rosa, L. Dam, M. H. Evans, I. Flores Cervantes, N. Fong, M. Gamez-Djokic, A. Glenz, S. Gordon-McKeon, T. J. Heaton, K. Hederos, M. Heene, A. J. Hofelich Mohr, F. Högden, K. Hui, M. Johannesson, J. Kalodimos, E. Kaszubowski, D. M. Kennedy, R. Lei, T. A. Lindsay, S. Liverani, C. R. Madan, D. Molden, E. Molleman, R. D. Morey, L. B. Mulder, B. R. Nijstad, N. G. Pope, B. Pope, J. M. Prenoveau, F. Rink, E. Robusto, H. Roderique, A. Sandberg, E. Schlüter, F. D. Schönbrodt, M. F. Sherman, S. A. Sommer, K. Sotak, S. Spain, C. Spörlein, T. Stafford, L. Stefanutti, S. Tauber, J. Ullrich, M. Vianello, E.-J. Wagenmakers, M. Witkowiak, S. Yoon, B. A. Nosek, Many analysts, one data set: Making transparent how variations in analytic choices affect results. *Advances in Methods and Practices in Psychological Science*, 1(3):337–356, 2018.

[285] Amit Singhal, Chris Buckley and Manclar Mitra. Pivoted document length normalization. In *ACM SIGIR Forum*, volume 51, pages 176–184. New York, NY: ACM, 2017.

[286] Peter Smit, Sami Virpioja, Stig-Arne Grönroos, Mikko Kurimo. Morfessor 2.0: Toolkit for statistical morphological segmentation. In *Proceedings of the Demonstrations at the 14th Conference of the [E]uropean Chapter of the Association for Computational Linguistics*, pages 21–24. Gothenburg, Sweden: Aalto University, 2014.

[287] Jasper Snoek, Hugo Larochelle and Ryan P. Adams. Practical bayesian optimization of machine learning algorithms. In *Advances in Neural Information Processing Systems*, pages 2951–2959, 2012.

[288] Irwin Sobel and Gary Feldman. A 3x3 isotropic gradient operator for image processing. In R. Duda and P. Hart, editors, *Pattern Classification and Scene Analysis*, pages 271–272. New York: Wiley, 1973.

[289] Samuel Thomas Sriram Ganapathy. Tutorial: The art and science of speech feature engineering. www.clsp.jhu.edu/~samuel/pdfs/tutorial.pdf, 2014. Accessed: 2018-06-11.

[290] Tavish Srivastava. A complete tutorial on time series modeling in r. www.analyticsvidhya.com/blog/2015/12/complete-tutorial-time-series-modeling/, 2015. Accessed: 2019-01-15.

[291] Contributors StackExchange. What is the difference between ZCA whitening and PCA whitening? https://stats.stackexchange.com/questions/117427/what-is-the-difference-between-zca-whitening-and-pca-whitening, 2014. Accessed: 2018-09-15.

[292] Contributors StackExchange. Feature map for the gaussian kernel? https://stats.stackexchange.com/questions/69759/feature-map-for-the-gaussian-kernel, 2015. Accessed: 2018-08-27.

[293] Contributors StackExchange. Relationship between svd and pca. how to use svd to perform pca? https://stats.stackexchange.com/questions/134282/relationship-between-svd-and-pca-how-to-use-svd-to-perform-pca, 2015. Accessed: 2018-09-10.

[294] Contributors StackExchange. Deriving feature map formula for inhomogeneous polynomial kernel. https://datascience.stackexchange.com/questions/10534/deriving-feature-map-formula-for-inhomogeneous-polynomial-kernel, 2016. Accessed: 2019-01-15.

[295] Contributors StackExchange. How to perform feature engineering on unknown features? http://datascience.stackexchange.com/questions/10640/how-to-perform-feature-engineering-on-unknown-features, 2016. Accessed: 2018-06-11.

[296] Contributors StackExchange. How does lda (latent dirichlet allocation) assign a topic-distribution to a new document? https://stats.stackexchange.com/questions/325614/how-does-lda-latent-dirichlet-allocation-assign-a-topic-distribution-to-a-new, 2018. Accessed: 2018-09-9.

[297] Carsten Steger. Machine vision algorithms. In Alexander Hornberg, (ed.), *Handbook of Machine and Computer Vision: The Guide for Developers and Users, Second, Revised and Updated Edition*, chapter 9. Hoboken, NJ: Wiley, 2017.

[298] Jonathan A. C. Sterne, Ian R. White, John B. Carlin, Michael Spratt, Patrick Royston, Michael G. Kenward, Angela M. Wood and James R. Carpenter. Multiple imputation for missing data in epidemiological and clinical research: Potential and pitfalls. *BMJ*, 338:b2393, 2009.

[299] Hervé Stoppiglia, Gérard Dreyfus, Rémi Dubois and Yacine Oussar. Ranking a random feature for variable and feature selection. *Journal of Machine Learning Research*, 3(Mar):1399–1414, 2003.

[300] Fabian M. Suchanek, Gjergji Kasneci and Gerhard Weikum. Yago: A core of semantic knowledge. In *Proceedings of the 16th International Conference on World Wide Web*, WWW '07, pages 697–706, New York, NY, USA, 2007. New York, NY: ACM.

[301] Michael J. Swain and Dana H. Ballard. Indexing via color histograms. In Arun K. Sood and Harry Wechsler (eds.), *Active Perception and Robot Vision*, pages 261–273. New York, NY: Springer, 1992.

[302] Kei Takurita. Paper dissected: "GloVe global vectors for word presentation" explained. http://mlexplained.com/2018/04/29/paper-dissected-glove-global-vectors-for-word-representation-explained/, 2018. Accessed: 2018-12-22.

[303] David Talbot and Thorsten Brants. Randomized language models via perfect hash functions. *Proceedings of ACL-08: HLT*, pages 505–513, 2008.

[304] Lappoon R. Tang and Raymond J. Mooney. Using multiple clause constructors in inductive logic programming for semantic parsing. In *European Conference on Machine Learning*, pages 466–477. New York, NY: Springer, 2001.

[305] Robert Tibshirani. Regression shrinkage and selection via the lasso: A retrospective. *Journal of the Royal Statistical Society: Series B (Statistical Methodology)*, 73(3):273–282, 2011.

[306] Andreas Töscher, Michael Jahrer and Robert M Bell. The bigchaos solution to the Netflix Grand Prize. Report from the Netflix Prize Winners, 2009.

[307] Matthew Tovbin. Meet TransmogrifAI, open source AutoML that powers einstein predictions. SF Big Analytics Meetup. www.youtube.com/watch?v=93vsqjfGPCw&feature=youtu.be&t=2800, 2019. Accessed: 2019-7-13.

[308] Martin Tschirsich and Gerold Hintz. Leveraging crowdsourcing for paraphrase recognition. In *Proceedings of the 7th Linguistic Annotation Workshop and Interoperability with Discourse*, pages 205–213, Sofia, Bulgaria, August 2013. Stroudsburg, PA: Association for Computational Linguistics.

[309] Virginia Goss Tusher, Robert Tibshirani and Gilbert Chu. Significance analysis of microarrays applied to the ionizing radiation response. *Proceedings of the National Academy of Sciences*, 98(9):5116–5121, 2001.

[310] Franklin Ursula. *Real World of Technology*. Toronto, Ontario: House of Anansi Press, 1989.

[311] Laurens van der Maaten and Geoffrey Hinton. Visualizing data using t-SNE. *Journal of Machine Learning Research*, 9:2579–2605, 2008.

[312] James Van Hinsbergh, Nathan Griffiths, Phillip Taylor, Alasdair Thomason, Zhou Xu and Alex Mouzakitis. Vehicle point of interest detection using in-car data. In *Proceedings of the 2Nd ACM SIGSPATIAL International Workshop on AI for Geographic Knowledge Discovery*, GeoAI'18, pages 1–4, Seattle, WA, USA, 2018. New York, NY: ACM.

[313] Ashish Vaswani, Noam Shazeer, Niki Parmar, Jakob Uszkoreit, Llion Jones, Aidan N Gomez, Łukasz Kaiser and Illia Polosukhin. Attention is all you need. In *Advances in Neural Information Process Systems*, pages 5998–6008, 2017.

[314] Ragav Venkatesan, Vijetha Gatupalli and Baoxin Li. On the generality of neural image features. In *2016 IEEE International Conference on Image Processing (ICIP)*, pages 41–45. San Diego, CA: IEEE, 2016.

[315] Celine Vens and Fabrizio Costa. Random forest based feature induction. In *2011 IEEE 11th International Conference on Data Mining*, pages 744–753. San Diego, CA: IEEE, 2011.

[316] Ruben Verborgh and Max De Wilde. *Using OpenRefine*. Birmingham, UK: Packt Publishing, 1st edition, 2013.

[317] Pascal Vincent, Hugo Larochelle, Yoshua Bengio and Pierre-Antoine Manzagol. Extracting and composing robust features with denoising autoencoders. In *Proceedings of the 25th international conference on Machine learning*, pages 1096–1103. New York, NY: ACM, 2008.

[318] S. Vichy N. Vishwanathan, Nicol N. Schraudolph, Risi Kondor and Karsten M. Borgwardt. Graph kernels. *Journal of Machine Learning Research*, 11(Apr):1201–1242, 2010.

[319] Trang VoPham, Jaime E. Hart, Francine Laden and Yao-Yi Chiang. Emerging trends in geospatial artificial intelligence (geoai): Potential applications for environmental epidemiology. *Environmental Health*, 17(1):40, Apr 2018.

[320] Eric W. Weisstein. Frobenius norm. From MathWorld–A Wolfram Web Resource. http://mathworld.wolfram.com/FrobeniusNorm.html, 2018. Accessed: 2018-12-17.

[321] Tsung-Hsien Wen, Milica Gasic, Nikola Mrksic, Pei hao Su, David Vandyke and Steve J. Young. Semantically conditioned lstm-based natural language generation for spoken dialogue systems. In *EMNLP*, pages 1711–1721. Stroudsburg, PA: The Association for Computational Linguistics, 2015.

[322] Laura Wendlandt, Jonathan K Kummerfeld and Rada Mihalcea. Factors influencing the surprising instability of word embeddings. In *Proceedings of the 2018 Conference of the North American Chapter of the Association for Computational Linguistics: Human Language Technologies, Volume 1 (Long Papers)*, volume 1, pages 2092–2102, 2018.

[323] Marc Wick. Geonames ontology. www.geonames.org/about.html, 2015. Accessed: 2015-04-22.

[324] Hadley Wickham. Tidy data. *Journal of Statistical Software*, 59(1):1–23, 2014.

[325] Wikipedia. Akaike information criterion. https://en.wikipedia.org/wiki/Akaike_information_criterion, 2018. Accessed: 2018-06-04.

[326] Wikipedia. List of common coordinate transformations. https://en.wikipedia.org/wiki/List_of_common_coordinate_transformations, 2018. Accessed: 2018-08-27.

[327] Wikipedia. Multinomial theorem. https://en.wikipedia.org/wiki/Multinomial_theorem, 2018. Accessed: 2018-08-27.

[328] Wikipedia. Multivariate adaptive regression splines. https://en.wikipedia.org/wiki/Multivariate_adaptive_regression_splines, 2019. Accessed: 2019-01-10.

[329] Wikipedia. tf-idf. https://en.wikipedia.org/wiki/Tf-idf, 2019. Accessed: 2018-01-10.

[330] W. John Wilbur and Karl Sirotkin. The automatic identification of stop words. *Journal of Information Science*, 18(1):45–55, 1992.

[331] Ian H. Witten and Eibe Frank. *Data Mining: Practical Machine Learning Tools and Techniques with Java Implementations*. San Francisco, CA: Morgan Kaufmann Publishers, 2000.

[332] David H. Wolpert and William G. Macready. No free lunch theorems for optimization. *IEEE Transactions on Evolutionary Computation*, 1(1):67–82, 1997.

[333] Yuk Wah Wong and Raymond J Mooney. Learning for semantic parsing with statistical machine translation. In *Proceedings of the Main Conference on Human Language Technology Conference of the North American Chapter of the Association of Computational Linguistics*, pages 439–446. Stroudsburg, PA: Association for Computational Linguistics, 2006.

[334] Xindong Wu, Kui Yu, Hao Wang and Wei Ding. Online streaming feature selection. In *Proceedings of the 27th International Conference on Machine Learning*, pages 1159–1166, 2010.

[335] Robert H. Wurtz. Recounting the impact of Hubel and Wiesel. *J Physiol*, 587(12):2817–2823, 2009.

[336] Jingen Xiang. Scalable scientific computing algorithms using mapreduce. Master's thesis, University of Waterloo, 2013.

[337] Weizhong Yan. Feature engineering for PHM applications. www.phmsociety .org/sites/phmsociety.org/files/FeatureEngineeringTut orial_2015PHM_V2.pdf, oct 2015. Accessed: 2018-05-01, linked from www.phmsociety.org/events/conference/phm/15/tutorials.

[338] R. K. Rao Yarlagadda. *Analog and Digital Signals and Systems*, volume 1, chapter 2. New York, NY: Springer, 2010.

[339] Annie T. T. Ying, Gail C. Murphy, Raymond Ng and Mark C. Chu-Carroll. Predicting source code changes by mining change history. *IEEE Trans. Software Engineering*, 30(9):574–586, September 2004.

[340] Chun-Nam John Yu and Thorsten Joachims. Learning structural svms with latent variables. In *Proceedings of the 26th Annual International Conference on Machine Learning*, pages 1169–1176. New York, NY: ACM, 2009.

[341] Hsiang-Fu Yu, Hung-Yi Lo, Hsun-Ping Hsieh, Jing-Kai Lou, Todd G McKenzie, Jung-Wei Chou, Po-Han Chung, Chia-Hua Ho, Chun-Fu Chang, Yin-Hsuan Wei, Jui-Yu Weng, En-Syu Yan, Che-Wei Chang, Tsung-Ting Kuo, Yi-Chen Lo, Po Tzu Chang, Chieh Po, Chien-Yuan Wang, Yi-Hung Huang, Chen-Wei Hung, Yu-Xun Ruan, Yu-Shi Lin, Shou-de Lin, Hsuan-Tien Lin, and Chih-Jen Lin. Feature engineering and classifier ensemble for kdd cup 2010. In *KDD Cup*, 2010.

[342] Zdenek Zabokrtsky. Feature engineering in machine learning. https://ufal .mff.cuni.cz/~zabokrtsky/courses/npfl104/html/feature _engineering.pdf, 2014. Accessed: 2018-06-10.

[343] Matei Zaharia, Mosharaf Chowdhury, Michael J. Franklin, Scott Shenker and Ion Stoica. Spark: Cluster computing with working sets. In *Proceedings of the 2Nd USENIX Conference on Hot Topics in Cloud Computing*, HotCloud'10, pages 10–10, Berkeley, CA, USA, 2010. Berkeley, CA: USENIX Association.

[344] Ce Zhang, Arun Kumar and Christopher Ré. Materialization optimizations for feature selection workloads. *ACM Transactions on Database Systems (TODS)*, 41(1):2, 2016.

[345] Sheng Zhang, Weihong Wang, James Ford and Fillia Makedon. Learning from incomplete ratings using non-negative matrix factorization. In *Proceedings of the 2006 SIAM International Conference on Data Mining*, pages 549–553. Philadelphia, PA: SIAM, 2006.

[346] Tian Zhang, Raghu Ramakrishnan and Miron Livny. Birch: An efficient data clustering method for very large databases. In *ACM Sigmod Record*, volume 25, pages 103–114. New York, NY: ACM, 1996.

[347] Kang Zhao, Hongtao Lu and Jincheng Mei. Locality preserving hashing. In Carla E. Brodley and Peter Stone, (eds.), *AAAI*, pages 2874–2881. Cambridge, MA: AAAI Press, 2014.

[348] Shenglin Zhao, Michael R. Lyu and Irwin King. *Point-of-Interest Recommendation in Location-Based Social Networks*. SpringerBriefs in Computer Science. Singapore: Springer Singapore, 2018.

[349] Shichen Zhao, Tao Yu, Qingyan Meng, Qiming Zhou, Feifei Wang, Li Wang and Yueming Hu. Gdal-based extend arcgis engine's support for hdf file format. In *Geoinformatics*, pages 1–3. San Diego, CA: IEEE, 2010.

[350] Alice Zheng. *Evaluating Machine Learning Models: A Beginner's Guide to Key Concepts and Pitfalls*. Sebastopol, CA: O'Reilly, 2015.

[351] Alice Zheng. *Mastering Feature Engineering*. Sebastopol, CA: O'Reilly Early Access, 2016.

[352] Alice Zheng and Amanda Casari. *Feature Engineering for Machine Learning: Principles and Techniques for Data Scientists*. Sebastopol, CA: O'Reilly Media, Inc., 2018.

[353] Hui Zou and Trevor Hastie. Regularization and variable selection via the elastic net. *Journal of the Royal Statistical Society: Series B (Statistical Methodology)*, 67(2):301–320, 2005.

Index